The Sonic Gaze

Living Existentialism

Series Editors: T Storm Heter, East Stroudsburg University, LaRose T. Parris, Lehman College, the City University New York, and Devin Zane Shaw, Douglas College

Existentialism is a living, practical philosophy, engaged in contemporary events and responsive to other currents of philosophy across the globe. It can be instrumental to an individual's understanding of themselves as well as to examinations of political, societal, and ecological phenomena.

This series focuses on creative, generative scholarship that expands discussions of existentialism in order to foster an intellectual space for articulating the diverse lineages of existentialism—from Beauvoir's feminist philosophy, to the anticolonial, black existentialism of thinkers like Frantz Fanon and Angela Davis who composed their views of freedom, self, and other from the lived experience of racism and colonialism.

Existentialism has often been miscategorized as a European tradition, limited by the gravitational pull of a few thinkers. Part of the work of this series is to dismantle this incorrect impression of where Existentialism comes from and what its potential is. Existential thought offers a valuable vocabulary for expressing the lived perspectives of colonized, indigenous, and othered peoples. As such, it is increasingly relevant to the ongoing struggle for human freedom the world over.

Philosophy of Antifascism: Punching Nazis and Fighting White Supremacy
Devin Zane Shaw

Sartre on Contingency: Antiblack Racism and Embodiment
Mabogo Percy More

Black Nihilism and Antiblack Racism
Devon Johnson

The Sonic Gaze: Jazz, Whiteness and Racialized Listening
T Storm Heter

The Sonic Gaze

Jazz, Whiteness, and Racialized Listening

T Storm Heter

ROWMAN & LITTLEFIELD
Lanham • Boulder • New York • London

Published by Rowman & Littlefield
An imprint of The Rowman & Littlefield Publishing Group, Inc.
4501 Forbes Boulevard, Suite 200, Lanham, Maryland 20706
www.rowman.com

86-90 Paul Street, London EC2A 4NE

Copyright © 2022 by T Storm Heter

All rights reserved. No part of this book may be reproduced in any form or by any electronic or mechanical means, including information storage and retrieval systems, without written permission from the publisher, except by a reviewer who may quote passages in a review.

British Library Cataloguing in Publication Information Available

Library of Congress Cataloging-in-Publication Data

Names: Heter, T Storm, author.
Title: The sonic gaze : jazz, whiteness, and racialized listening / T Storm Heter.
Description: Lanham : Rowman & Littlefield, 2022. | Series: Living existentialism | Includes bibliographical references and index. | Summary: "This book argues that whiteness is not only a visual orientation; it is a way of hearing. Inspired by formulations of race and whiteness in the existential writings of Frantz Fanon, Simone de Beauvoir, Jean-Paul Sartre, W.E.B. Du Bois, Richard Wright, Lewis Gordon, Angela Davis, bell hooks and Sara Ahmed, this book introduces students to the notion of the white sonic gaze"— Provided by publisher.
Identifiers: LCCN 2021046342 (print) | LCCN 2021046343 (ebook) |
  ISBN 9781538162613 (hardback) | ISBN 9781538162620 (paperback) |
  ISBN 9781538162637 (ebook)
Subjects: LCSH: Jazz—Social aspects. | Listening (Philosophy) | Music and race. | Blacks—Social conditions. | Whites—Race identity.
Classification: LCC ML3918.J39 H47 2022 (print) | LCC ML3918.J39 (ebook) |
  DDC 781.65—dc23
LC record available at https://lccn.loc.gov/2021046342
LC ebook record available at https://lccn.loc.gov/2021046343

For Kate

Contents

Acknowledgments		ix
Preface		xi
1	Aural Orientations	1
2	The Jazz Problem: Patterns of White Bad Faith Listening	27
	Listening Exercises for Chapter 2: The Jazz Problem	61
3	Listening to Difference: Creole Critiques of White Listening	67
	Listening Exercises for Chapter 3: Listening to Difference	99
4	The Ears of a Guilty People: Africana Critiques of White Listening	103
	Listening Exercises for Chapter 4: The Ears of a Guilty People	141
Afterword: Say Their Names: Breonna Taylor, George Floyd		151
Notes		159
References		183
Index		191

Acknowledgments

This book was written while I was living and teaching in *Lenapehoking,* the unceded land of the Lenni Lenape people, the Delaware Nation, the Delaware Tribe, the Stockbridge Munsee Community, the Seneca-Cayuga Nation, and others.

Thank you to the North American Sartre Society, the Caribbean Philosophical Association, the Phenomenology Roundtable, the Frederick Douglass Institute, the Diversity Dialogue Project, and the Frederick Douglass Debate Society.

Thank you to Michael Monahan, Craig Matarrese, Devin Z. Shaw, La Rose T. Parris, Lewis R. Gordon, Sara Ahmed, Veronica Watson, Patricia Graham, Tim Connolly, Frankie Mace, Anna Mendoza, Eduardo Navas, Cem Zeytinoglu, James D. Wallace, and Zohreh T. Sullivan.

Thank you to my students, debaters, and dialogue facilitators.

I thank my family: Jean and Tom Heter, Annette Boardman, Marjorie and Marvin Heter, Aileen and Byron Minter, Kate Bullard, and Miriam and Iris Heter.

I dedicate this book to my life partner, Kate, who let me borrow all of her books so I could write this one.

Preface
A Note on Jazz Pedagogy

Listen actively! This phrase encapsulates what I hope my readers get out of these pages. My experiences in teaching philosophy, coaching debate, and directing an intergroup dialogue project led me to believe in the pedagogical power of active listening. Active listening is a skill to be cultivated, like the skill of playing a musical instrument or the skill of public speaking. In traditional classrooms, listening is not given the same pride of place as reading, speaking, and writing. Universities have departments of reading, rhetoric and communication, and literature, but few have departments of listening. Music schools are a different story. The homepage of the Ear Training Department at the Berklee School of Music explains why musicians must study listening: "Ear training, one of Berklee's core requirements, teaches students how to hear and apply melodic, rhythmic, and harmonic musical forms.... Ear training assists listeners in understanding what they are hearing."[1]

This book was inspired by the idea that just as musicians need *ear training* as part of their musical education, so do students of rhetoric, science, literature, reading, philosophy, culture, language, and other disciplines, in order to "understand what they are hearing." Listening to music and listening to speech (orally and in print) are related types of listening. Active listening, in the sense used in this book, is a wide-ranging, transferable skill that fosters empathy,[2] inquiry, dialogue,[3] and perhaps most importantly, respect.[4] In the language of existential philosophy, listening actively is important because it is an act of *human recognition*.

Drawing on Marc Lamont Hill's notion of "Hip Hop Pedagogy,"[5] one could call the project of nurturing active listening in the classroom a "Jazz Pedagogy." Jazz music thrives on spontaneity, improvisation, and call-and-response. Recognizing the potential of jazz as a model for teaching, Amiri Baraka writes, "If we used Afro-American Improvised Music (American

Classical Music) in the classroom, we would see big changes."[6] The main change I foresee is that classrooms modeled on jazz performance would be *noisy spaces* where calls-and-responses between and among teachers and students would thrive. Jazz Pedagogy emphasizes a learning experience based on mutual listening.

The Sonic Gaze argues that active listening is performative, not observational. Active listening requires improvisation. Usually improvisation is treated as exclusively a feature of what musicians do, especially jazz musicians. Few have studied improvisation as part of the listening process. Existential philosophy, with its attention to freedom and inter-subjectivity, allows us to rethink the role of listening.

Many students come to university having been trained by their primary school teachers to be passive, still, and quiet—all in the name of being "good listeners." Countless drummers got their start, not through a band teacher's recognition of their talent, but by entertaining their classmates beating out rhythms on desks. Most of these young drummers were disciplined by their teachers for being too noisy. Jazz Pedagogy would un-discipline students, encouraging them to become active listeners by speaking, clapping, singing, gesturing, and moving—in body and mind.

Influenced by hands-on music books like *The Art of Bop Drumming* by John Riley, I have created listening exercises and playlists to accompany chapters of this book.[7] The exercises blend traditional musical ear training (listening for pitch, melody, and rhythm) with the expanded sense of active listening described above (listening to others speak in conversation, dialogue, and debate; and listening to others through written texts). In the spirit of improvisation, I encourage my readers to develop their own exercises and to create their own playlists to listen to while reading this book.

Chapter 1

Aural Orientations

The main argument of *The Sonic Gaze* is that we make race with our ears. I study how Whites in the United States "became White" not only by distinguishing themselves visually from those they classified as non-White but also by marking them as sonically different.[1] Being White has been and continues to be a way of listening to others. Or more precisely, being White in the United States has been a way of *not* listening, and *not listening well*, to those individuals whom Whites hear as "people of color," especially Indigenous, Black, Creole, and mixed-race people.

Most current discussions of Whiteness, like most discussions of race, focus on the visual. But there is an older tradition of Critical Whiteness Studies initiated by Black, mixed-race, Indigenous, and Creole philosophers in the United States. Critiques of Whiteness have circulated in Black and Creole print and sound culture since the nineteenth century. Oral critiques of Whiteness—sung or spoken or danced—go back to the first points of contact between Europeans and those they colonized. Colonized people resisted European speaking and listening patterns by creolizing the European languages forced upon them. The category "White" emerged, in part, when European colonizers distinguished "sound" from "noise," attributing the latter to the colonized and the former to themselves. Jodi A. Byrd explains that "Colonial logic . . . renders some subject positions visible and heard, and others absent and silent."[2] In particular, "new world indigenous peoples . . . within the literatures of empire, have been relegated to inarticulate savages."[3] "White" has come to mean "articulate" and "consonant," while "non-White" has come to mean "inarticulate," "noisy," and ultimately, not-human.

Just as Whiteness was a late discovery for Whites, the critical study of Whiteness has been a late discovery for mainstream academics. As La Rose T. Parris argues, "Africana thinkers have written works of great philosophical

1

import, yet the enduring legacy of racist thought has led these thinkers' intellectual productions to be marginalized or negated."[4] It is paradoxical, but not surprising, that White people have become White by listening selectively to the sonic productions of Indigenous, mixed-race, Creole, and Black people who were critical of White racism and cultural hegemony.

The Sonic Gaze problematizes Whiteness by placing a spotlight on the collective listening habits of White people in the United States. My notion of problematizing Whiteness is derived from the critical sociological and existential thought of W.E.B. Du Bois. Du Bois instructs us to problematize Whiteness by asking, *How does it feel to be a White problem?*[5] Du Bois's attention to the phenomenological "feeling" of being a problem is another example of how Africana thinkers anticipated themes of European philosophy, such as freedom, being, and intersubjectivity.[6] As Lewis R. Gordon argues, Western philosophers have been late to recognize the existence of, much less the importance of Africana philosophy.[7] When I first began teaching Africana philosophy, I remember being met with skepticism from a well-meaning White colleague who asked, "What Africana philosophy? Is that really a thing?" As Mabogo P. More writes in *Sartre on Contingency: Antiblack Racism and Embodiment,* "In the eyes of such philosophers there is either no black philosopher in the whole world or very few worth knowing and even reading."[8]

White authors writing about jazz and listening in the United States have often written from a position of colorblindness and power. Nevertheless, there is a growing interest in what Linda Martín Alcoff calls "the future of Whiteness."[9] As the academic field of Critical Whiteness Studies grows, it is important that the historical origins of the field be located not just in the writings of such important scholars as David Roediger, George Lipsitz, or Richard Dyer, but in the Africana thinkers who proceeded them, like Du Bois and so many others.[10]

By raising the problem of White listening, I hope to open up new space for theorizing race and combating racism in the United States. As More reminds us, hearing race is not unique to the American experience: "The problem of jazz and racism was not simply an American peculiarity."[11] Yet, in the United States, anti-Black racism structures everything from driving down the street, to applying for a job, to which radio station one listens to. For U.S. Americans,[12] hearing race is a mundane and pervasive feature of life. White folks here talk all the time about how the Black people they encounter "sound Black," or "sound White," or "are articulate." Most of us Whites have detailed ideas about Black music, but go mute if asked to describe the qualities of White music. You would be hard pressed to find a U.S. American who hadn't heard much Black music or who could not name ten Black musicians. Black musicians are both hyper-visible and hyper-audible in Unites States culture, where the White "love" of Black music is, to paraphrase Sartre, "a national pastime."[13] I agree with Tendayi Sithole that the White "marking" of Blackness in music and sound lies at the heart of the Western imperial project: "The labelling of black music as exotic, primitive, ethno, ghetto, inferior, and so on, has been the Westernized-racist-colonial-imperial mark, which seeks to settle itself at the center to deny anything musical that comes from blackness."[14]

What it means to hear race has received less attention than what it means to see race. There is scholarship on what it means to *talk* White, but little on what it means to *listen* White.[15] I challenge the tendency to prioritize vision over hearing by studying the collective, racialized listening orientations that were developed in response to early jazz music in the United States, and which have persisted. I contend that jazz listening orientations are among the most important mechanisms by which Whites in the United States have created and navigated their racial identities.

Our language is so saturated with visualist assumptions that I have had to resort to a mixed metaphor to name my topic. Rather than "the gaze" as traditionally understood in existential literature, I study *the sonic gaze*. We experience the sonic gaze when we feel alienated by how others listen to us. The sonic gaze refers to the active, othering dimension of hearing. In the language of musician Charles Mingus, my thesis is that White listeners have "clogged ears," which distort how we hear.[16]

Existentialism is a fruitful theoretical perspective from which to address race and its auditory dimensions. European existentialists Simone de Beauvoir and Jean-Paul Sartre were among the first to name "the gaze." Frantz Fanon's Africana existentialist thought modified and creolized European existentialism, ferreting out Eurocentric assumptions and providing a decolonial agenda. The existential thinking advanced in this book is indebted to Beauvoir, Sartre, and Fanon in particular, and also to the work of Lewis R. Gordon, who has been steadily advancing the Africana existential agenda for over twenty-five years, and who has written extensively on sound.[17] One of the key ideas of Africana existentialism is that philosophy can be articulated in a diversity of geographies and through a diversity of expressive cultures. The pedigree "philosopher" is not necessary for one to be an Africana existentialist.

In *The Sonic Gaze*, I collect vignettes about the existential encounter between audience and performer. By "existential encounter," I allude to Fanon's discussion of the "Look! A Negro," phenomenon, Sartre's case of the voyeur in the hallway, and Beauvoir's observation that, "He is subject; He is the Absolute—she is other."[18] An existential encounter is usually dramatized as a face-to-face reckoning, but it also points to a whole set of social relationships. When Fanon writes in *Black Skin, White Masks* that "After all that has just been said, it will be understood that the first impulse of the Black man is to say *no* to those who attempt to build a definition of him,"[19] he is commenting on the existential encounter between colonized peoples and their colonizers. My Fanonian approach to listening prioritizes the voices of musicians, philosophers, and writers who "say no" to how they have been defined by the White sonic gaze. The novelty of my approach is that I attend to how colonized peoples have been heard, not only how they have been seen.

The question of whether and how colonized peoples are heard is far from new. In 1986 Gayatri Spivak elaborated on her celebrated question, "Can the subaltern speak?" by challenging the "benevolent imperialism" of White, colonial ears. Spivak writes:

> For me the question "Who should speak?" is less crucial than "Who will listen?" "I will speak for myself as a Third World person" is an important position for political mobilization today. But the real demand is that, when I speak from that position, I should be listened to seriously, not with that kind of benevolent imperialism.[20]

Feminist philosophers have frequently "complained," in Sara Ahmed's sense, about being ignored, misheard, and not listened to properly. Beauvoir states in the introduction to *The Second Sex* that "the most mediocre of males thinks himself a demigod compared to women," noting that this male arrogance is expressed though listening to women "on a tone of polite indifference."[21] Inspired by these decolonial and feminist thinkers, I pursue the question they initiated: Who will listen?

Like Mabogo P. More, I have long been drawn to the philosophies of sound and philosophies of listening found in existential thought, particularly that of Sartre, who was a good listener in the sense that "Unlike many white philosophers of his time and even after, Sartre gave a sympathetic ear to the writings and voices of black thinkers."[22] Sartreanism is fundamentally and unapologetically indebted to Black thinkers including Fanon, Wright, Alioune Diop, Leopold Senghor, Aimé Césaire, Albert Memmi, Patrice Lumumba, and others. More reminds us that White thinkers who sympathetically cite and build on Black thinkers do not escape their Whiteness. In fact, "Speaking on behalf of blacks by 'whites of goodwill' has always been a major problem among blacks struggling for freedom in an antiblack world."[23] Souleymane Bachir Diagne goes as far as saying that that Sartre's famous preface to *Black Orpheus* plastered "*a kiss of death* on Senghor's anthology" by overshadowing and distorting the views of the authors it was meant to "introduce" to European ears.[24] In *Black Orpheus*, Sartre addresses himself to a White public: "Here are black men, standing, looking at us, and I hope that you—like me—will feel the shock of being seen."[25] *The existential "shock" of being seen and heard as White is the subject of the current work.* Learning from Spivak, More, and Diagne, White thinkers should choose to engage with Black sound and print culture, with the understanding that in doing so, we are not becoming less White, but rather modifying our "being-White-in-the-world," as Chabani Manganyi might put it.[26]

Reframing race as an aural rather than visual problem threatens to be a one-trick pony. If we replace hearing with vision, then we might fall into abstract ideas about what it means to be "othered" or "gazed at." To develop a phenomenology of listening that is concrete, I have expanded my research outside philosophy, in particular to the fields of sound studies and remix studies. I also draw on a host of jazz writers. The historical and sociological specificity that is routine in studies of listening coming out of these fields has been of the utmost importance to me as I have struggled to "un-discipline" my thinking about jazz, listening, and being-White-in-the-world.

In this book, I am speaking mostly to other White people. By "White" (which I capitalize throughout), I mean the category of personal identity that gives economic, social, political, and cultural power to those light-skinned, European-descended people in the United States (and elsewhere in the West) who are implicitly seen and heard as White by other Whites. I do not think of Whiteness as a form of privilege, but a form of power.[27] Emphasizing the connection between Whiteness and imperial control of land and material resources, Du Bois calls Whiteness "ownership of the earth."[28] Fanon reminds us that in our colonial world, the fundamental division is "first and foremost what species, what race one belongs to. . . . You are rich because you are white, you are white because you are rich."[29] In his recent existentialist defense of antifascism, Devin Z. Shaw outlines why anti-racist activists of the twenty-first century must acknowledge that the "economic hegemony of settler-colonial societies rests on a white hegemony"[30] Being White means having White power, although Whites habitually obscure this fact, adhering to corrosive myths of colorblindness, meritocracy, and exceptionalism.

One last biographical point: I am a philosopher and a musician, and I write as such. If I were not a performer, I don't think it would have occurred to me to write a book about bad listening habits and being misheard by an audience. I don't ever remember not being a musician, but as far back as I can remember, playing improvised music has involved developing critical listening habits. Jazz musicians in particular engage in ear training to become proficient in their craft. Jazz is one kind of improvised music, and I contend that active listening is required of both the jazz performer and the jazz listener. Jazz is the context for most of my theorizing, but my insights about how White people listen are not limited to jazz. I generalize beyond the case of jazz listening to cases like listening in conversations and reading authors in print. I have focused on discourses of jazz in the United States in and around the 1920s because there I have found a robust and informative conversation about mishearing across the color line.

HEARING RACE THROUGH "CLOGGED EARS"

In 1989, Angela Davis published the seminal study of U.S. American blues and jazz women of color: *Blues Legacies and Black Feminism*.[31] In that book, Davis argues that "the recording industry implicitly instructed White ears to feel repulsed by the blues."[32] Davis pioneered a Black feminist phenomenology of the sonic gaze. The White sonic gaze is imposed, as she says, by "White ears." While it may be strange to think of someone else's *ears*—those ugly little blobs of wrinkled flesh that sit on the sides of our heads—as imposing anything, on a phenomenological level, listening is just as active as seeing. As Tendayi Sithole writes, the ear is not passive but takes part actively in "cutting, mixing, and repeating" sound.[33] Listening and looking are both forms of consciousness that reach out into the world. Listening is "intentional" in Edmund Husserl's sense. Sithole proffers: "Listening does not mean being at the receiving end, but being engaged with what is listened to."[34]

Davis shows that White listening practices in the United States were formed through a constellation of "implicit instructions" that have positioned Whites to hear jazz and blues music as "primitive and exotic." Inspired by Davis, I examine how jazz musicians (and others) speak about their experiences of being cast into the role of the "primitive" by Whites who gaze at them with their ears.

The somewhat medical-sounding phrase "clogged ears" is mixed-race jazz musician Charles Mingus's metaphor for his experience of the White sonic gaze. The case of Mingus is a good starting point for thinking about how racialized listening orientations have been formed and contested in American jazz culture. In 1959, while performing at the Five Spot in New York, Mingus was dissatisfied with the way his White audience was listening.[35] From the bandstand, Mingus shouted: "You're phonies. You're here because jazz has publicity . . . and you like to associate yourself with this sort of thing. But it doesn't make you a connoisseur of the art because you follow it around. . . . A blind man can go to an exhibition of Picasso and Kline and not even see their works. And comment behind dark glasses, Wow! They're the swingingest painters ever, crazy! Well, so can you. You've got your dark glasses and clogged-up ears."[36]

This existential encounter at the Five Spot dramatizes the negotiation of phenomenological space between performer and audience. Mingus was describing his experience of the White sonic gaze and saying "no" to it. He accused his audience of being fakes, inverting the role of critic and audience.

This encounter is a Fanonian refusal: Mingus feels misrecognized by his audience's White listening habits. He charges the White hipsters in the audience with listening badly because they are listening Whitely.[37]

As Fumi Okiji shows, Mingus's outburst is an example of a musician giving his audience ear training.

> Mingus shows us—in fact he embodies—the paradox of hypervisibility and mis- or nonrecognition. He exposes his audience as blind to black America and deaf to its music. The audience's ears are "clogged up," keeping them from the "truths" that the music could tell. . . .[38]

While Mingus's metaphor is objectionably ableist (being "deaf" is not a deficit, nor is being "blind"), his point stands. By telling the audience they need ear training, Mingus challenges the assumption that listening is passive. To feel objectified by others' listening practices is to feel them as acts of power. Mingus's comments reveal the intersubjectivity of listening. Listening can be reciprocal or nonreciprocal. Mingus, in other words, has an existential account of listening. He posits that listening is an act of creation. Because the audience is part of the performance, and because listening is performative, the audience's listening may need to be guided, not unlike an auxiliary member of the band.

While all of us know the experience of being misheard, it can be difficult to articulate why or how the other is mis-listening. We say, "You are not listening," but what exactly does this mean?

Mingus has a sonic understanding of the existential gaze. His statement that his White audience has clogged ears is a dramatic example of how artists instruct their public to listen. Such listening instructions are discussed throughout this book. I compile voices of people who have felt alienated by their experiences with the White sonic gaze. These voices reveal that being misheard is a fundamental type of social misrecognition. The first-person experience of sonic misrecognition might be expressed in the sentiment: "I do not hear myself in the way you are listening to me."

My project of hearing race will be organized around three questions, which also constitute the three main chapters of this book. Chapter 2 asks: What phenomenological descriptions of the White sonic gaze have emerged from White theorists? Chapter 3 asks: What phenomenological descriptions of the White sonic gaze have emerged from Creole theorists? And chapter 4 asks: What phenomenological descriptions of the White sonic gaze have emerged from Black theorists?

My answers are not comprehensive, whether philosophical or historical. Most of the effort of this book consists in weaving together source materials that have otherwise not been placed in relationship to each other.

WHITENESS AS SONIC ORIENTATION

The central argument of this book—that there are racialized listening orientations that form the background of experience—would be inconceivable without the writings of Sara Ahmed. It is from Ahmed that I borrow the notion that Whiteness is a phenomenological orientation. She writes: "Whiteness could be described as an ongoing and un-finished history, which orientates bodies in specific directions, affecting how they 'take up' space."[39] In *Queer Phenomenology: Orientations, Objects, Others*, Ahmed shows how White orientations are "styles, capacities, aspirations, techniques, [and] habits."[40] In my usage, a "White orientation" is a conscious, embodied position from which the world unfolds to an agent. Being oriented whitely includes the full spectrum of senses: tasting, touching, smelling, seeing, and of course, hearing. Like Ahmed's feminist analysis of smiling, my goal is to take a mundane experience—listen to music—and peel back the obvious until we get at how sexism, Whiteness, and heteronormativity are "lived as a background" to the experience of listening.[41]

My trope of "the sonic gaze" references the racialized listening habits that have formed the background of auditory experiences in the United States. The idea of a *sonic* orientation is an extension of Ahmedian thinking. Ahmed's work is rich with provocations about listening, and her recent work conducting oral interviews with diversity workers models a feminist politics of listening. The orientational approach is well-suited to describing the social, institutional spaces where we listen.

Ahmed's work on orientations—and her work on feminism, race, and queer theory—is compelling in part because of her skill in creating phenomenological archives of experiences that speak to her audiences. In *The Promise of Happiness*, Ahmed weaves together personal stories with analyses of literary and theoretical texts. In *On Being Included* she fashions a phenomenological, archival method that prioritizes the first-person perspective of women of color. On her blog *feministkillljoys* in a post titled "Complaint as Diversity Work,"[42] Ahmed begins with a powerful feminist act, that of listening. "I am listening . . ." is the first line of that entry. The importance of Ahmed's "I am listening" is that it positions feminist ears to listen to the sound, speech, and voices of other women. In thinking about what distinguishes feminist listening from nonfeminist listening, we can consider to whom we are listening as well as how we are listening. "I am listening to those who have made complaints," Ahmed writes.[43]

The feminist practice of listening gives feminist complaints somewhere "to go." The feminist archive is a resonator for voices that are otherwise buried by the very institutions they were meant to challenge. The feminism of feminist archives has to do with the community of listeners and their collective engagement. Ahmed writes, "Feminism: living with consequences. A complaint: when a collective is necessary to bring something about. Complaint as diversity work: what we have to do to dismantle the structures that do not accommodate us. We are with you; we hear you. Feminism is about giving a complaint somewhere to go."[44] The current work is inspired by the idea of "giving a complaint somewhere to go," in that it aims to restate critiques of Whiteness that have been ignored by traditional philosophical and popular approaches to jazz, sound, and music.

EXISTENTIAL PHENOMENOLOGY

The Sonic Gaze tells the story of musicians and writers who have felt alienated by how White audiences listen to them. Critiques of White listening exist in various cultural sites, including Black abolitionist literature, Black journalism of the teens and twenties, Creole autobiographies, and also within the lyrics and sonic content of jazz and blues music.

I document how Black and Creole authors call out the Whiteness of dominant listening practices in the United States. Critiques of voyeuristic and primitivist White listening practices can be found in the work of Black anti-slavery writers Frederick Douglass and Harriet Jacobs. Critiques of White listening blossomed in the Black press of the teens and twenties. Harlem Renaissance writers Alain Locke and Zora Neale Hurston studied performance contexts for Black music, spelling out philosophical critiques of authenticity. A classic critique of White listening can be found, for instance, in Alain Locke's 1928 article, "Art or Propaganda," where he encourages fellow Black artists to stop trying to correct White mishearing.[45]

Critiques of White listening in Creole sources are also plentiful. I analyze the work of Creole jazz pioneer Sidney Bechet, showing how his autobiographical writing constitutes a phenomenology of "listening to difference." I also draw on the Creole music of Kid Ory and the Original Creole Band.

In conducting my research, I have been struck by how often what I thought were new insights into White listening turned out to be well-known observations within communities of color. A common dynamic is that writers and musicians in Black, mixed race, and Creole communities write and perform *for each other*, while noting how their work is misheard by Whites.

In my chapter on Whites talking about Whiteness, I examine popular writings from *The Etude* (an early music magazine), as well as the writings of Paul Whiteman and Mezz Mezzrow, who contributed to the emergence of White listening habits in the early days of jazz. I study contemporary White writers, arguing that they often fail to thematize their White racial embodiment. I challenge White thinkers who propose that disembodied, colorblind listening is the best way to hear music.

The Sonic Gaze comes out of the tradition of existential phenomenology. I understand phenomenology as a philosophical approach that describes reality from the perspective of the first person. In the words of Jacqueline M. Martinez: "Both a theoretical perspective concerning the nature of human existence and an applied research procedure for explicating features of human existence, phenomenology offers a rich field of discourse and practice. . . . As a theoretical perspective, phenomenology focuses our attention on the lifeworld and lived experiences of persons."[46]

Martinez's conception of the existential task of phenomenology is particularly apt to the study of listening. I draw frequently on the idea of a listening encounter, that is, the intersubjective experience of listening that reveals how we are "always already part of a social and cultural momentum."[47] Phenomenology allows us to move from the face-to-face experiences to those structures "in which every human consciousness is situated."[48] A phenomenology of listening attunes us to the deep structures of sonic experience.

Martinez articulates the importance of the connecting phenomenology and autobiography. "The autobiographical emphasis . . . has been an essential space within which I have struggled with these conflicting and ambiguous experiences of consciousness."[49] Martinez's Chicana-feminist phenomenology instructs us how "to focus the autobiographical account on . . . consciousness of lived experience and identify key events that generated . . . conscious awareness of race, ethnicity, cultural heritage, privilege, and power."[50] The autobiographical perspectives that I consult fall into three broad racial categories: White, Black, and Creole voices.

Finally, Martinez's conception of Chicana phenomenology has influenced my thinking about who counts as a phenomenologist. She notes that a genuine commitment to phenomenology will force the theorist to begin listening in new ways. The phenomenologist will listen to voices that speak to experience, regardless of pedigree. "Encountering the critical perspective taken by Chicana lesbians and other women of color has had a far greater effect in my developing capacity to describe my experiences of race, ethnicity, and sexuality than my formal study of semiotics and phenomenology."[51] Like Martinez, I have found it important to have one foot in philosophy and one foot outside of philosophy. It has taken me a long time to write this book, in part because I have struggled to untrain myself from some of the bad philosophical habits I learned in the academy. For example, it has taken me a long time to articulate why I think the jazz musician Sidney Bechet is a phenomenologist.

I draw on philosophers canonically associated with existentialism, new philosophical approaches to existentialism that are emerging from the Caribbean and Global South, my own intuitions as a living existentialist, as well as the inchoate existentialism of various expressive cultures in the United States associated with jazz music and culture.

VISUALISM

As Don Ihde,[52] Jacques Attali,[53] Martin Jay,[54] and Jonathan Sterne[55] have shown, philosophers have taken vision to be the default sense. Philosophers writing about race have shown similar tendencies. *Blackness Visible: Essays on Philosophy and Race*[56] by Charles W. Mills describes the visual features of racial identity. In his classic article "But What Are You Really: The Metaphysics of Race,"[57] Mill notes the "evasion" of race in mainstream American philosophy: "Race has not traditionally *been seen* as an interesting or worthy subject of investigation for White Western philosophers, although it has, of course, been the central preoccupation of Black intellectuals in the West."[58] Analyses of racial identity in the United States need to be placed in a global context. As readers outside the United States are quick to recognize, the American racial system is largely based on a Black/White binary that obscures our thinking about mixed-race, Creole, Latinx, and other racially nonbinary peoples.[59] It is binary racial logic produces the question: "But what are you *really*?" This racial logic is also strongly visualist, as revealed by the persistence of "the eye-ball test."[60]

While Linda Martín Alcoff agrees with Mills's claim that in the United States the eye-ball test dominates, her work *Visible Identities* moves away from reductive visualism. [61] By naming some social identities as "visible," Alcoff recognizes the presence of nonvisual racial identifiers. Alcoff has shown how "Race and gender operate as our penultimate visible identifies," while also opening up the category of identity to the fuller spectrum of phenomenological differences, including auditory difference.[62] Alcoff's theorizing is particularly attuned to the problem of reducing mixed-race categories to the Black/White binary familiar in the United States.

Paul C. Taylor's *Race: A Philosophical Introduction* takes racial discourse or "race talk" as its entry point, thus avoiding an immediate appeal to the visual.[63] Like Taylor, I also take discourse as an entry point, though I am interested in how language reveals and structures experience. In *Black Is Beautiful: A Philosophy of Black Aesthetics*, Taylor challenges visualism by "theorize[ing] the (in)visible."[64] He critiques "ocularcentrism" and concludes that "visuality must be essentially racialized."[65] Taylor demonstrates that within Black aesthetics, vision has usually been treated critically—it has been noticed as a particular form of conscious experience and social control. Black invisibility and hypervisibility are a major theme of African American literature.[66] In passing, Taylor articulates with clarity the dynamic that I have taken as my subject in *The Sonic Gaze*: "I will in what follows focus on . . . racial misperception. As it happens, misperceiving Blacks is a danger for both Whitely and anti-Whitely forms of expressive culture. 'Whitely' refers here to the ways of interpreting, navigating, and inhabiting the world that are consistent with or that follow from White supremacist ideology. . . . Interestingly, opposition to Whiteliness does not guarantee a commitment to Black visibility."[67] Taylor and I both treat the term "whitely" as an adverb for how White folks "interpret, navigate, and inhabit" their world. Taylor and I both take "racial misperception" to be a fundamental fact of aesthetic experience that needs unpacking. Where Taylor and I diverge is more a matter of emphasis than principle: I prioritize Black and Creole authors who speak to the combined feeling of being invisible and inaudible.

STUDYING SOUND

My existentialist approach to listening is indebted to an interdisciplinary body of scholarship on sound. I note my debt to scholars working in the areas of sound studies, remix theory, and philosophy of music.

Scholars working in the field of sound studies have opened new discussions about the political economy of sound and the connections between seeing, hearing, technology, and reality. The collection *Sound Clash: Listening to American Studies*,[68] edited by Kara Keeling and Josh Kun, brings together innovative methods for challenging "sound's marginality."[69] Keeling and Kun note: "More and more scholars across a variety of disciplines are beginning to not only take the culture, consumption and politics of sound seriously but are making it the centerpiece of their research, publishing and pedagogy."[70] My existential account of White listening is also a way of "listening back" to "foundational moments in American political history."[71] Nina Sun Eidsheim's recently published *The Race of Sound*[72] confronts us with the fact that listening is a form of social power: "No ear is innocent."[73]

Jonathan Sterne's *The Audible Past* is one of the original texts of sound studies. In that book, Sterne is critical of phenomenology, which he describes as the attempt to find "trans historical description[s] of human listening experience."[74] Sterne proposes to study sound by exploring what he calls "audile techniques," or "sets of practices of listening."[75] Like Sterne, I have found historically specific accounts of listening to be the most informative. My use of vignettes is consistent with Sterne's project of describing a "genealogy of new constructs of sound and hearing."[76] As an existential phenomenologist, I agree that "the emergence of sound-reproduction technologies" should be studied along with the "dynamic history of the body."[77] Technology and habit are indeed intertwined, and Sartre even had a phrase for this intertwinement: "the practico-inert."[78]

Sterne urges us to treat listening as an embodied experience: "An appeal to the 'phenomenological' truth about sound sets up experience as somehow outside the purview of historical analysis. This need not be so—phenomenology and the study of experience are not by definition opposed to historicism."[79] I show that the habits of listening to jazz in the United States are racialized, gendered, and tied to particular spaces and times. My study corroborates one of the central ideas in *The Audible Past*—that of the "audio-visual litany." The audio-visual litany "idealizes hearing (and, by extension, speech) as manifesting a kind of pure interiority."[80] The White sonic gaze is indebted to the audio-visual litany, while criticisms of White listening often challenge the assumption that listening is passive. The critiques of White hearing below all argue for active listening. The phenomenological approach can draw on and expand the way sound studies theorists have shown that "sounds makes us re-think our relation to power."[81]

Philosophers interested in music and sound would benefit from exploring the field of remix studies. In his 2012 book *Remix Theory: The Aesthetics of Sampling*,[82] Eduardo Navas articulates a theory of sound that is responsive to the cultural shifts that have accompanied changes in mechanical sound reproduction. Remix theory has aided me in thinking about the interaction between bodies, machines, background noises, and those noises we foreground as "music." Remix theory is an extended discussion of active listening. As Navas shows, theorizing sound in the twenty-first century requires us to admit that "To remix is to compose."[83]

Dick Hebdige's *Cut-n-Mix: Culture, Identity and Caribbean Music* argues that remix is not just a way to think about DJ culture, but a philosophical approach to sound, mass culture, and music.[84] What Hebdige and remix scholars call "versioning" can be a powerful tool for thinking about jazz, and for contextualizing it as one among many creolized New World music forms.[85] Versioning refers to the Caribbean practice of releasing many separate versions of the same track, each with a variation and comment on the other. Versioning is connected to sampling, which Navas defines as a "meta-activity that follows early forms of sound capturing."[86] In my contribution to *Keywords in Remix Studies*, edited by Eduardo Navas, Owen Gallagher, and xtine burrough, I argue that jazz musicians employed a proto-version of the remix when they repurposed their turntables to learn music from records.[87] The broad implications of this specific practice—jazz musicians repurposing turntables—is that a phenomenologically and historically sensitive approach to theorizing sound must treat machines, bodies, and backgrounds as active ingredients in our perceptions of sound. As Tashima Thomas has shown, there are many sonic and visual texts that we can read through remix theory:

She has studied the Casta paintings of Creole elites in Mexico in the colonial period as a form of remix.[88] Thomas exhibits a synesthetic approach to "the aesthetics of race," reading visual and auditory texts for how they disclose messages about racial mixture between African, European, and Indigenous peoples in the New World.

In addition to sound studies and remix studies, I have been influenced by recent work in the philosophy of music. The philosopher of music Robin James has written extensively about the conjunction of aesthetics and politics. In *The Conjectural Body: Gender, Race, and the Philosophy of Music*,[89] James articulates an important premise of race-critical aesthetics: "[T]he relationship between music and race is not just one of exemplarity; rather, in the West, the concepts of music and race/culture are related at a more fundamental level."[90] James demonstrates that race, gender, class, and sound do not "intersect," for if they did, there would also be a point at which sound could be considered raceless, genderless, and bodiless.[91] I also borrow ideas from James's *Resistance and Melancholy*, a book that offers an "upgraded" approach to the existential gaze.[92] James brings to light how "resistance" has become the new narrative about how to navigate the damaging effects of the colonial gaze.[93]

With respect to theorizing jazz listening, James's work moves us away from the "over-simplistic opposition of European musician conventions and African/African-American musical conventions."[94] She identifies the importance of the relationship between audience and performer in Black music when she writes that "the blues requires cooperation."[95] In "Oppression, Privilege, & Aesthetics," James argues that jazz aesthetics—swing rhythm and blue notes in particular—were "racially unruly."[96] This unruliness was lost when the music was modified to satisfy White mainstream commercial tastes.[97] Engaging Ahmed, Alcoff, and phenomenology, James had led the way for theorizing Whiteness as an aural orientation: "Treating race and gender as horizons or orientations foregrounds the role of the aesthetic."[98]

James's most recent monograph, *The Sonic Episteme*,[99] is an exploration of sound and neoliberalism that argues that we are witnessing "versions of the same updated relations of domination and subordination."[100] One point of convergence between James's rich work and my own is that we both draw on cultural studies, sound studies, and philosophy to develop a mixed methodological approach to sound. I agree with James that "the sonic episteme misrepresents sociohistorically specific concepts of sound and vision as their universal, 'natural' character."[101] In studying White U.S. American listening habits, it is important to study cases at length. The existentialist term for this is "situational" thinking.

Other approaches to music that have been important to me include the work of Ingrid Monson, beginning with her book *Saying Something: Jazz*

Improvisation and Interaction.[102] I appreciate Monson's mixed methodology and her attention to race. Anticipating my central argument, she articulates "a striking American cultural paradox," namely, "White Americans have taken up Black musical styles in the twentieth century while at the same time failing to address the cultural implications of this process."[103] In *Freedom Sounds*,[104] Monson analyzes public discourse about jazz in the 1950s and 1960s, locating a key example of White colorblind listening. She hits the nail on the head, revealing that White critics wrote from a position of "White fear of exclusion (by the excluded)."[105] However, Monson's conclusions in *Freedom Sounds* are different from my own. While Monson treats colorblind White discourse as an act of power that is fed by White fears of exclusion, I think she may end up with a position that is not much different from the one she critiques, which I will call, following Robin James's use of the term, "upgraded" colorblind listening. *Freedom Sounds* concludes with the sentiment we must move beyond the "rhetorical gridlock" between colorblind jazz critics and the supposed cultural protectionism of Afrocentric jazz critics. I am unconvinced that speaking about fixing a "gridlock" is productive. Such a framework posits White voices and Black voices on jazz as two equal partners engaged in a discussion where there can be a friendly agreement to disagree. The power dynamic of White philosophers and critics offering to "settle" historical debates elevates them (us) to a position of arbiter.

Similarly, my work diverges from recent philosophical discussions of jazz by Bruce Ellis Benson, Lee E. Brown, and Theodore Gracyk. Benson's *The Improvisation of Musical Dialogue: A Phenomenology of Music* is a useful starting point for gaining conceptual clarity over the terms "jazz" and "improvised music."[106] Benson's main point is accurate, but not surprising to those whose philosophical orientation is phenomenological: Some jazz is nonimprovised, and some classical music is improvisatory. I agree that improvised music cannot be mapped onto the jazz/classical distinction.[107] By my lights, the deeper issue is exposing the Eurocentric assumptions that underlie the jazz/classical distinction.[108] What is the political economy of this distinction?

The philosopher Theodore Gracyk has written extensively on jazz. Gracyk has a historically informed approach, but unlike Monson, his view of race is flawed at the outset. For example, in their 2018 title, *Jazz and the Philosophy of Art*,[109] Gracyk, Lee Brown, and David Goldblatt argue that "postmodern" and "Afrocentric" jazz writers have constructed a cultural myth that "Whites 'took' Black music and made it their own: that music that is somehow essentially Black was co-opted by Whites."[110] In a pattern common among authors who advocate racial colorblindness, they cite examples of Black jazz musicians who have been influenced by White musicians, believing these cases are evidence against structural anti-Black racism in jazz. These authors write wistfully about "The tendency of many well-meaning White people to identify with the plight of Black people. Is this identification doomed to failure just because the White person will never get it?"[111] In this passage, Gracyk, Lee, and Goldblatt unintentionally describe one of the forms of White listening I explore in depth. Both White hipster listeners and the White revivalist listeners are "well-meaning White people" who love jazz and who listen to the music "to identify with the plight of Black people." Further, when Gracyk, Brown, and Goldblatt draw on the history of Congo Square, they appeal to "one eyewitness account of a ritual that took place around 1825 and describes a strongly Dionysian scene."[112] These authors cite a long passage from this White "eyewitness," whose language is typical of White colonial onlookers whose mix of fascination and fear with Black culture has been the subject of so much discussion in Africana thought.[113] Brown, Goldblatt, and Gracyk take this description at face value, failing to note its colonial, racist language. By contrast, Martin Munro is highly critical of the imperial, White sonic gaze.[114] His study of the history of rhythm shows how colonial descriptions of the practices of Black, Creole, and other non-White people were (and are) political instruments. Munro traces the White fascination with Africana culture to M.L.E. Moreau, whose 1796 writings on dances in Haiti reported a "magnetism" that "had been felt by Whites spying on the ceremony."[115] As Munro articulates, the colonial sonic gaze has been a way to "beat back darkness."[116] The White fascination with Voodoo is part of a long history of the "envy" and "dread" Whites have described in their encounters with racialized others. While authors such as Kathy Ogren[117] and Ted Gioia[118] have detailed discourses of primitivism surrounding jazz in the 1920s, Munro's work demonstrates that the association of Black rhythm with ecstasy, Dionysianism, and a "hypnotic" power over Whites has an earlier tie. Moreau's imperial gaze that looked upon the Voodoo dance was transmuted into an imperial gaze that looked upon improvising jazz musicians as "entranced" performers of wild, jungle music.

Beyond the few titles listed above, I have been influenced by theorists from a wide variety of backgrounds who have taken up the relationship of sound to race. My inquiry builds on the enlivening work of Jon Cruz,[119] Ronald Radano,[120] Guthrie P. Ramsey Jr.,[121] Alex Weheliye,[122] Karl Hagstom Miller,[123] and others.

I will also mention Eric Lott's 1993 treatment of Blackface minstrelsy *Love and Theft*,[124] which shifted scholarly understandings of the genre of the minstrel show and provided a framework for analyzing White investments in non-White music, culture, and experience. Lott transformed how many of us think about the tradition of Blackface minstrelsy by turning away from questions of authenticity to the question of why White U.S. Americans identified or even "disidentified" with Blackness.[125]

Patrick B. Mullen's *The Man Who Adores the Negro: Race and American Folklore* also takes up the question of why Whites in the United States "adore" Blackness.[126] Mullen draws his title from Fanon's powerful insight that "To us, the man who adores the Negro is as 'sick' as the man who abominates him."[127] Mullen is a White folklorist who spent his life studying Black culture; at the end of his career, he reflects on the pathological, systematic misrepresentation of Blackness within folklore studies, a field he helped build. Mullen, however, like Monson, ends his book with ideas on how to "fix mistakes" and work "collaboratively across racial lines."[128] This move shows how the listening orientation of a well-intentioned White ethnographer can end in bad faith. Mullen's book is a sincere account of a White expert who is aware of critiques of Whiteness. But Mullen does not accept the necessary steps for challenging the White love of Blackness, which include: rethinking the basic methods in the fields of folklore studies and jazz studies; turning from the study of Blackness to the study of Whiteness; and avoiding the logic of "inclusion" that reproduces racism against people of color. Mullen shows that American music archives were created through a colonial White love of Blackness. But Mullen's book is disappointing because it attempts to return self-critical Whites to a happy place, where they can listen to jazz archives in peace and treat colonialism a thing of the past.

Robin D. G. Kelley's extensive work on jazz and Africana aesthetics has been an inspiration for the current work. From *Africa Speaks, America Answers*[129] I have tried to learn how to bring together a group of different musicians, writers, and theorists under one cover, even when "They shared neither a common agenda nor a common culture, though they recognized and often embraced cultural commonalities, 'jazz' being one."[130] Kelley's writing is phenomenologically rich, and blends first-person observations, synesthetic thinking, and an agenda of freedom. In the preface to *Thelonious Monk: The Life and Times of an American Original*,[131] Kelley describes how he formed his jazz listening orientation as a young musician by learning Monk's masterpiece "Evidence."[132] Kelley thinks and writes with his ears. As a musician, philosopher, and writer, he is in a particularly good position to teach us how to be better in our attempts to write about something that we can only hear—sound.

At one point, I considered calling this book *Black Noise/White Ears* as a riff on Tricia Rose's amazing title *Black Noise*.[133] In that work, and also in *The Hip Hop Wars*, Rose established a framework for analyzing sound, race, and U.S. American culture.[134] Her discussion of the noisiness of Black noise points to how listening and audience participation are central to hip-hop culture. A key insight I take from Rose is that music theorists should not reduce "Black cultural signs and codes" to the "White voyeuristic pleasure of Black cultural imagery."[135]

In sum, there is a rich literature on the subject of Whiteness and listening. My own basic theoretical commitment is to existentialism, which I treat as a vocabulary for describing human freedom, human consciousness, and relations to others. Existentialism is a flexible approach that must be continually "upgraded" (to use Robin James's term) if it is to remain a living theory.

THE SONIC GAZE

As mentioned, Francophone existentialists Frantz Fanon, Simone de Beauvoir, and Jean-Paul Sartre were among the first to make the gaze a crux of their analysis. As Sterne notes, the gaze has subsequently taken on a life of its own, beyond phenomenology, in areas like film studies, feminism, critical race theory, and poststructuralism.[136] I suggest how the existential notions of intentionality, recognition, intersubjectivity, and freedom can be rethought by prioritizing sound. How we listen to other people is a fundamental aspect of who we are.

The phrase "sonic gaze" is awkward. I take it as a sign that Sterne is correct about the audio-visual litany that in our language we have no good name for the objectifying, othering, alienating effects of being misheard. Using Sartre's notion of existential shame—being frozen by the consciousness of the other—we might speak of sonic shame. Once again, the label is bad, although the phenomenon is clear. Just as another person can stare at me and turn me into stone, a person can listen to me and turn me into stone. It should be remembered that in Sartre's classic example of the voyeur in the hallway, it is the *sound* of the other's footsteps that triggers existential shame.

Fanon is especially attuned to the sonic dimensions of the White gaze. In chapter 5 of *Black Skin, White Masks*, "The Fact of Blackness," he explains the dynamic of the racialized White gaze with the unforgettable line: "'Dirty ni****!' Or simply, 'Look, a Negro!'"[137] Fanon goes on to express the effects of the racial gaze: "The glances of the other fixed me there, in the sense in which a chemical solution is fixed by a dye." "For not only must the Black man be Black; he must be Black in relation to the White man."[138] Fanonian thinking asks us to theorize looking and listening as colonial forms of power. As an existential thinker, Fanon treats Whiteness and Blackness as social categories that are relational. As he states, to "be Black" is to be so in relation to others, especially Whites.

Glen Coulthard's *Red Skins, White Masks*[139] and Hamid Dabashi's *Brown Skin, White Masks*[140] are evidence of the ongoing relevance of decolonial, existential approaches to White culture. Coulthard and Dabashi refigure Fanon's criticism of White gazing for two related contemporary struggles: the decolonial efforts of Indigenous peoples in Canada (and globally), and the decolonial efforts of Muslims in North America, Western Europe, and globally.[141] Dabashi's anti-imperialist view challenges us to notice how sound colonizes; in particular, he studies how the "accents from targeted cultures and climes Orientalize, [and] exoticize." Meanwhile from a privileged position, the colonist "no longer hears [his] own imperial accent."[142]

Aaron Oforlea's Fanonian, decolonial reading of the American folklorist Alan Lomax also shows the relevance of a living existentialist approach to Whiteness and sound. His article "[Un]veiling the White Gaze" starts from the existential idea that "Black culture [is] continually constructed by the White gaze."[143] Oforlea uses Africana existentialism to "fruitfully critique" the work of White American writers. This critique requires that we attend to both language and experience. Language is important, for, as Fanon showed, the term "Negro"—along with other modern versions "Black" and "African American" and "person of color"—"embody and represent a history of Othering."[144] The White gaze uncritically adopts Black cultural objects, instead of treating White and Black as relational social categories. The White gaze covers up its ideological work by insisting that it is a neutral and natural.

Criticizing the Eurocentrism of Sartre's and Beauvoir's notions of the gaze is not a primary purpose of the current work, though it is an ongoing task for any creolizing, living existential philosophy. Sartre's *Anti-Semite and Jew*[145] with its claim that anti-semites "create the Jew," still holds up more or less, but the conversation has expanded significantly. Two points are important. First, Fanon showed how Sartre failed to understand the lifeworld of the marginalized people he celebrated and romanticized. Regarding the main thesis of *Anti-Semite and Jew*, Lewis Gordon notes that "Those who adhere to Abraham's covenant have lived long before anyone decided to hate them. What anti-Semites make, or in phenomenological language, *constitutes* is the pejorative conception of being Jewish."[146] I would add that Sartre had a romanticized and often phenomenologically thin idea about the experiences of women, Jews, Black people, and queer people, all of whom he wrote about. While Sartre owned his Whiteness and insistent that his aim in *Anti-semite and Jew* was to expose the White liberal and the White anti-semite from within, his White critique of Whiteness (like all White critiques of Whiteness) threatens to reinscribe the power it names. Naomi Zack has argued that Whites who write about Whiteness in the effort to deconstruct their racial identities sometimes reinforce White power.[147] Naming the White gaze can be a roundabout way of placing White experiences back at the center. My historical discussion of White listening deals with this problem by acknowledging that theorizing Whiteness is a long tradition in communities of color, and a new tradition among Whites. To highlight the diversity of these traditions, I examine three cultural perspectives on White listening: White, African American, and Creole.

One of the dynamics of White listening that I hope to short-circuit is the willed ignorance of White writers who believed that they are "damned if they do and damned if they don't" speak about Whiteness. This logic holds that if we White writers do not mark our Whiteness and speak to issues of race, then we will be accused of colorblind racist thinking and White privilege. The flipside of this White logic is that White writers who cite non-White theorists and incorporate them into their perspective will be accused of appropriation. I believe this assumption of "damned if I do and damned if I don't" reflects the growing pains of philosophy and other disciplines that have allowed their White majorities to go unnoticed. White theorists (myself included) must learn to navigate philosophical conversations that place us at the margin and turn us into objects of study. We must learn to *listen differently* as we study the long history of critiques of the White sonic gaze.

CREOLIZING LISTENING

Mainstream and academic jazz writing is full of White scholars stating what they think about Creole people of color in New Orleans. By Creole people of color, I mean those mixed-race, often French-, Spanish-, English- and/or Creole-speaking people who have self-identified as Creole in the context of New Orleans and its surrounding areas. In 1803, when Louisiana became part of the United States, it was—in the words of Martinican creolist writer Édouard Glissant—"a land of creolization."[148] Following Glissant, I will treat New Orleans as a creolizing space, in the sense that its basic cultural patterns are not unlike those of Port-au-Prince, Havana, San Juan, or Port of Spain, from architecture to food to the struggle of mixed-race, Africana people against colonialism.

The absence of Creole voices in contemporary discussions of jazz is worrisome. White scholars sometimes talk to themselves, without a consciousness of being gazed at or listened to from non-White vantage points. As I argue in chapter 2, White discourses about Creole people of color mainly follow the pattern set out by ethnomusicologist Alan Lomax (1915–2002) in his best-selling biography *Mister Jelly Roll* (1950).[149] Lomax is a paradigm case of a White listener who "gazes" as he listens. His gaze is loving, not hateful, and yet it "creates" its object in Sartre's, Fanon's, and Gordon's sense. In the subsequent chapter, I explore how Creole theorists have theorized White listening. I study the work of Creole composer, musician, and writer Sidney Bechet, arguing that his autobiography *Treat It Gentle* (1960) is a creolizing corrective to what we could call, following Spivak, the "benevolent imperialism" of Lomax.[150]

In speaking of a creolizing corrective in philosophy, I mean to build on the work initiated by not only Glissant, but also more recently by Jane A. Gordon,[151] Michael J. Monahan,[152] and others. Neil Roberts and Jane A. Gordon are editors of the Rowman & Littlefield International book series *Creolizing the Canon*, which has published numerous works articulating the project of creolization.[153]

These creolist scholars implicitly point to a practice of *creolizing listening*. I will argue that Glissant's notion of "digenesis" is important for theorists of sound. Digenesis is a neologism. I use the concept to mean a style of thinking about culture that does not reduce cultural patterns to single origins. Everyone is familiar with single-origin (or "genetic") accounts of jazz—nearly all of which point to Congo Square. The digenetic account of jazz I offer suggests multiple origins of jazz, including well-known places like St. Louis and Kansas City, as well as smaller, forgotten spaces like Joplin, Missouri.[154] Digenetic thinking is a complement to phenomenological thinking about jazz, for it provides a historically, culturally thick treatment of roots. Creolized aesthetic forms, like jazz and other Caribbean music, cannot best be described with appeals to authenticity such as those found in Lomax. Instead of the narrative that "jazz could only have happen in the United States," the digenetic approach insists that jazz is closely related to other syncopated music across the Americas and especially in the Caribbean.

Glissant is relevant for White Americans who want to critically reappraise their listening habits. He developed the notion of digenesis through an engagement with the prose of American writer William Faulkner. The pattern Glissant notices in Faulkner is the pattern that I notice in American jazz discourse—many American writers are committed to an exceptionalist logic that presents the United States as the "only place" where jazz could have been born. This narrative is pervasive—just check Ken Burns's popular television series *Jazz*. Exceptionalist thinking about jazz places Americans outside of time and space, outside the influence of colonialism, and outside the transnational forces of White supremacy.

As a corrective to the nationalistic assumption that jazz is uniquely American, digenetic cultural explanations point to "circularity" and "halting attempts at creation."[155] As La Rose Parris argues, "Jazz reflects a larger Africana expression of dissent against empire and Western hegemony while still, ineluctably, reflecting the influence of Western and Africana culture."[156] Drawing on Kamau Brathwaite, Parris shows the deep connections between jazz and Caribbean music, language, and culture. The digenetic account of jazz does not treat styles of performance and listening practices as replacing one another in a logical order. Jazz culture in the United States did not "progress" toward a fixed goal. We find, for example, an unevenness about ideas of Black belonging and Creole belonging depending on era, geography, and gender. On the flipside, White rhetoric linking jazz to primitiveness, drugs, crime, and race-mixing has not changed much, but has been recycled across different periods of American discourse.

Creolization is an intellectual posture that is skeptical about appeals to cultural authenticity. Glissant writes: "It is no longer valid to glorify 'unique' origins that the race safeguards and prolongs."[157] My work links Glissantian digenesis with phenomenological descriptions of space and race. I study how the physical space of the plantation was the background geography for musical production in early jazz performance and listening. Just as plantation systems repeated themselves across the Caribbean—as Benítez-Rojo masterfully shows in *The Repeating Island*—Afro-diasporic musical styles repeat themselves.[158] As jazz emerged from the minstrel show, performers' references to the plantation lifestyle shifted. I examine how Creole artists referenced the plantation in their performances through the names of their bands and their repertoire. Creole artists who used the sounds and images of plantation life in their performances were both entertaining Whites and articulating a musical a response to White racial terror.

My three main chapters—one each on White, Black, and Creole perspectives on listening—would suggest that I think of Creole as a third racial categorical that can be added to the American Black/White binary. However, treating Creole as a third category of race is problematic on historical and conceptual grounds. Creolizing thought will "deconstruct . . . the category of 'creolized' that is considered as halfway between two 'pure' extremes."[159] Historically, one of the elements of Creole racialization in New Orleans has been that subjects raced as Creole have strategically occupied, challenged, or straddled other racial categories, as Angel Adams Parham has shown.[160] In *Blues People*, Amiri Baraka tells how Creole musicians—he mentions Jelly Roll Morton—sometimes emphasized their Whiteness and European-ness in order to shield themselves from anti-Black racism.[161] The experiences of the members of the Original Creole Band, Sidney Bechet, and Kid Ory reveal different ways of living Creole identity. Bechet's autobiography is about being both Creole and Black. As will become clear, the phenomenology of Creole experience has multiple variations. The implications for writing a philosophy that is responsive to these variations in Creole identity claims is that we must be willing to suspend the assumption that someone simply "is" or "is not" Creole, given that being Creole (in New Orleans, and also elsewhere in the Caribbean) has meant challenging binary racial logic. We must learn how to treat the category of Creole digenetically, rather than relying on the dominant codes of race that appeal to the concept of authenticity and single genesis.

The projects of hearing race and creolizing listening are complementary. I will treat creolizing as a strategy, a tactic, an epistemological frame, and a philosophical orientation toward experience. Most of the cases of White listening I describe are about how audiences interact with jazz music, although I also explore other contexts of White listening. I will conclude this introductory chapter with a nod to one of the central Black feminist writers of the Jazz Age, Alice Dunbar-Nelson, whom I discuss in greater detail in chapter 4.

"UNE FEMME DIT" (A WOMAN SPEAKS)

In 1926, Alice Dunbar-Nelson, a prominent journalist, poet, and fiction writer associated with the New Negritude movement, announced that she would no longer bother herself with challenging the White sonic gaze: "Why should all of us or any of us waste perfectly good time, type, paper, or energy frothing at the pen over what our White contemporaries think or write of us? We will rush into print . . . to prove that these statements made by the Nordics are all wrong. And to whom do we prove them? To our own dear selves. For said Nordic never sees our answers, or our papers or our statements. Wouldn't read them if he did."[162] With these words, Dunbar-Nelson expressed a fundamental critique of White writers of the Jazz Age: *Whites wrote frequently about Black culture, especially Black aesthetics, Black music, and Black dance; yet Whites failed to read the responses of Black authors replying to White misrepresentations of Blackness.*

Dunbar-Nelson offered this critique of Whiteness in her transformative column "Une Femme Dit" (A woman speaks), which was the most well-known among the four she wrote in the 1920s. Dunbar-Nelson had a thirty-year career in the Black press and was the premier Black writer of regionalist, Creole fiction. Not only was Dunbar-Nelson offering a criticism of the one-way nature of the White investment in Black and Creole cultures, she was staking out a Black feminist speaking position. By announcing that she wrote as a Black woman—"Un Femme Dit"—Dunbar-Nelson returns us to the issue raised by Spivak: The question is not whether colonized people have spoken, but who will listen when they do?

In this book, I focus on the contributions of Dunbar-Nelson, as well as other Black feminists, queer theorists, musicians, phenomenologists, and critical race scholars. What draws together this wide-ranging cast of voices is that they all have criticized the White sonic gaze. As I noted at the outset, little of what I'm saying is new. Indigenous peoples in the Americas have theorized White listening from the beginning of their contact with Europeans. For instance, Denise Low argues in her fascinating collection *Natural Theologies: Essay About Literature of the New Middle West* that the listening and speaking styles in Kansas and other Midwestern states represent a creolization of Indigenous and European styles. "Writers of this region inherit a 'frontier' legacy from Indigenous and American settler communities, which persists."[163] Such Indigenous "commentaries" on how Europeans spoke and listened were not, of course, written commentaries, but consisted in praxis such as slow speaking and using "compressed, experienced-based language," which transformed how European settlers came to use language.[164]

Critiques of White listening emerging from Afro-diasporic populations are also as old as contact. Again, the first "commentaries" on Whiteness from Afro-diasporic peoples were not written, but spoken and sung. As Parris emphasizes, Black people radically transfigured the languages of their European colonizers, Africanizing them, creolizing them, and hence *resisting* them. The "words, songs, *and* music of the African oral tradition as a diasporic cultural system . . . has irrevocably altered the sound and diction of (imperial) English."[165] While my focus is on critiques of Whiteness in and around the Jazz Age in the United States, the origin of these critiques is hundreds of years earlier at the point of contact between Europeans and those they colonized.

I will repeatedly affirm that the Jazz Age was also the age of the Harlem Renaissance. While nearly all Harlem Renaissance writers were aware of jazz, it is not the case that White writers of the Jazz Age were aware of the Harlem Renaissance. To this day, this pattern persists, with many jazz theorists preferring to engage jazz music though the lens of Theodore Adorno (and other European theorists) rather than the Black, mixed-race, and Creole authors of the Jazz Age. It is important to remember that even a canonical text such as Zora Neale Hurston's *Their Eyes Were Watching God* was out of print for nearly forty years, until 1978. Academia has been slow to recognize that America's Jazz Age birthed not only a musical revolution, but also, in the words of A. Shahid Stover, an "aesthetic-ontological rebellion," as well.[166]

Since the 1980s, poet and writer Akahsa Gloria Hull has been writing about the importance of the Black feminist writers of the Jazz Age, Dunbar-Nelson in particular.[167] Hull's work has shaped Black feminist traditions in the United States and globally. It is through my engagement with feminists such as Hull, Parris, Dunbar-Nelson, Sara Ahmed, Angela Davis, Jacqueline Martinez, bell hooks, Veronica Watson, Kris Sealey, Linda Martín Alcoff, Kathryn Sophia Bell, Nathalie Nya, Kate Kirkpatrick, Debra Berghoffen, Nathifa Greene, Sonia Kruks, Linda A. Bell, Margaret A. Simons, Sarah Hoagland, Gail Weiss, Anika Simpson, Christine Daigle, Constance L. Mui, and others that I have learned the importance of rethinking the philosophical canon I was taught as an undergraduate, graduate, and young professional in the field of philosophy.

Dunbar-Nelson's Black feminist complaint—"said Nordic never sees our answers, or our papers or our statements. Wouldn't read them if he did"—suggests a pessimistic approach to the problem of White listening.

Dunbar-Nelson did not write for White U.S. Americans because they refused to read her. One hundred years later, are we White Americans willing to engage such Black feminist critiques of the White sonic gaze? I am optimistic enough to have written this book. I believe that we White people can benefit immensely from reading critiques of Whiteness that structures our perceptions—especially the ways we see and the ways we hear. The hope in writing this book is that I have provided a partial archive, a partial resonator, for oft-ignored criticisms of listening whitely.

Chapter 2

The Jazz Problem

Patterns of White Bad Faith Listening

White listening is a problem. But most Whites are neither aware of themselves as Whites nor aware of themselves as listeners. Problematizing Whiteness requires us Whites to confront our collective bad faith. White bad faith, like all forms of existential bad faith, is a flight from freedom. Phenomenological thought is a way to confront bad faith by examining first-person experience critically and attending to the social conditions of agency. Phenomenological thought is guided by what Du Bois called "second sight," or the ability to see *and hear* oneself from the point of view of others. White Americans are not gifted with second sight because they are a dominant majority and do not normally experience racial double consciousness. White culture protects Whites from the existential shame of being seen, heard, and judged as White. As a matter of habit and custom, Whites direct their gaze outward toward those whom they problematize as "not-us." Confronting "the White problem" means addressing the irony that Whites in American have formed White identities largely through stories, beliefs, and assumptions about others whom they lump into the category of "non-White people."

    Inspired by the existentialist formulation of the White problem in the writings of Fanon, Beauvoir, Sartre, Du Bois, Richard Wright, Lewis Gordon, and Kathryn Sophia Belle, I examine Whiteness concretely by presenting six patterns of White listening or sonic gazing: White minstrel listening, White savior listening, White hipster listening, White revivalist listening, White colorblind listening, upgraded White colorblind listening, and White ecstatic listening. White listening orientations are habits of perception that structure how Whites experience space and time. The when and where of White perception matters. A historically, geographically informed approach helps cut through the fog of White bad faith that deters Whites from understanding that Whiteness is both a system and a choice. The basic dynamic of existential

White bad faith is that Whites know that Whiteness is a "fatal invention,"[1] but they do not take responsibility for acting White. White patterns of bad faith listening have one thing in common: They invert reality and turn this inversion into something normal. White sonic gazing constitutes what it hears while pretending it is a passive, neutral, force. This is exactly why Du Boisian existentialism is needed: to problematize White hearing by treating it as active, collaborative, and therefore problematic.

The vignettes below, culled from White print and sound culture, speak to the experiences of listening Whitely. American Whites live their Whiteness through their ears. I focus on how Whites train their ears to jazz because of the enormous cultural capital they have invested into being good jazz listeners. Jazz listening is such an important part of White identity that the 1920s are widely known as the Jazz Age. It would be just as accurate to describe the 1920s in America as "the age of the Harlem Renaissance" or "the age of New Negritude," but our history texts favor a narrative that centers White people's experience of Black culture rather than Black people's experience of Black culture. Jazz listening is a principle means through which Whites negotiate their relationships with other White and non-White Americans. Jazz figures prominently in White mythologies about the American nation state. The debate over whether jazz is "America's classical music" is a case in point.[2]

Jon Panish's insightful book, *The Color of Jazz*, shows how distinct White and Black discourses have been regarding their construction of jazz as a symbol of Americanness.[3] The dominant jazz narrative is "a racial discourse, controlled by white Americans." Panish notes: "Jazz was one field on which the assaults, responses, exchanges, challenges, inversions, and rejections between blackness and Whiteness were launched, issued and played out..."[4]

The listening orientations explored below begin in the teens and end in the present. These snapshots into the first-person experiences of White listening are genealogical and analytical. The historical emphasis is necessary because Whiteness is not a stable category. By taking us back to the period when jazz music emerged from ragtime, the blues, and the minstrel show, we learn how American Whites crafted their sense of White selfhood by listening to music of non-White others, especially Black and Creole musicians. White minstrel listening is one of the oldest and most powerful White technologies of sonic gazing. Its roots are much older than jazz and extend to the plantation. Its branches stretch across the entire twentieth century and are present to this day.

Similarly, White savior listening, White hipster listening, White folk revivalist listening, White colorblind listening, and White ecstatic listening are historically specific orientations that have been recycled in a variety of periods, including the present.

HOW DOES IT FEEL TO BE A
WHITE AURAL PROBLEM?

I frame the phenomenological issue in this chapter as an auditory version of Du Bois's question in *Darkwater*: How does it feel to be a White problem?[5] To address their collective bad faith, Whites must understand that White culture directs them to look and listen outwardly. Just as Whites think that race is something others have, White listeners think about sound as something that is produced by the other. But sound is a form of mediated reciprocity; sound is a negotiation among agents. "Sounding Black" is a category imposed by White listening, though White listeners evade this fact, searching for Black qualities within music and musicians.

For more than one hundred years, Whites have been fascinated with jazz, reading into the music an entire theory of Black America. White writers have approached jazz as a substance. They have frozen the music. A dominant myth is that Black people make music naturally, not through effort, practice, skill, or agency. White listeners have foisted a phony politics of authenticity onto Black, Creole, mixed race, and non-White musicians. Many American myths about Blackness emerged from the long tradition of minstrelsy, which stretched from the 1840s all the way through the early twentieth century. White tropes about Blackness came from minstrel show characters like Old Black Joe and Jim Crow. White popular opinions about Blackness were and are drawn from the entertainment industry.

In the 1920s, where my analysis begins, we find the White press analyzing the newly emerging improvised, syncopated Black and Creole music as a problem. I take as my first case study a popular musical periodical called the *Etude*. It was read mostly by music educators and provided pedagogical advice, sheet music, as well as articles on music history and theory. The *Etude* was an important early site of the White public discourse in America about how Whites should listen. Following the work of jazz scholars Ted Gioia and Kathy Ogren, I locate one origin of White listening in White print culture of the Jazz Age. Like Kara Keeling and Josh Kun, I ask: "What role have hearing and listening played in 'American' formations of race, ethnicity, sexuality, gender, community, and class, and how has the birth of recorded sound in the late nineteenth century informed those formations?"[6]

In 1924, the *Etude* ran a front-page splash: "The Jazz Problem: Opinions of Prominent Public Men and Musicians." Jazz was framed as a "problem" for White American listeners in the 1920s because Whites were fearful of, yet fascinated by, Black culture and Black people. To Whites, jazz was a symbol of everything Black. While the *Etude* claimed to speak for a national audience, the specific fears expressed about jazz were rooted in White anxieties brought on as northern, metropolitan Whites began seeing and hearing more

Black people in their everyday lives as well as through the emerging technologies of mass-distributed sound and print. In the early 1920s, as a result of the Great Migration, the explosion of Black print culture, and the boom in recordings of Black blues artists, northern White audiences had more opportunities to hear jazz. New Orleans musicians toured nationally, and there were Creole, Black, and mixed-race musicians playing syncopated, improvised music throughout the Midwest, especially in Chicago, Kansas City, St. Louis, and Memphis.

Ragtime music had been on the minds of the *Etude* editors since Scott Joplin's 1889 hit "Maple Leaf Rag," which was distributed across the nation in the form of written sheet music. Pianist and composer W.C. Handy had published the sheet music for his "Memphis Blues" in 1912. Handy's sheet music was inspired by the dirty blues style, with its characteristic blue notes—flattened thirds and sevenths. Handy was a major musical innovator who would arrange and notate for keyboard a blues style that had been developed by Black musicians using mostly guitar, voice, and percussion. Joplin and Handy were raced as "Negro" musicians, and they wrote music in what people of the time considered two related and emerging Black styles—ragtime and blues. But their music—highly technical piano music, scored and distributed to thousands of middle- and upper-class White, mostly female, parlor players in America—did not create a problem.

It was after Joplin and Handy, in the period from 1919 to 1927, when White music educators and moral reformers began to call jazz music a problem.[7] The technology of distributing music shifted with the birth of records. During the Great Migration, six million Black people would move to northern urban centers. Formulating the jazz problem in White print culture was a way for northern Whites to negotiate imaginary and physical space with a cultural minority whom they had previously ignored.

White writers in the *Etude* used the metaphors of "infection" and "contagion" to describe the perceived power of jazz rhythms. The specter of live jazz frightened and thrilled mainstream White audiences. In the live setting, there would be close physical proximity and mixture among racially diverse individuals. In the late teens and early twenties, when the Creole musician Edward "Kid" Ory moved to Los Angeles to perform for mixed audiences in Black-and-tans, the police raided these clubs and shut them down because Black men were dancing with White women. "Black-and-tan" clubs were so named because they were venues where both Black and White patrons formed the audience for jazz music and dancing. These clubs were found in Black commercial districts in major cities such as Los Angeles, Chicago, and New York.[8] In some Black-and-tan clubs (clubs that allowed both Black and White patrons), Whites danced with Black patrons; in other clubs, they were separated by a rope or a physical barrier.

At the same time that Whites expressed their fear of jazz in White print culture, a generation of young White hipsters emerged. These hipsters wanted to learn the language of jazz. The fact that the music was associated with dancing, drugs, and race-mixing was part of the allure. The White music education industry as represented by the *Etude* warned against jazz, in part because they saw themselves becoming irrelevant. If young Whites could learn music from records, they wouldn't need to pay for professional music lessons. The *Etude* was, in a sense, far ahead of the curve in spotting the cultural changes that the Jazz Age was bringing—among them learning music from records and hearing live music rather than taking lessons or going to conservatories. The dominant tone of the *Etude* was rearguard: It was anti-jazz at a time when the popularity of this music was growing among Whites.

That the White press would couch a discussion of jazz in terms of a problem is not surprising, given that Americans had spoken for years about "the Negro problem." As Kathy Ogren shows, the *Etude* took a strongly unfavorable view of jazz, linking it to sensuality, sex, lack of training, African-ness, and primitiveness. The journal used the metaphors of drugs, the jungle, disease, and sex to characterize jazz. "Jazz . . . is an unforgivable orgy of noise, a riot of discord, usually perpetrated by players of scant musical training."[9] Perhaps sensing that new generations of White youth would be drawn to the music no matter what moral warnings the magazine offered, the *Etude* characterized some types of jazz as bad and dangerous, while leaving space for the possibility of good jazz. "Good Jazz can be a wholesome tonic; bad Jazz is always a dangerous drug."[10] Once again, the music was characterized in terms of drugs. The *Etude* positioned itself as a White guardian who could separate out the good Black culture from bad Black culture. As it would turn out, supposedly good jazz—the "wholesome tonic"—would be jazz played by Whites. Drawing on the Eurocentric idea that European classical music is more ordered, precise, and harmonic, the *Etude* suggested that White players improved jazz by writing it down. The White press refused to note that Joplin and Handy were master composers and master musicians who wrote out their music and who used harmonic techniques not unlike those of, say, Béla Bartók and Darius Milhaud.

Writing in the 1940s, the sociologist Morroe Berger was one of the first authors to give an academic account of the jazz problem. His article, "Resistance to the Diffusion of a Culture-Pattern," published in 1947 in *The Journal of Negro History*, surveyed writing about jazz from mainstream presses in the 1920s, 1930s, and 1940s, finding that overwhelmingly jazz was associated with vice, sensuousness, dance, and Blackness.[11] Berger's academic techniques were similar to Du Boisian sociology of forty years prior. Like Du Bois, Berger's sociology was a way of "flipping the script" on the White gaze, to borrow George Yancy's metaphor.[12] Berger was a sharp critic of the White press, which, he showed, treated Black culture as a symbol and a symptom, not a complex reality.

Berger reveals that music periodicals such as *The Musician* and *The Musical Quarterly* also wrote unfavorably about jazz in the 1920s, usually on moral grounds. Jazz was perceived as a moral threat because listening to jazz supposedly led to miscegenation. The White press discussed how Whites were not just reading sheet music written by Black people; nor were they simply listening to jazz music on records. The presence of Black people in the North was experienced by Whites as a bodily threat to their space. The participatory, improvisational nature of the jazz experience was oppositional to mainstream White norms that promoted the physical separation between races.[13]

The White press' statement of the jazz problem is important phenomenologically because it reveals how Whites, at the dawn of the mass distribution of recorded sound, problematized Blackness; they did not problematize their listening habits or their Whiteness. White discourse subscribed to the audio/visual litany, treating listening as passive, natural, and neutral. White print culture supported listening practices that made Whiteness invisible and inaudible.

WHITE MINSTREL LISTENING

In addition to the discourse of the jazz problem in music journals of the 1920s, there was a steady stream of stories about jazz in the mainstream White press. Lawrence Gushee has shown that the mid-to-late teens were a critical period in the formation of White attitudes toward jazz. The term "jazz" entered the national White vocabulary around 1917 mostly as a result of the widely covered, back-to-back national tours of the Original Creole Band during 1914–1917. It would be difficult to overstate the importance of the Original Creole Band in the story of how White Americans learned to listen to jazz. The Original Creole Band was the first New Orleans band to tour extensively outside of Louisiana and the American South. The audiences at the Original Creole Band performances forged a national White taste for jazz. White readers of White newspapers were contributing to a national public that defined itself through mass consumption of jazz sounds, words, and images.

The White print culture of the 1920s is a significant phenomenological resource for understanding White listening orientations. From period reports, we learn about the demographics, size, and behavior of White audiences. Whites writing about and listening to the Original Creole Band and other early jazz acts forged what I will call a White minstrel listening orientation. The distinctive element of White minstrel listening is that it conflates actors with their minstrel roles. Minstrel listeners imagine that they are in the presence of "authentic" Black, Creole, and mixed-race people whose onstage personas are not personas at all, but natural expressions of selfhood. Mark Twain, a White minstrel listener, famously praised what he called "the genuine ni**** show."[14]

The term "minstrel" should be clarified. The association of minstrelsy with Blackface is not inaccurate, but it can be misleading. Black and Creole bands of the late nineteenth and early twentieth centuries often called themselves the "So-and-so Minstrels," sometimes placing in a geographic qualification such as "The Georgia Minstrels." These acts used minstrel not primarily to signal Blackface, but variety. The minstrel variety show consisted in music, dance, acting, comedy, theater, juggling, and, in the case of the Original Creole Band, a trained rooster. The performances of the band were short and quick paced. The minstrel show was a mashup of styles and genres: There might be opera music, sentimental and patriotic tunes, and comedy numbers, all in the space of thirty minutes. White audiences expected mixed pleasures, from levity, to contemplation, to guttural laughter, to sacral contemplation.

Minstrel variety acts did involve Blackface comedy, and the Original Creole Band was no exception. But the term "minstrel" would have had different connotations to a White northern audience hearing jazz for the first time, than it would have to someone familiar with Black vaudeville performance styles. White northerners hearing jazz for the first time conflated minstrel with Blackface comedy, as evidenced by the White press' fascination with calling jazz musicians "plantation darkies."

The case of the Original Creole Band demonstrates how early jazz performances were indebted to minstrelsy in both senses: They contained both variety and Blackface comedy. It is an uncomfortable truth—which is evaded to this day by some White jazz critics—but jazz began, in part, with Black, Creole, and mixed-race performers who wore Blackface, performed in "plantation" settings, and drew on the repertoire of plantation songs from the middle nineteenth century.

How did Whites in the North describe listening to the Original Creole Band, and why have I called this "minstrel listening"? Whites were minstrel listeners to the extent that they imagined themselves as hearing the authentic sounds of Southern slavery plantations. Similar to how White Americans in the 1990s consumed hip-hop as the authentic sound of the "ghetto," Whites in the teens experienced a voyeuristic high when they listened to syncopated music played by non-Whites. White audiences liked listening to the Original Creole Band because they were excited by experiencing a real, true, representative other.

Unsurprisingly, what caught White ears was the Southern-ness and Blackness of the new music. Press reports repeatedly suggested that the Original

Creole Band brought Whites in contact with Southern plantation culture. Whites imagined they were hearing an unfiltered, untutored folk. They imagined that Creole and Black performers—even in costume—were being themselves. Unlike the Black press of the period, which carefully distinguished actors from their roles, the White press conflated them.

In 1914, on their first tour, the *Winnipeg Telegram* described the band as playing "real old time Southern melodies."[15] The *Telegram* found the Creole Band to be "a most welcome diversion from the usual run of ragtime and present-day songs. . . . These people have a style all their own."

The *Indianapolis Star* in 1915 described the Original Creole Band as an "old time plantation act."[16] The review of the performance commented on the settings, which showed "the South before the war, with cotton fields in full bloom, the negro quarters and the 'big house.'" From the same tour, the *Manitoba Free Press* singled out the Original Creole Band as "the oddity of the bill,"[17] describing "New Orleans Creole Musicians" as "a collection of colored performers on various instruments who temper with a pretty touch of pathos singing of the old time darky songs."[18]

The *Calgary Morning Albertan* (1914) described the visual appearance of the performers: "This band of ragtime musicians is composed of mulattos and quadroons of distinctive types."[19] Another description of the group held them to be a "mixed orchestra" consisting of "mulattos" who were "characteristically dressed as typical plantation darkies."[20]

Some in the White press were disappointed that the band members "appear to be colored men and not Creoles."[21] These audiences were participating in what Neil Harris has called the "humbug."[22] At the turn of the century, popular entertainment was not sharply distinguished from edification or scientific curiosity. Harris describes how White audiences viewing P.T. Barnum's Fiji mermaid felt the thrill of being amateur scientists distinguishing the real from the fake. Similarly, Whites were thrilled by getting to judge for themselves whether Creole musicians were really Creole, whether they were really Southern, whether they really knew the experiences of the plantations that they acted out in their roles.

The White press was also fascinated with the newness of jazz. The terms "Creole" and "jazz" entered the national White vocabulary at the same time: around 1917. Indicating linguistic instability, the term was spelled variously as "jaz," "jas," "jass," and eventually "jazz." One newspaper noted that "jaz" is "a vaudeville word denoting the putting of speed, ginger or pep into an act."[23]

Whites heard jazz as continuous with and yet different from existing music, including ragtime. "Jazz music of the players with real ragtime swing of way-down-South-darkies."[24] "The feature is the jazz music of the players."[25] As the term "jazz" began to catch on, it was used sometimes interchangeably with "ragtime," as when the press called TOCB a "New Orleans creole rag band."[26]

The term "jazz" emerged in part to describe sounds heard under the tents of Black vaudeville. The new sound of the Original Creole Band was "known in vaudeville circles as a 'jas' band."[27] And the primary reference was rhythmic: "You 'got to feel' jass. The time is syncopated."[28] It was said that the "New Orleans Creole rag band had the feet of those in the audience itching to try the 'chicken-wing' clog."[29]

The White press coverage of early jazz bands reveals a White minstrel listening orientation. The White press encouraged listening practices that conflated Black performers with their onstage persona, for instance commenting that Black actors were naturally able to play syncopated music, because it was "born in the bone."[30]

The listening orientations emerging from the White press during the time of the Original Creole Band show that White minstrel jazz listeners were neither facing themselves nor listening to their Whiteness. Whites imagined they were hearing unfiltered, folk sounds of authentic "plantation darkies." They listened to jazz and asked one another: Have we been humbugged? White minstrel listening has its roots in the 1840s, when Whites in Blackface dominated the minstrel stage. In the teens, when early jazz emerged from ragtime, the blues, brass band traditions, and the minstrel theater, a new iteration of White minstrel listening was birthed. White Americans turned their ears toward people of color, some of whom were in Blackface, listening for the new syncopated rhythms and the melodic and harmonic improvisation that they heard as jazz.

WHITE SAVIOR LISTENING

Another foundational form of White listening emerged in the late 1920s and early 1930s when White jazz orchestras became popular. The orientation of White savior listening is expressed in the music and writings of Paul Whiteman (1890–1967). Hailed by the White press as the "King of Jazz," Whiteman crafted a national White audience for jazz music based on the assumption that he, and other White musicians, could "bring jazz out of the jungle."[31] Whiteman figured himself as a savior who could elevate Black music by adding European harmony and discipline.

At his concert "An Experiment in Modern Music" (1924) and in his book, *Jazz* (1926), Whiteman argued that jazz music before him was primitive. He purported that White arrangers and big band leaders were the real genius of jazz. Whiteman arrogantly assumed that Black and Creole jazz musicians couldn't read music. He thought that written arrangements would improve jazz by creating order and control. His style of jazz minimized improvisation. The White musicians in his band were allowed short, "hot breaks," not elaborate solos.

Whiteman outlined his message to the White public in a press statement released before the 1924 concert:

> The experiment is to be purely educational. I intend to point out, with the assistance of my orchestra, the tremendous strides which have been made in popular music from the day of the discordant jazz, which sprang into existence about ten years ago from nowhere in particular to the really melodious music of to-day which—for no good reason—is still called jazz.[32]

Whiteman literally began his concert with a lecture to his White audience about how to listen. By arguing that early jazz was primitive, he encouraged other Whites to think of Black and Creole music as a thing of the past that had led to his current greatness. Whiteman was a White vanguard who would interpret Black culture for the mediocre tastes of the White mainstream. Whiteman intended orchestral jazz to become a musically distinct and racially White genre.

Whiteman's "purely educational" efforts in 1924 were part of a social trend that began forty years earlier in a different musical context. In the 1880s, the White critic and social reformer John Sullivan Dwight (1813–1893) wielded influence among wealthy music lovers in the northeastern United States. In part through his efforts writing in *Dwight's Musical Journal*, and his successful campaign to create a Boston Symphony Orchestra, the notion of a symphonic orchestra took shape. Dwight complained that "bands in the streets and gardens and on every steamboat, hand organ grinders, whistlers of Pinafore, keep the air full of melodies that cross each other in all directions."[33] The White savior mentality insists on distinguishing mere bands from orchestras. Bands are noisy (i.e., Black), while orchestras are musical (i.e., White).

Orchestral jazz, Whiteman believed, would prioritize the written score, ensuring order, control, and fidelity to the composer. Since the jazz composer's intentions would be written into the score, only trained, professional musicians would be legitimate interpreters of the music. These values of professionalism and control had also animated Dwight's notion of an authentic symphony orchestra. In Whiteman's orchestra, instrumentalists were not expected to improvise, either individually or collectively, unless a section in the score indicated a break. A break would be a short solo, perhaps of a few bars. Summarizing the new role of the White orchestrator, music critic Sigmund Spaeth wrote in 1928: "The real artists of jazz in the popular field have been the arrangers and masters of orchestration."[34]

As Whiteman distanced himself from the Black and Creole jazz traditions, he insisted on a parallel between his jazz and Europe. Whiteman styled himself after Antonín Dvořák, Béla Bartók, and Darius Milhaud. These composers became well known for incorporating Indigenous and folk elements into their compositions. Dvořák's 1893 Symphony No. 9, "From the New World," commissioned by the New York Philharmonic, had incorporated some aspects of Black spirituals and Indigenous American music. Placing himself in the same imaginary space as these European composers fed Whiteman's missionary-like attitude to jazz: "All the years I had been playing . . . I never stopped wanting to go into the concert halls and in some measure remove the stigma of barbaric strains and jungle cacophony."[35]

Whiteman crafted a particular audience for his music. By combining his musical performance with a lecture, he encouraged White people to think of listening to music as a serious endeavor, distinct from mere entertainment. At some venues, like Chicago's Club Trianon, his pseudo-intellectualism flopped. Audiences who expected to dance didn't like the music, which they found un-danceable. Meanwhile, the upper-middle-class White audience he cultivated "refused to patronize a dance hall and mingle with the masses."[36]

The social context against which Whiteman was crafting a new listening public was the jazz problem. He claimed that White, orchestral jazz was good jazz. If Whites feared that listening to jazz meant dancing, drugs, and contact with non-Whites, then segregated White listening spaces would be the solution. Whites could attend segregated concerts with all-White bands and audiences, experiencing in part the thrill they associated with Black music, while staying safely within their White comfort zone.

Whiteman's listening instructions were Eurocentric, not least of which because he taught audiences to associate complex harmony with Europe and Whiteness. Whiteman perpetuated the myth that Black music focuses on rhythm while White music focuses on harmony. At the 1924 concert, Whiteman's orchestra began with a satirical version of a tune that had been recorded by a White New Orleans band seven years earlier, the now infamous "Livery Stable Blues." Their rendition of "Livery Stable Blues" was informed by and drew upon the Blackface minstrel tradition. When Whiteman had first worked with George Gershwin on the ill-fated opera "Blue Monday" two years earlier in 1922, performers onstage blacked up. In 1924, there was no burned cork. Nonetheless, Whiteman himself described the performance as a racial burlesque. He experienced temporary discomfort when he thought the White audience failed to understand that his band was mocking the musical style of New Orleans. "I had for a moment, the panicky feeling that they hadn't realized the attempt at burlesque—that they were ignorantly applauding the thing on its merits."[37] Whiteman's performance was a White caricature of Black and Creole culture, performed for a segregated, White audience. The band performed "Livery Stable Blues" to demonstrate what bad jazz sounded like—it was supposedly primitive, discordant, and lacked sophisticated melody and harmony. That night and others, the band leader would use metaphors of the "jungle" and the "savage" to characterize New Orleans–style, syncopated, improvised music.

Whiteman was one of the most commercially successful musicians of his day. During the Club Trianon date in Chicago, his orchestra was paid an unbelievable $25,000 for six nights. For reference, a new car in 1924 cost around $265, and a new house around $8,000. For comparison, the Black band leader Fletcher Henderson was making $300 a week in 1923 and $1,200 a week in 1925.[38] Whiteman's astounding economic success can be attributed to his carefully crafted racial message: White jazz is good jazz.[39] The economic opportunities for White bands were systematically different from those open to Black and non-White bands. Speaking about the economic situation that would emerge in the 1930s big band era, Paul Allen Anderson writes:

> African American bands never shared equally in the popular vogues' financial rewards. The crowded field of White bands enjoyed too many commercial and social advantages, while Black big bands suffered institutionalized barriers to media exposure, commercial support, and access to various hotel ballrooms, dance halls, nightclubs, and concert stages.[40]

Whiteman was a major voice informing the emergence of White public opinions about how to listen to jazz. Two years after the Aeolian concert, his 1926 book, *Jazz*, was serialized in the *Saturday Evening Post*, the most widely circulated magazine in the United States. The book brought Whiteman's racialized views of jazz to a massive White audience and paved the way for the White big band craze of the 1930s. His educational mission succeeded in priming a White public who pointed their ears toward White "geniuses" and "kings." Whiteman's model of listening gave Whites permission to enjoy a music that they heard as thrillingly exotic while safely staying within their self-conception as Whites.

White savior listening was not limited to Whiteman's efforts. George Gershwin, for instance, promoted the view that jazz was an American folk music that was a natural resource that all Americans, including himself, could play authentically. "Jazz I regard as an American folk music; not the only one, but a very powerful one which is probably in the blood and feeling of the American people."[41] White musicians like Whiteman and Gershwin were cultural outsiders to jazz, which was primarily a Southern and Midwestern Creole and Black music. As outsiders, these Whites could not appeal to their geographic or racial experiences to bolster an "authentic" relationship to the music. Jazz was not their music, not originally. But they could lay claim to a new, better style of jazz, one that was not the product of Black and mixed-race communities, but one that was the product of a White national American culture, which they represented. The ideological position assumed by the White savior listener allowed Whites to benefit from their ambivalent status—they could imagine themselves immune to the bodily temptations they associated with jazz, like sex, drinking, dancing, prostitution, and marijuana.

White savior listening was an orientation that responded to the supposedly problematic nature of jazz. For Whites, jazz was a problem because it was too Black. Threatened and thrilled, White savior listeners cultivated listening habits they associated with European classical music. Against the noisy, humbug listening of vaudeville, White saviors listened as a form of White crowd control. These White listeners collaborated with White musicians like Whiteman, who taught them to think of themselves as intellectuals whose sophisticated tastes and still bodies would elevate the noisy, primitive jazz of Creole, Black, and mixed-race musicians.

WHITE HIPSTER LISTENING

In this section, I describe a listening orientation associated with White hipsterism. The figure of the White hipster has received attention from Robin James,[42] Andrew Ross,[43] Ingrid Monson,[44] and others. These authors point to Chicago clarinetist Mezz Mezzrow (1899–1972) as a classic example. I add to these existing accounts by attending to the listening instructions issued by Mezzrow. The White hipster believes that White listening is a neurotic condition that can be unlearned if Whites immerse themselves fully and sincerely in Black culture. Unlike the White savior, the hipster expresses feelings of White estrangement, longing to become non-White through honorary membership in a Black community. The hipster hears White culture as corny, cold, stiff, and boring. The hipster is critical of minstrel and savior listening because they are shallow perspectives that lead to imitative, derivative jazz.

I treat *Only the Blues* (1946), Mezzrow's memoir, as a phenomenology of estranged White listening. Mezzrow presents two types of White listening. Un-estranged White listening is corny, neurotic listening. Mezzrow associates corny listening with the middle-class values he was raised with. By contrast, estranged, hip White listening requires an immersion in the lifeworld of non-Whites. What Mezzrow calls his conversion away from Whiteness took place in South Side Chicago nightclubs, where he learned to copy the sounds of musicians from New Orleans.

Like Whiteman, Mezzrow was a successful musician and writer who influenced the way other Whites listened to jazz. *Only the Blues* is a popular, backward-looking memoir composed in the 1940s. The book is a first-person glimpse into the lifeworld of a group of White musicians known as the Chicago School. Mezzrow and his friends learned their style of jazz by listening to and imitating the live, improvised music played by Louis Armstrong, Joe Oliver, Sidney Bechet, and Kid Ory.

According to the phenomenology in *Only the Blues*, Whiteness is unlearnable. Whiteness consists in a style of playing and listening that is stiff, uptight, and neurotic. Mezzrow describes himself as unlearning Whiteness by studying the live and recorded sounds of New Orleanians. What he calls his White "education" required work, practice, and study—the same discipline that musicians would expect to put into their instruments. Mezzrow studied Black culture, claiming to learn to speak, think, live, and love like a Black person. Mezzrow thought that his love of Blackness was distinct from the cross-racial desires he associated with the Blackface minstrel traditions. He believed that shedding the neurotic skin of Whiteness was an anti-racist act.

Hipster listening consists in learning not to "mess up" White hearing. Mezzrow explains:

> Any white man, if he thought straight and studied hard, could sing and dance and play with the Negro. You didn't have to take the finest and most original and honest music in America and mess it up because you were a white man; you could dig the colored man's real message and get in there with him.[45]

The experience of unlearning Whiteness is laid out in musical terms, as a change in phrasing, intonation, and shedding of sonic harshness.[46] White sounds are coded as harsh, cold, and prickly, while Black sounds are coded as fuzzy, soft, and warm.

Mezzrow describes hipster listening as a feeling of White estrangement. Denying that he merely loves Black people, he imagines that he has become Black through proximity: "The Southerners had called me a 'ni****-lover' there. Solid. I not only loved those colored boys, but I was one of them—I felt closer to them than I felt to the whites, and I even got the same treatment they got."[47] Around White people, Mezzrow felt alienated; around non-White people he felt joy. Using the language of passing to describe his experience unlearning Whiteness, Mezzrow is pleased with the idea that Black musicians might think that he's a light-skinned Black person passing as White. Imagining a dialogue with young fans in Harlem, he writes, "To this day those girls probably believe that I was passing . . . 'If you ain't one of us,' they argued, 'how in the hell could you play that horn the way you do?' How I wished they were right."[48] For the White hipster listener, hearing White jazz brings on feelings of shame and disgust. These feelings are attenuated if the hipster receives recognition of their hipness from non-Whites.

Mezzrow rarely relates his Jewishness to his feelings of White estrangement. When he does talk about his Jewishness, he describes it as a visible identity, imposed by the gaze of Southern White racists. "We were Jews, but in Cape Girardeau they had told us we were Negroes. Now, all of the sudden, I realized that I agreed with them."[49] As a young man slumming in Chicago clubs, Mezzrow's Jewishness faded into the background—he felt himself a White person, not a White Jew. Later in life, when he was playing and traveling with Black and Creole musicians in the South, he experienced his Jewishness in the foreground, as an identity that allied him with Black people and gave him partial insight into anti-Black racism, which was simultaneously antisemitic.

Mezzrow's phenomenology of Whiteness can be summed up in one sentence: "Why are White musicians so corny?"[50] "Corny" is Mezzrow's favorite word for describing pre-critical, un-hip Whiteness. As a Google N-gram shows, there was a huge uptick in the use of the word "corny" from 1935 to 1945.[51] The invention of this word suggests that White hipsterism was a growing, collective form of White listening. "Corny" is derived from the phrase "corn-fed," meaning old-fashioned, sentimental, country, or folksy.[52] Mezzrow describes corny sounds as stiff and square. Corny Whites are mediocre players and listeners who emerge from the "killjoy world" of the White middle class.[53] Striking an existential note, Mezzrow diagnoses White corniness as a neurosis. "The White man is a spoiled child, and when he gets the blues he goes neurotic."[54]

Mezzrow was a musician, writer, and flamboyant spokesperson for a particular mode of White estrangement that emerged among middle-class youth in northern urban centers during the Great Migration. White hipsters were responding to what they thought were the corny, phony practices of White saviors and White minstrel listeners. Against Whiteman's notion that White people would bring order, control, and intelligence to jazz, Mezzrow rooted a Black "philosophy" in jazz.[55] He blasted the "hyped-up words and theories" of White jazz critics. Mezz was also developing habits of listening that would oppose White minstrel listening; calling out White audiences who listened to Sophie Tucker, Al Jolson, and Eddie Cantor; and offering an economic critique of White taste. White taste is boring and derivative; that is precisely why it sells to White killljoys.[56] Mainstream White jazz listeners cannot hear the phoniness of White jazz musicians such as Tommy Dorsey, Benny Goodman, and Paul Whiteman.

But for all of Mezzrow's sincere attempts to escape his own corny, neurotic Whiteness, he failed. He failed because, as Fanon observes, the White person who loves Black people is as sick as the White person who hates Black people. The intense identification Mezzrow felt with Black and Creole jazz musicians led him to believe that he had escaped being White.

Mezzrow was a White race traitor, but like all White race traitors, he took his Whiteness with him. The psychological trajectory of the hip White listener is quite understandable: Confronted with the disappointing truth that White culture is imitative, derivative, corny, and racist, the hipster turns to non-White culture seeking joy, vitality, strength, and humanity. Perhaps nothing is more White than thinking that moving to Harlem, marrying a Black woman, and playing the blues with Louis Armstrong makes one Black.

WHITE REVIVALIST LISTENING

The American Folk Music Revival began in the 1940s and reached its height in the 1960s.[57] Folk revivalism is a common and powerful technique of White listening. Alan Lomax's 1950 book *Mister Jelly Roll: The Fortunes of Jelly Roll Morton, New Orleans Creole and "Inventor of Jazz,"* was a bestseller that motivated and encapsulated the revivalist attitude of White audiences who reevaluated Black and Creole music. Like his father, John Lomax (1867–1948), Alan (1915–2002) was a proud ballad hunter. Ballad hunters were White, amateur folklorists who traveled to rural areas to record the music of nonprofessional musicians. Similar to the early "A&R men" (artist and repertoire agents who were talent scouts for record labels), ballad hunters unashamedly engaged in the project of discovery. They recorded musicians they believed were forgotten, overlooked, or lost. They traveled through the American South, driving on rural backroads, showing up uninvited to Black homes, houses of worship, workplaces, and most troubling of all, prisons.

John Lomax's proudest accomplishment had been his self-described "discovery" of blues composer, singer, and instrumentalist Huddie William Ledbetter (1888–1949), better known as Leadbelly. Leadbelly was a self-taught master of the twelve-string guitar. As Nolan Porterfield's biography shows, John Lomax made a habit of recording Black musicians in prisons.[58] Flashing paperwork from the Library of Congress or a letter of support from a governor, John Lomax found his way into incarceration facilities across the South, where he "hunted." In one penitentiary, he was served food cooked by female inmates while he waited for male prisoners to complete their day of hard labor before he recorded them with his mobile studio. John Lomax was so struck by Leadbelly's financial potential that he became Leadbelly's manager—I use the term "manager" loosely—taking him on multiple tours, even bringing him to a meeting of the Modern Language Association at Swarthmore College on December 27, 1934. Lomax's presentation on "Negro Folksongs and Ballads" was part of an academic panel discussion in the discipline of comparative literature. The committee chairman told Lomax,

"We welcome your generous suggestion that your talented aborigine 'ni****' sing for the guests.'"[59]

White revivalist listening is a colonial technology. White folk revivalists, as the name indicates, orient their ears toward those they consider a "folk"—a group of people, usually rural, often with a long oral history, and usually non-White or marginally White. These "folk" are treated as members of a decaying culture in need of resuscitation. The revivalist listener imagines folk music as an antidote to the ills of modern, urban, White life. Mirroring claims of the ballad hunters and A&R agents, White revivalist audiences engage in a vicarious emotional fantasy of ballad hunting and discovery. They believe they are amateur folklorists who are unearthing music that mainstream Whites ignore. The revivalist listener arrogantly assumes that music performed in rural, local, or noncommercial settings will be enhanced if it is staged for countercultural and mainstream White consumption.

In the Folk Revival period, Whites organized huge folk festivals where White businessmen promoted Black and non-White performers who were billed as fading resources and ignored gems. The Wikipedia entry for blues guitarist, composer, and singer Nehemiah Curtis "Skip" James (1902–1969) still has an entire heading titled "Rediscovery," listing James's performance at the 1966 Newport Folk Festival as the moment when he was "rediscovered by blues enthusiasts."[60] The White "rediscovery" of James turned his 1931 Paramount record "Drunken Spree," a 78 rpm race record, into a valuable collector's item among middle-class Whites. The same was true for thousands of other 78 rpm race records released four decades earlier by Okey, Emerson, Vocalion, and the Victor Talking Machine company. Race records were first recorded in the 1920s by Black and Creole artists like Bessie Smith, Gertrude "Ma" Rainey, King Oliver, Louis Armstrong, Lonnie Johnson, Ethel Waters, Leroy Carr, Robert Johnson, Alberta Hunter, Charlie Patton, Blind Lemon Jefferson, and many others. Race records became hot commodities for White collectors in the 1960s. These White revivalist listeners were disenchanted with the music available in White mainstream markets, which they believed to be too commercial and therefore inauthentic. These countercultural Whites were crate digging. But they were on a personal White journey, that of discovering Black culture for themselves for the first time. At this point in their journey, it did not occur to them that race records were also commercial products, and that many of the musicians they thought were nonprofessional, untutored, and thus pure "folk," were in fact seasoned performers and trained musicians who played in churches, at house parties, at blues jook joints, for family gatherings, and in myriad other contexts to which northern White outsiders had little access or understanding. Many of these musicians had navigated the White entertainment industry, cut multiple records, and performed live for non-White audiences for years. They were professionals, not amateurs. The identity of "folk" was thrust on them by the White sonic gaze.

While the colonial slumming of John Lomax might have seemed a long way off to those Whites who attended folk festivals and collected race records, it was not. These folk listeners in the 1940s, 1950s, and 1960s did not drive South to knock on the doors of Black homes, but they participated in a White racial fantasy that treated Black, Creole, and non-White musicians as noble savages and beautiful primitives, whose music would be the salve for their feelings of estrangement from White commercial culture.

Mister Jelly Roll was central to the practices of the American Folk Revival. Lomax's portrait of the Creole composer, pianist, and singer Ferdinand Joseph LaMothe, known professionally as Jelly Roll Morton (1890–1941), is among the most influential texts informing White public opinions about Creole music and Creole identity. While the book is narrated from Morton's perspective, calling it an autobiography is a stretch, since Lomax's ears are not the innocent repository they pretend to be. The book is a mashup of ethnography, biography, and White fantasy.

Katy Martin has recently argued that *Mister Jelly Roll* "reveals more about Lomax than about Morton."[61] My analysis builds on Martin's, while also cautioning against any attempt to decouple Morton's voice from Lomax's White sonic gaze in the text. Lomax's project of recording the words and music of Morton is so driven by what Michael Monahan[62] calls the "politics of purity" that it is more useful to read *Mister Jelly Roll* as an autobiography of Lomax, the White ballad hunter and colonial listener.

Lomax's listening orientation is White ethnographic slumming. He begins the second edition of *Mister Jelly Roll* with a romantic description of his role: "I had learned to realize that what these people had to say and their way of saying it was as good as their songs."[63] He positions himself as "backing up" his subject's history, by recording, arranging, and organizing sound. Lomax introduces, explains, qualifies, records, and transmits the experiences of Morton. Like his father, Lomax thought of himself as a lover and protector of Black and Creole culture. He even credited himself with creating the craze for oral history that would animate the American Folk Revival.

Aaron Ngozi Oforlea's excellent piece, "[Un]veiling the White gaze,"[64] uses the critical phenomenology of Fanon to dissect Lomax's techniques of listening. Oforlea contrasts Fanonian dialectical thinking with the undialectical, Lomaxian project. Fanonian dialectics studies the category "Negro" as an identity imposed by Whites. The terms "Negro" and "Creole," when utilized in White discourse, "embody and represent a history of Othering."[65] Oforlea distinguishes the White revivalist listening orientation of Lomax from Black listening orientations crafted by Harlem Renaissance writers like Du Bois, Alain Locke, and Zora Hurston who also formulated ideas about Black folk culture. Drawing on Eric Lott, Oforlea points to the "dialectic of misrecognition" that animates Lomax's corpus, concluding that "Lomax's writing could be seen as a record of how a particular White man constructs Black culture. . . . Once this has been established, one can find room to discuss Black culture as continually constructed by the White gaze."[66]

A significant problem with White revivalist listening is that it produces unreliable, unhappy sound and print archives. A cruel irony is that many of the recordings and interviews of Black and Creole musicians that were produced in the Folk Revival were conducted by Whites who thought that they were doing the world a favor by preserving dying cultures. The race-critical, decolonial listener of today must confront both the sound archive as well as how it was created. In *Archive Stories: Facts, Fictions, and the Writing of History*, Antoinette Burton describes a form of "archival pleasure" that is based on the colonial logic of discovery.[67] Historians, folklorists, and ballad collectors experience archival pleasure as they "wax rapturously about the capacity of archival discoveries to bring one into contact with the past."[68] Burton asks us to "talk about the backstage of archives—how they are constructed, policed, experienced and manipulated."[69] If today's listeners are not to replicate the violence of discovery, they must treat sound archives as "technologies of imperial power, conquest and hegemony."[70]

When Lomax recorded the music and stories of Morton, he engaged in archival pleasure. "I knew that Jelly Roll had given me, as Woody and Leadbelly had earlier, the living legend of his existence."[71] Lomax positioned his White body as the recipient of a gift. This gift was the false promise that Whites could invisibly and inaudibly participate in Black experience. Lomax imagined himself as passing on to other White folks the gift of privileged access to Black and Creole existence.

In *The Man Who Adores the Negro: Race and American Folklore*[72] Patrick Mullen argues that Lomax had "an emotional bond to Black people" that drove his fieldwork.[73] Mullen's book is extraordinary. It narrates the regrets and shame of a White folklorist who for most of his career followed in the footsteps of the Lomaxes. Mullen describes his White shame, admitting that he, like the Lomaxes, suffers from the sickness of a toxic love of Blackness. Mullen's White self-critique ends with a romantic White gesture of reconciliation and apology. But this is just more "romance of the dust." Burton insists: "Archives are not just sources or repositories as such, but constitute full-fledged historical actors as well."[74]

The archival instabilities that Lomax wanted to place in the background—his own position as White, as cultural outsider, as male, as expert and lover of folk culture—threaten to become the foreground, destroying White innocence and White pleasure. Once archive users—in this case the readers of *Mister Jelly Roll*—take the decolonial turn and begin to question "the history of the archive itself,"[75] we will begin to hear ourselves "if only figuratively, [as] thieves."[76] White archival pleasures are blocked, disrupted, and muted by the noisy politics of archival use.

When Lomax released *Mister Jelly Roll*, he thought he had captured essential Creole qualities. Lomax thought Creole experiences, whatever they turned out to be, would be the key to explaining jazz. This was the hope of the White folk listener. Lomax, a cultural outsider to New Orleans Creole people of color, entered and observed the lifeworld of musicians with the ambition of authentically recording and communicating their experiences to other White outsiders. As Oforlea argues: "Unlike Fanon, Lomax writes for a normative audience like himself (White, male and liberal) who are interested in his subject and perspective on rural southern blues music and culture."[77] Lomax's approach motivated White listeners into a White delusion that suggested that by turning on the microphone and letting the tape roll, unmediated sounds would be captured. After all—they believed—the microphone doesn't lie; it has no race, no gender, and no sexual orientation.

One reason the revivalist orientation has driven popular and academic culture is its promise to provide knowledge. Articulating a list of the features of Creole people, culture, and music preoccupies White jazz writers. The problem is that these White writers background the relationships that produce their knowledge, privileging single, supposedly authentic encounters with others.

White revivalist listeners orient themselves toward Creole and Black performers, but the relationship is not mutual. Revivalists imagine themselves as joyful discoverers and preservers. They foist onto others a politics of purity. The sound archives produced by White listening are productive, but unhappy. The archive offers knowledge in the form of sound recordings. But these recordings are fraught with the tensions of the colonial project. The colonial daydream that the sound archives of Black and Creole musicians were freely offered "gifts" to the White world, is an obvious and ongoing form of bad faith that allows Whites, to this day, to fantasize that they have discovered Black culture.

WHITE COLORBLIND LISTENING

In his 1957 work, *The Book of Jazz*, critic, composer, and musician Leonard Feather (1914–1994) recounted a bet he made with trumpeter, composer, and jazz master Roy Eldridge (1911–1989). Eldridge was a swing musician who modified Armstrong's trumpet lines, adding harmonic variations in the form of tri-tones and other sophisticated harmonies that foreshadowed bebop. Feather challenged Eldridge to a blindfold test. Once blindfolded, Feather would drop the needle on a cut, let it play, and ask Eldridge a series of questions, testing his ears. Could he name each soloist? The rhythm section? What was his opinion of the song? Feather was specifically interested in finding out whether Eldridge could identify the race of the players. The blindfold test would become a staple of *Downbeat* magazine, the American jazz periodical.

Feather's motives were not benign. An aggressive advocate of colorblind White listening, Feather tried to discredit Eldridge. Eldridge had said something to the White press that offended Feather. Sick of suffering from years of White racist violence he had experienced on the road with White bands, Eldridge vowed only to play with other Black musicians. The fact that Eldridge's vow offended Feather tells us a great deal about how fragile his ego was. Using the largest platform he had, the massively popular *Downbeat* magazine, Feather set out to demonstrate that nobody, not even the most accomplished jazz trumpeter of the time, could hear differences between Black jazz and White jazz. Feather wanted to advance his personal agenda of listening whitely by spreading it to the thousands of readers of *Downbeat*. His colorblind agenda, like that of colorblind thinking more generally, was to delegitimize Black voices critical of White violence. The colorblind listener operates from a position of White bad faith, styling himself as an anti-racist.

True to form, Feather claimed Eldridge was the real racist. He railed against the "Hitlerian" musicians and critics of his era, called race a "myth," and pompously suggested that because he didn't see or hear race that he could not be racist. When he argued that "there are no jazz genes,"[78] he was not rejecting racism, but airing a White grievance that bothered White musicians and critics. He was upset that anyone would challenge his ability to play jazz because he was White. White colorblind jazz listeners are motivated by a sense of White shame in being told (or imagining being told) that Whites don't play good jazz.

Feather couched his notion of good jazz in White tropes initiated in the *Etude*. Good jazz is mature, technical, and classical. Feathers described New Orleans jazz as an "aesthetic failure" liked by fans with "adolescent" tastes.[79] In the White big band music of the 1930s, Feather heard "progress."[80] He condescendingly described drummer Jo Jones, who anchored the pioneering rhythm section of the Count Basie Orchestra section from 1934 to 1948, as an adolescent player who took a "long step towards maturity."[81] By contrast, White Chicago school drummer, composer, and band leader Gene Krupa is called a "master technician" with "knowledge of the history and nature of percussion."[82] Feather repeatedly described Black and Creole players as childlike, and Whites as mature. White guitarist Eddie Lang "was the first to elevate the guitar to the stature of horns and piano as an *adult voice*."[83] Feather, like Whiteman thirty years before, propounded that jazz musicians of the 1920s, the very musicians who invented the genre that he copied and imitated, lacked "general knowledge."[84] They were the Black children; he was the White adult.

In Feather's words, what prompted the blindfold test was that "Eldridge at that time, embittered by his experiences with White bands, vowed never again to play in one."[85] Incredibly, Feather goes on to cite a long list of White violence experienced by Eldridge, who was often the only non-White member of the big bands in which he performed. In 1941, Eldridge had joined the all-White Gene Krupa Orchestra, becoming one of a handful of non-White musicians to work as a permanent member of a White big band. By 1944, he had joined Artie Shaw's predominantly White big band, but he left abruptly, owing to, he said, frequent racism.

According to Eldridge, touring with White big bands in the 1940s was exhausting and traumatizing. Onstage, he was a star of the show; offstage, he couldn't stay in the same hotels as the White band members, couldn't eat with the band members, couldn't go out publicly with the band, and at times had to pretend he was a porter for the White musicians in the group. Eventually, Eldridge suffered a nervous breakdown from the prolonged effects of White violence. "It was a lonely life . . . one night the tension got so bad I flipped. I could feel it right up to my neck while I was playing *Rockin Chair*; I started trembling, ran off the stand, and threw up. They carried me to the doctor's. I had a 105 fever; my nerves were shot."[86] Reflecting on his many years of being the only Black member of White big bands, Eldridge insisted: "Man, when you're on the stage you're great, but as soon as you come off, you're nothing. It's not worth the glory, not worth the money, not worth anything . . . just as if I had leprosy."[87]

Feather's colorblind listening had the effect of erasing Eldridge's experiences with White violence. Feather was the White adult, Eldridge the Black child in need of education. In bad faith, Feather thought of colorblindness as tough love—as though to say,

> Yes, Eldridge, you've experienced anti-Black racism, but the only way to cure racism is to stop thinking about race. In vowing to play only with Black musicians *you* have become a racist. Your immature ears cannot hear Blackness because there is no such thing. There are no Black or White musicians, just good and bad ones.

UPGRADED WHITE COLORBLIND LISTENING

White colorblind listening such as that advocated by Leonard Feather in the 1950s is still with us today. Presenting itself as anti-racist and anti-essentialist, upgraded White listening is a reactionary tool invented by Whites who experience Black looks.

Two contemporary books articulate what Robin James might call an "upgraded" version of White colorblind listening. Richard Sudhalter's *Lost Chords: White Musicians and Their Contributions to Jazz*[88] and Randall Sandke's *Where the Dark and the Light Folks Meet*[89] are rearguard White texts that explore the authors' feelings of White loss, White exclusion, and White marginalization. These authors feel overlooked and misheard by non-Whites. In response to the emotions of White estrangement, they craft a listening orientation that apprehends White jazz as a "lost" resource, under attack and in need of recovery.[90]

Given the absurdity of trying to orient a contemporary White public toward the "lost sounds" of a maligned and forgotten White jazz tradition, one wonders: What is the situation such that books defending White jazz as a fading resource are published and reviewed?

Can we treat upgraded White colorblindness as an ally of White supremacy advocated by Whites who believe they are progressive? Who are these supposedly progressive White readers, imagined and real, who feel attacked by Black looks? The *Atlantic Monthly* ran a positive review of *Lost Chords*, suggesting that its central thesis was credible: "a peculiar form of racial discrimination was thus, for a time at least, imposed on White bands by the record companies."[91] By contrast, the responses from Branford Marsalis and Amiri Baraka were harsh. Marsalis said the book didn't "dignify a response,"[92] and Amiri Baraka laughed when asked about it.

I don't think Sudhalter or Randke have a case that is even remotely plausible. But in describing Whiteness as a feeling of "laboring against a current," doing battle, and "saving" White culture, and in describing White listening as a "counterweight" and "corrective" to the "Black creationist canon,"[93] these authors articulate a contemporary pattern of White bad faith. Upgraded colorblind listening is aggressively White and aggressively anti-Black.

The upgraded colorblind listener denies that jazz is Black music, denies the history of White violence in jazz, and asserts that colorblind listeners are the real anti-racists. Incredibly, Sudhalter writes, "Jazz, says the now accepted canon, is Black."[94] He calls this claim a "noble lie," which he believes was created by Black radicals and White liberals. On this view, Black culture is not culture, and even if Black culture does exist, it is not part of America.[95]

In point of fact, colorblind listening is a White technique for erasing Black humanity, as revealed in sentences like this: "I should make it clear that nowhere in this book do I question the existence of Black culture."[96] When upgraded colorblind listeners assert that the history of Whites listening to jazz is "a Black-White symbiosis,"[97] they adopt a nostalgic, whitewashed attitude that obscures coercion, present and past. Sudhalter's assertion that racial symbiosis "flourished within the jazz world from the mid-thirties onward"[98] is a dangerous fantasy that allows today's White colorblind listeners to imagine themselves as anti-racists who reject the politics of purity.

WHITE ECSTATIC LISTENING

White ecstatic listening is a cousin of colorblind listening, but its motivations are different. Colorblind listeners are reactive; they develop raceless orientations in response to feeling seen and heard as White. Ecstatic listening is White, but it is not necessarily reactionary. The ecstatic listener I describe is attuned to phenomenological embodiment, but not racialized embodiment. Early Sartre is an ecstatic listener, as is the philosopher Don Ihde. The ecstatic listener makes a simple mistake: elevating classical listening to a universal. Ecstatic, or classical, listening refers to the type of listening exhibited by Americans and Europeans who attend symphony halls with the expectation that they must remain still and quiet so that they, and those around them, can be transported beyond the material. Notions of ecstatic listening can be found in various cultural contexts, including, of course, Greek theater. The version I describe is ecstatic *classical* listening, the American version of which emerged in the middle and late nineteenth century as a technology for separating music from noise. White ecstatic classical listening was a racialized technology that coded Black people as noisy, fleshy, and embodied, and coded Whites as disembodied intellectuals who could transcend the flesh by closing their eyes and quietly entering a trance.

I read the American philosopher Don Ihde as a White ecstatic listener. His path-breaking 1976 book, *Listening and Voice*, articulated a phenomenology of listening in an era when most mainstream philosophers were debating the definition of art. But even the updated 2007 edition of *Listening and Voice* is problematic because it offers a raceless and genderless account of listening. Ihde simultaneously values embodied philosophy and obscures the Whiteness and masculinity of the ecstatic view he offers.

The problem with the White ecstatic listener is that he or she elevates still, quiet, and nonparticipatory listening above noisy listening. Noisy listening acknowledges the call-and-response among musicians and audiences, whether mediated by sound recordings or in live performance. While theorists like Henry Lewis Gates,[99] Amiri Baraka,[100] and Paul Gilroy[101] have established the African roots of the practice of call-and-response and traced its development in Black diaspora sonic cultures, the place of call-and-response in White sound culture has received less attention. In White Baptist church music of the early Americas, for instance, there were no hymnals, no instruments, no trained song leaders, and many White parishioners were illiterate. Lay congregants would "line out" or state the "time and tune" of a hymn by singing one line at a time, to be repeated by the congregation.[102] By the late 1700s, however, the White Baptist church began eliminating such "lining out"—that is, call-and-response—because it was perceived as too noisy, and I would add, too Black. One commentator praised the elimination of lining out, which caused "an horrid Medly [sic] of confused and disorderly Noises."[103] A fuller genealogy of White ecstatic listening would involve studying a variety of such cultural moments in secular and religious musical practices when Whites modified or abandoned call-and-response in the name of separating sound from noise. As I have argued throughout, the distinction between sound and noise is a political, not an ontological distinction.

Ihde summarizes the White ecstatic view of listening when he writes about spinning a record of J.S. Bach on a turntable, alone in his living room. "In ecstasy I would listen to the disciplined, artful, magnificence as this music filled the room and my consciousness. However, it took little time to note a flaw. Any scratch, any barely audible hum, any interference became annoying and threatened the enchantment of the experience."[104] The White ecstatic listener argues that musical listening requires shutting out noise. But, in fact, hearing noise is one of the most important elements of embodied listening.

As Vivian Sobchack[105] writes, Ihde's autobiographical approach to phenomenology is appealing because it utilizes "the familiar as a methodological tactic."[106] This appeal becomes concerning when Ihde fails to note that his ecstatic listening orientation is gendered, raced, and geographically situated. The race-neutral description of listening is problematic within the terms Ihde offers, that of a "flesh[ed] out" phenomenology and a "grounding [of] the body."[107] He shows how to start from the mundane, using autobiography, engaging the flesh—but by not marking his flesh, he passively assumes the position of Whiteness, and misses the opportunity to theorize the White, male body as a form of technology. Ihde is not sufficiently attuned to the body as a practico-inert-orienting technology that changes over time.

Listening practices are historically contingent. White ecstatic listening is a technology with a time and date stamp. As Lawrence W. Levine has shown in *Highbrow/Lowbrow: The Emergence of Cultural Hierarchy in America*, ecstatic listening emerged in the United States in the nineteenth century as a form of social control.[108] Ecstatic listening habits were crowd control measures created by White elites in response to the noisy listening practices of vaudeville. The ecstatic White listener sharply differentiated music from noise. Eliminating noise in theaters and controlling the bodies of listeners was a whitening, segregationist technology. Ecstatic listening orientations were cultivated by White American elites like John Sullivan Dwight, who were anti-vaudeville and wished to make theater-going a sacred experience, like going into an all-White segregated church. Failing to understand the history of White efforts to shut out what Tricia Rose calls "Black noise" leads today's White ecstatic listener to think that White perspectives of listening are universal.[109]

Ihde builds his phenomenology around personal listening situations. These include taking a hike in the woods, walking through a city, listening to a record, sitting at a chair in his home, listening to music through a set of headphones, and his favorite case, going to hear Western classical music in concert halls. Ihde's most frequent reference point is listening to Bach, a passion I also share. However, when I listen to a Bach record, I do so noisily, often with my guitar in hand, playing along and interrupting the sound recording frequently, engaging in a type of remix. I am also used to catching glares from my White colleagues when I spontaneously verbalize and vocalize my reactions to performances in White classical music halls. When I am shushed in the symphony hall, I am experiencing the White sonic gaze.

Ihde describes listening as the creation of a phenomenological field where music emerges from noise, but he does not offer a political economy of the noise/sound distinction. He describes listening as an immersive, synesthetic experience of "musical ecstasy" where there is no will, or directionality, and no consciousness of an object.[110] In the ecstatic state, "I do not even primarily hear the symphony as the sounds of the instruments."[111] The ordinary relationship to things is suspended. But musical ecstasy is fragile, since the noise of the ordinary world constantly intervenes.[112] Ihde returns to the case of noise frequently: the scratched record, the squeaky bow, and the amateur who makes mistakes.

Ihde analyzes listening with a tool he inadvertently borrows from visual phenomenology—the foreground-background distinction. He argues that listening is like looking, since noise (background) must be separated from music (foreground). Music emerges through the exclusion of noise. Listening involves tuning out static, scratches, wrong notes, coughs, and ambient sounds. I submit that in Ihde's work, the visualist foreground-background distinction gets mapped onto a culturally specific set of listening practices. Ihde's case of listening to Bach is based on a White tradition of so-called "classical" music listening. I enclose the term "classical" in quote marks to note that the term is ideological, not neutral. The White classical listening orientation insists on shutting out noise from the listen spaces of the theater. At the political level, "noise" is aligned with Blackness, especially call-and-response, improvisation, and dance. Such Black noise is shut out because Black people are shut out. Within theaters and churches in particular, White Americans developed social practices that silenced and shushed their bodies. For instance, in White classical listening spaces, applause is highly regulated; those who applaud at the wrong time are censured through glares, ushers, and the passive-aggressive White shush, all various forms of the White sonic gaze. Knowing precisely when to applaud is considered a mark of highbrow sophistication. At a recent student concert where my daughter was performing on clarinet with an orchestra, the conductor painstakingly instructed the audience that they must not clap in between movements and must hold their applause to the end. In preparation for the concert, my daughter specifically asked me not to clap at the wrong time, lest I embarrass her. The social practice of White ecstatic listening is also cooked into the architecture of classical theaters, which are constructed to resonate the sounds of acoustic chamber instruments. But this acoustic environment backfires when small noises from the audience, like a cough, are amplified. On my view, White listening practices, as much as or more than repertoire and performance style of the musicians onstage, create what we think of today as the classical music experience.

In "Jazz Embodied: Instrumentation," written in 2001, Ihde updates *Listening and Voice* by offering brief thoughts about jazz. The "embodiment" of his title refers not to the human body, but the "body of the saxophone." Drawing on his broader writings on technology and science, Ihde suggests that the saxophone gave rise to jazz soloing, because the instrument was both loud and expressive. In point of fact, the tradition of soloing grew out of the collective improvisation of New Orleans brass players like Louis Armstrong who developed the practice of taking long solos rather than short, improvised breaks. Armstrong, not the trumpet he played, was the "body" that brought jazz soloing to White ears in the Jazz Age, long before saxophones were common in jazz bands.

The basic phenomenological limitation of Ihde's theory of listening is that it does not recognize the political economy of the noise/sound separation. In many musical situations, noise can be a part of the listening experience, for both players and audiences. Jazz listening is noisy and thrives on the call-and-response.[113] The ecstatic view fails to grasp the dynamic of noisy listening, a form of listening that is not based on shutting out noise, but on attuning the noises of the listening body with the noises of the performer. Noise has been an important part of jazz for the past hundred years in the United States at sideshows, theaters, cabarets, clubs, jooks, live recording sessions, rent parties, fish fries, and jam sessions.

WHITE EXISTENTIALISM AND THE WHITE PROBLEM

Having outlined six patterns of bad faith White listening, I conclude this chapter with reflections on the existential framework of the "White problem." I explore a tension in Simone de Beauvoir's thinking about Whiteness: She problematized White racism, especially in the United States, but she also exhibited the White sonic gaze.

In 1947, on a four-month tour of the United States, Beauvoir slummed in Black neighborhoods, churches, and jazz clubs in Harlem. I use the verb "slum" to mark the similarities between her travel memoir *American Day by Day* and the "genre of the slum narrative."[114] As Katharine S. Bullard argues, well-intentioned, White urban reformers in the Progressive Era wrote popular first-person accounts of walking through poor, immigrant neighborhoods. Styling themselves as anti-racists, Progressive Era Whites wanted the White world to open its eyes to "how the other half lived."[115] But their writings drew extensively on the observational techniques of colonial travel narratives that figured slum dwellers as "primitives." Colonial travel narratives, extremely popular in the eighteenth and nineteenth centuries, were written accounts of travel and exploration in parts of the world considered "exotic" by Europeans. Travel narratives fueled and rationalized European imperialism by bolstering public opinion in the metropoles that non-Europeans were fundamentally different from Europeans. Mary Louise Pratt has shown that travel narratives "created the 'domestic subject' of Euroimperialism," which is to say that Europeans created a sense of themselves as White and "civilized" through an imaginary contrast with the peoples, customs, and lands described by travelers and conquered by European powers.[116] While it is deeply ironic that Beauvoir, an avowed anti-imperialist, drew on a literary techniques that were used to justify imperial land grabs in the eighteenth and nineteenth centuries, the pattern is not unique to Beauvoir. Nathalie Nya's *Simone de Beauvoir and the Colonial Experience* directly connects the themes of anti-colonialism and existential feminism. Nya writes, "I refer to Beauvoir as a *colonizer women* or *colon*, in the French, in order to emphasize the weight of French colonialism on Beauvoir's identity as a white French woman."[117] This critique of Beauvoir is not personal; all of France's White citizens were colons, Nya notes.[118] As Bullard shows in the case of the American reformer Jane Addams, slumming was not uncommon among early White American (and European) feminists who believed proximity to the oppressed would allow them to advocate for those who had no advocates.[119] To describe the ironic juxtaposition of progressive politics on the one hand and use of imperial literary techniques on the other, Antoinette Burton has coined the useful phrase "imperial feminism."[120]

In *America Day by Day*, Beauvoir is swept away by the romance of Black America. She gives exoticized, essentialist descriptions of the Black people she encounters, drawing heavily on French primitivist tropes about jazz, especially those found in Hughes Panassié's *Le Jazz Hot* (1934). Beauvoir describes American White bad faith, but rarely thematizes her position as a White, French traveler. Though critical of American White gazes and American White bad faith, she listens Whitely, not because of malintent, but because, in the words of Jamaica Kincaid, "a tourist is an ugly human being."[121]

The most poignant illustration of Beauvoir's White bad faith is her "adventure" walking down Lenox Avenue. With a confused metaphor, she dimly admits she is slumming: "I was the Zulu afraid of a bicycle, the country woman lost in the underground."[122] Beauvoir is slumming because she goes to Harlem to prove that she is not afraid of Black people. Journaling the night after her "adventure" walking alone in Harlem, she gives a rich phenomenological account of White fear. "[I] asked myself just what I should have done to have had to flee from here, screaming towards the protection of an underground station; it seemed as difficult to provoke rape or murder as it would have been in Columbus Circle at midday. Strange orgies must take place in the minds of serious thinking people; as for me, this broad, gay, peaceful boulevard acted like a brake on my imagination."[123] Beauvoir writes about White fear as something that other Whites experience.

Beauvoir is slumming in the sense that she desires contact with Black people to ease her anxieties. White anxiety is not peculiar to her, but it is part of the tradition of White phenomenological orientations that treat non-Whites, and especially Black Americans, as sources of primal energy and truth. Unlike Progressive Era White slummers, Beauvoir was a critic of White bad faith and operated from within an understanding of the White problem. Ultimately though, as Margaret A. Simons notes, "Beauvoir's understanding of racism is central to her philosophical project in *The Second Sex*; but racism and ethnocentrism are also problems for her."[124] The same is true for *America Day by Day*.

In *The Second Sex*, Beauvoir writes:

> Women's entire history has been written by men. Just as in America there is no Black problem but a White one . . . just as anti-Semitism is not a Jewish problem, it's our problem, so the problem of woman has always been a problem of men.[125]

This incandescent passage, published seventy years ago, sets a prescient agenda for race- and gender-critical phenomenology. It is a classic statement of the White problem. But as Kathryn Sophia Belle shows in her extensive work on the relationship between White existentialism and critical theories of gender and race in Black existential thought, "Unfortunately, while Beauvoir and Sartre do recognize problems of White privilege, neither of them explicitly engages Black women intellectuals or a Black feminist analysis."[126] Across her writings, including "Fanon and Sartre 50 Years Later,"[127] "Sartre, Beauvoir, and the Race/Gender Analogy: A Case for Black Feminist Philosophy,"[128] and "'The Man Who Lived Underground': Jean-Paul Sartre and the Philosophical Legacy of Richard Wright,"[129] Belle shows that White existentialist critiques of Whiteness were influenced by and imbricated with the critiques offered by Black existential thinkers. Belle's work challenges the listening politics of White existentialist thinkers—like Beauvoir and like myself—raising the question of how we listen today, given that White bad faith is systematic, not just personal. White existentialists do not escape being White just by treating Whiteness as a problem.

In *Hannah Arendt and the Negro Question*,[130] Belle helpfully interprets Richard Wright's formulation of the White problem. When Wright asserts, "there isn't any Negro problem, there is only a White problem," he "negates the conceptualization of Black people as a problem *and* the notion that anti-Black racism is Black people's problem. Wright does this while simultaneously situating White people—or more specifically, White people's anti-Black racism as the problem."[131] Belle's argument exposes the logic that turns women, Jews, and Black people into a single problem. White existentialism sometimes conflates the struggles of the oppressed by reducing race and gender to the same othering force.

Beauvoir's conception of White bad faith in *American Day by Day* draws on Wright's formulation of the White problem.[132] She references his novel *Black Boy* and describes walking in New York with Wright, attending a Black church with him, and going together to the all-Black Savoy theater to hear jazz. Through her friendship with Wright, she negotiated her White love of Blackness. From him she says she learned that in America a Black person "can never forget that he is Black."[133]

Beauvoir experiences Harlem both alone and with Wright at her side. She struggles with her Whiteness—at times experiencing it as a "curse" imposed by the looks of Black people, especially children. Whiteness "weighs heavily no matter what I may think or say or do."[134] As a White woman with a Black man, she becomes a target of the gaze. When walking with Wright and his White wife, Ellen, Beauvoir experiences her Whiteness as a "stiffness," "guilt," and fear. At one point she and Ellen are catcalled. The male gaze is conveyed through sound. When Wright talks back to the catcaller, Beauvoir writes, "A White man never would have found just the right word and smile. . . . I climbed the steps with a light heart; Wright's friendship, his presence at my side, seemed to absolve me to-night."[135] Beauvoir feels that Wright's friendship absolves her of Whiteness.

Linda Martín Alcoff, in *The Future of Whiteness*, offers a different view of Beauvoir's visit to Harlem. Rather than focusing on Beauvoir's emotions of absolution, Alcoff highlights her feelings of White shame and estrangement. For Alcoff, Beauvoir's refusal to smile at Black children is a positive, antiracist step. "As she recounts experiences of shame and deep-seated discomfort, she was not simply commenting on the racism of others, but awakening to the deep and complicated nature of her own White subjectivity."[136] Alcoff portrays Beauvoir as starting down the path of White double consciousness. Beauvoir demonstrates a productive type of White shame in her smile "boycott," to borrow a concept from Shulamith Firestone, Lisa Milbank, and Sara Ahmed.[137]

Though I am in broad agreement with Alcoff's decisive analysis of Whiteness, I disagree that Beauvoir owned her fear. Beauvoir describes White fear as that of others: "I walk toward Harlem, but my footsteps are not quite as carefree as usual; this isn't just a walk but a kind of adventure. A force pulls me back, a force that emanates from the borders of the Black city and drives me back—fear. Not mine by that of others—the fear of all those Whites who never take the risk of going to Harlem."[138] *American Day by Day* is an unstable text. In one breath Beauvoir formulates the problem of White bad faith, and in the next breath she embodies it.

Beauvoir even notes with clarity that White bad faith is an orientation toward reality through which White people evade responsibility. As for whether she believes she is in White bad faith, the text does not seem to support this interpretation. Beauvoir opines: "White people can mask their responsibility thanks to the vicious circle we just mentioned: they see in the conditions of the Blacks they find an apparent confirmation of their behavior toward them. One of the reason that allows them to believe . . . in the inferiority of Blacks is that this inferiority exists—but it exists because they've created it, because they are still creating it, and this they refuse to acknowledge."[139] By failing to place herself in the category of "White," and instead thinking of herself as an observer and critic of American Whiteness, Beauvoir ironically creates a text that is ideological rather than self-reflective. To this day in France, a debate rages over whether "blanchité" (Whiteness) is a valid category.[140]

Given the modes of bad faith White listening I've adumbrated, where do Beauvoir's listening practices fall? Was Beauvoir a good listener? I think of her as part hipster, part revivalist, and part slummer. She is attuned to how listening practices create the musical object and sharply critical of mainstream White taste. Yet as a White voyeur in Black spaces, she cannot escape the shame of being an invader. Beauvoir's desire to be absolved of Whiteness through her proximity to Blackness is a form of slumming, as revealed in her time with Mezz Mezzrow, her trip to the Savoy with Wright, her experience hearing Bechet, and her two trips to Black churches in Harlem.

Beauvoir was a White revivalist listener. Believing that New Orleans style was authentic jazz, she sought to hear Louis Armstrong, Sidney Bechet, and Billie Holiday during her time in New York. She did not like modern jazz, describing bebop as "noise." Hearing Armstrong perform in Carnegie Hall, she was disappointed that he was "old," out of place, and performing for

Whites who applauded at the wrong places.[141] White mainstream audiences did not appreciate New Orleans jazz, the only "authentic jazz, so pure and moving." Beauvoir even called White American listening a form of murder: "Americans have more or less murdered jazz, but they still love it."[142]

Beauvoir criticizes White mainstream listening using the metaphors of death, dehumanization, and clogged ears. In White middle-class clubs, "treacly music filters through the radio or from a pick-up, *gums your ears and ends by clogging your brain.*"[143] Beauvoir is critical of White audiences with gummy ears who listen to radios, Muzak, and commercial White big bands. "That White Americans understand jazz less and less is evident."[144] Whites listen to "sugared melodies," and leave the radio on all the time, in the background.[145] She draws a parallel between White radio and "Muzak"—both pervade social space. Even White liberals at a "more or less *avant-garde* night club," where Josh White is performing, listen with gummed-up ears.[146] She is "uncomfortable" among these White liberals because they hypocritically applaud protest music but do nothing to fight racism.

Beauvoir distinguishes White liberal listeners from hipsters. In Harlem, she meets Mezz Mezzrow, who gives her a signed copy of *Really the Blues* and some records. She identifies with Mezzrow, and with the spirit of White hipsterism: "I knew they loved jazz and hated American capitalism, racism, puritan moralizing and indeed everything I most detest in America, the country to which they belonged."[147] Unlike the hypocritical White liberals among whom Beauvoir feels estranged, with White hipsters she feels at home. She and the hipsters hate the same things: White mainstream music tastes, racism, puritan morality, and capitalism. Reflecting on her conversations with Mezzow, she explains her dislike for bebop. Bebop is "noise and rhythm and nothing more."[148]

Beauvoir uses standard revivalist language when she describes Sidney Bechet as "one of the last musicians to play in the pure New Orleans style."[149] One significant part of Beauvoir's memory of hearing Bechet is her description of a Black female cook working in the back of the club. She gives a long physical description of the cook, a "woman with a Black face," who is "stout," "with a tired look but with indefatigable eyes."[150] As she watches her dance, Beauvoir imagines that the cook has a troubled life full of "misfortunes." The cook "danced, rooted to the spot, with a smile in her eyes not known to White men's faces."[151] Beauvoir watches the cook listening to Bechet and imagines her lost in an ecstatic state, "without past or future she was filled with joy, the music justified the whole of her difficult life."[152] The Black cook, under Beauvoir's pen, is reduced to a White trope of jazz ecstasy.

At the Savoy, Beauvoir trains her White gaze on Black dancers, outlining their bodies, describing what they're wearing, how they move, how they smile. Though not "pretty," these Black women are "alive," unlike "the stiff formality" of White Americas.[153] "Their animal life is not choked by the armor of puritan virtue."[154] Watching the dancers, Beauvoir ruminates on the sexual jealousy of White heterosexual men: "[Y]ou understand how sexual jealousy can enter into the hatred that White men in America carry within themselves."[155] Like her description of White fear, Beauvoir's description of White sexual fascination focuses on orientations of other White people, not her own. In reality, she is experiencing the White fear and sexual fascination she attributes to other Whites. Beauvoir does not highlight her White listening position, instead describing how Black dancers are listening. The Black dancers express a "truth" unknown to Whites.[156] Beauvoir contrasts the truthful dancing of Black Americans with the inauthentic dancing of Black people in France. Black Americans are "natural," "relaxed," and "possessed by the rhythm of jazz."[157]

So profoundly moved is Beauvoir by the truth of Black dancing, that she compares slumming at the Savoy to the philosophical conversion of exiting Plato's cave. "But to-night I felt its message, I touched on something which was linked to nothing but itself: I had emerged from the cave."[158] Listening to jazz and watching dancers "was the greatest miracle of my journey and it was never more dazzling than to-day."[159]

Beauvoir did not consider her trip to New York complete without a visit to a Black church. To be precise, she visited two Black churches. With Wright as her guide, she first visited the Abyssinian Baptist Church, and was struck by the call-and-response between the preacher, Clayton Powell, and congregants. But Beauvoir was disappointed. The Black congregants were too restrained, too "moderate," too "respectable."[160] She hungered for a more authentic experience of Black life that she thought she would find only in churches in poor neighborhoods. She asked Wright to take her to a different Black church and was more satisfied with the Black preacher's performance, describing it as a form of jazz: "It was a 'hot' improvisation, the most authentic jazz of all."[161]

The fact that Beauvoir went slumming in Harlem is not surprising given the long cultural history of the practice among Whites. Slumming in Black churches is a common form of White racial voyeurism that is with us today. In *Seeing a Colorblind Future: The Paradox of Race*,[162] critical race theorist Patricia J. Williams describes how White tourists in Harlem practice "gate-crashing." "In Black neighborhoods around the United States, but most particularly in well-known communities like Harlem in New York, busloads of tourists flock to Black churches on Sunday . . . gate-crashing."[163] Noting that "the real lives of Blacks unfold outside the view of many Whites," Williams suggests that racial voyeurism is an "obsessive indulgence" among curious Whites.[164]

Beauvoir was a hipster, revivalist jazz listener who felt that her friendship with Richard Wright absolved her—at least temporarily—of her Whiteness. She chipped away at the audio/visual litany by studying how White audiences listened. She articulated a version of the White problem that was gender critical and critical of antisemitism. Her critique of White bad faith was far ahead of its time by the standards of White, European philosophy. Beauvoir was estranged from her White skin and bristled at the hypocrisy of White liberals who listened to jazz music but did nothing to fight for Black lives.

Beauvoir described White bad faith philosophically and struggled with it personally. As Alcoff shows, reading Beauvoir today is an important part of formulating the future of Whiteness. Whites experiencing White double consciousness have an existential choice. "Like Beauvoir, Whites may come to realize the social meanings of Whiteness, its unearned privileges and moral collusion, once they begin to intuit how they are viewed by non-white others."[165] Alcoff's project for the future of Whiteness strikes a more optimistic tone than my own. Our basic conclusion, however, is the same: "Even those Whites who come to participate in the coalition for social change . . . come to the group or event *as Whites.*"[166]

From the plantation to the academy, White Americans have made race with their ears. White listening is a colonizing technology, an orientation in space and time, through which Whites have controlled listening spaces by distinguishing music from noise.

White minstrel listening, which conflated actors with their roles, allowed Whites to transfer images and sounds of the stage into egregious stereotypes of Black people. The minstrel images and sounds of Black people became stock components of White psychology. In 1924, the "jazz problem" was first articulated in White print culture. By describing Blackness as a problem, Whites expressed their anxieties about sexuality, self-control, drugs, dancing, and cross-racial desire. In the big band era, White jazz saviors were crowned "kings" by a White public that was fascinated with Black music and Creole rhythms, but who preferred all-White spaces. Hipsters and revivalists balked at the White commercial big band music of their parents' generation, and fetishized Black and Creole folk musicians. Desiring contact with non-White others, hipsters slummed in Black neighborhoods, fantasizing about becoming Black, and leaving the White killjoy world behind. Revivalists collected race records, organized festivals, and experienced archival pleasure in rediscovering lost sounds. Colorblind jazz listening materialized as White musicians, critics, and jazz audiences felt, looked at, and listened to jazz music as Whites. Ecstatic White listening is not aggressively pro-White like colorblind listening, but by not marking the embodied position from which ek-stasis is experienced, the results can be the same.

It has been one hundred years since Du Bois formulated the White problem in *Darkwater*. Today, no self-critical White American listener can ignore the fact that our collective listening habits are racist and sexist.

Listening Exercises for Chapter 2
The Jazz Problem

Rhythms are stories, as are melodies and harmonies. Rhythms are also concepts—they express ethical truths and social facts. Rhythms serve as open-ended instructions. Broadly speaking, our bodily orientation to rhythmic instructions can be observational (passive) or participatory (active). Jazz Pedagogy emphasizes experimentation with different bodily and mental orientations to sound, and using phenomenological self-reflection to make explicit the stories and concepts we experience musically.

To explore the notion that musical meaning is established by *how we listen*, we will need to learn to hear musical pulses as variable. A fun and important place to begin is by learning the ur-text of all Afro-Caribbean music, *the clave beat*. "Clave" is Spanish for "key," and it names both an instrument and a rhythmic pattern. The clave pattern is considered the "key" because it is used as the touchpoint for organizing musical ensembles. In ensembles, musicians listen for the high-pitched click of the clave (two hardwood sticks struck against one another) to organize their accompaniment. The fundamental dynamic of the clave pattern (there are many variants) is three-against-two polyrhythm. Polyrhythm is what gives Afro-Caribbean music such a danceable, fluid, interactive feel. It allows dancers and musicians to hear endless numbers of pulses and inflection points within a short, usually two-bar, repeating phrase. Europeans hearing these rhythms for the first time often described them as hypnotizing and trance-inducing. The same language that of infection, characterized the first period of the White American reception of jazz.

Polyrhythm refers to multiple rhythms occurring simultaneously. Speaking broadly, and with many notable exceptions, especially in folk music,[1] European music is either in duple meter or triple meter. Triple meter is "waltz time," counting in three (one, two, three//one, two, three).

Duple meter is felt in groups of two (one, two//one, two) or four (one, two, three, four//one, two, three, four). *The clave rhythm is simultaneously felt in groups of three and four,* hence, the name "three-against-two" polyrhythm. Even if you don't know these terms, you are familiar with the *clave feel*, which is prominent in such music as calypso (Barbados), Danzon and son (Cuba), merengue (Dominican Republic), salsa and reggaeton (Puerto Rico), reggae, and ska (Jamaica), and of course, jazz (New Orleans). I like to use the polyrhythm exercises below in group settings, especially classrooms, to help establish community and the fun of listening together. Encourage members of the group to listen noisily by clapping, stomping, or singing along. Learning the three-against-two polyrhythm of the clave beat is a way of synesthetically grasping how the "jazz problem" was a form of contact between Eurocentric ears and the rhythms of the Afro-Caribbean traditions.

POLYRHYTHM EXERCISES

Listen to any recording that has a syncopated or polyrhythmic feel and clap along. Listen for difference. At first, select any song that has polyrhythm and have members of the group clap wherever they feel the pulse. Have them compare where they feel the pulse with others in the group. Note how different people feel the pulse in different places. (You can find suggested playlists on my YouTube channel.) Next, use the Figures included here to build up to clapping a three-against-two polyrhythm.

To avoid the complication of teaching standard Western musical notation, I have modified a notation system from the contemporary drummer Billy Martin in his book *Riddim: Claves of African Origin.*[2] Each "x" is a clap and has equal value. Underneath the notation, I have written out the words that drummers usually sing to accompany their clapping (or playing). The first "x" is the "one," and the second "x" is the "and." In other words, each "x" would be equivalent to an eighth note in standard Western music notation. The bolded "x" signifies an accent. An accent is a beat that is played louder than other beats. The patterns should be repeated over and over without stopping. Start very slowly at first. (You can find a video on my You Tube channel to guide the group exercises listed in figures 2.1–2.4.)

XX|XX|XX|XX

|1 and 2 and 3 and 4 and|

Figure 2.1 Polyrhythm Clapping Exercise One.

XX|XX|XX|XX

|1 and 2 **and** 3 and 4 and|

Figure 2.2 Polyrhythm Clapping Exercise Two.

XX|**XX**|XX|XX

|1 and **2** and 3 and 4 and|

Figure 2.3 Polyrhythm Clapping Exercise Three.

XX|XX|XX|XX||XX|XX|XX|XX

||**1** and 2 **and** 3 and 4 and |||1 and **2** and 3 and 4 and||

Figure 2.4 Polyrhythm Clapping Exercise Four.

WHITE MINSTREL LISTENING EXERCISE

Add a content warning before introducing these exercises. Evaluate how White minstrel listening conflates actor and role. Try to imagine a period White listener who projects the degraded characters ("Sambo," "Jim Crow," the "coon") onto the performer. Occupy the mindset of "hokum" authenticity, in which period listeners asked themselves, "Is this singer a fake or real?" Describe a White minstrel and humbug orientation toward the music of George W. Johnson's song "The Whistling Coon" (1891) and "The Laughing Song." Focus on Johnson's vocal technique and musicianship. Think of the role of the trickster. For a visual tie-in, watch portions of the Duke Ellington film *Black and Tan* (1929) and the Amos N' Andy film *Check and Double Check* (1930). For a contemporary tie-in, explore musicians who challenge minstrel listening. One good example is the Pharcyde's production "It's Jigaboo Time" from their album *Bizarre Ride II* (1992).

WHITE SAVIOR LISTENING EXERCISE

Clap and sing along to Paul Whiteman's 1920 recording of "Whispering." Listen to how Whiteman's attempt to "tame" swing makes it rhythmically stiff, less syncopated, less polyrhythmic than other versions. The call-and-response to the audience is muted and discouraged. Note the tempo of "Whispering" and sing the first part of the melody. Compare "Whispering," Whiteman's first hit, which sold two million copies, to other hits of 1920s such as Al Jolson's "Swanee" (Jolson was a White Jewish singer famous for his Blackface performances), Mamie Smith's "Crazy Blues" (the record that created the vocal blues craze), and the Ted Lewis Orchestra's tune "When My Baby Smiles at Me." Appraise the Paul Whiteman film *King of Jazz* (1930) as a narrative of White uplift, especially the "King of the Jungle" vignette, which opens the film, and the "Voodoo Drum" vignette, which introduces Gershwin's "Rhapsody in Blue." Duke Ellington credits Whiteman with introducing syncopated music by making it "Whiter."[3] What do you think Ellington meant by "Whiter"?

WHITE HIPSTER LISTENING EXERCISE

Mezz Mezzrow treated White listening as a neurosis that could cured by immersion in non-White culture. Unlike the savior, the hipster experiences White estrangement and wants to participate in the call-and-response. Study Mezzrow's "loving" White imitations of Louis Armstrong and Sidney Bechet in the song "Sendin' the Vipers" (1934). Compare Mezzrow's version of "I Found a New Baby" (1928) with Ethel Waters's version. White hipsters slum in Black spaces. Conduct a White "space invader" self-assessment.[4] If you identify as White, have you ever been to a musical space where you were the ethnic minority? Was this space a church, mosque, concert hall, club, party, or sports event? Describe your feelings in these spaces. Did you feel "estranged" from your Whiteness? Conduct a White shame self-inventory on the topic of White listening and the "N-word." If you identify as White, do you listen to music that has the N-word in the lyrics? Do you sing along? Is your experience different at a party? Alone in your room? With other people? With other White people? Among non-White people? Explore the story and politics of "Sukka Ni**a" by *A Tribe Called Quest* (1993).

WHITE REVIVALIST LISTENING EXERCISE

Based on Sidney Bechet's critique of revivalist listening in his autobiography, *Treat It Gentle*, there are three elements of White revivalist listening: nostalgia for the past, an appeal to authenticity, and a feeling of discovery. Explore nostalgia by listening to the music of contemporary composer and pianist Robert Glasper and reflecting on his "We're the only genre of music that competes with people that aren't here anymore."[5] Look at the list of ten episodes of Ken Burns's mega-hit miniseries documentary *Jazz*. The final episode of the film only goes up to 1961. Did jazz end in 1961? Episode One opens with Marsalis and a narrative voice-over: "Jazz is America's music . . . born of a thousand negotiations . . . between having and not having . . . between Black and White

... between the old Africa and the old Europe."⁶ Why is it problematic to depict jazz music as a force that *unified* Black and White Americans in the 1920s?

Explore discovery listening by reading the Wikipedia entry for Skip James and the heading "Rediscovery." Listen to James performing "Devil Got My Woman" at the Newport Folk Festival in 1966. Why is it dubious to claim that James had been "discovered" and then "rediscovered"? Listen to Jelly Roll Morton being interviewed by Alan Lomax in 1938.⁷ Explore the "archival pleasure" that Lomax would have felt in conducting this interview. Explore your own feelings of archival pleasure. In Morton's voice and story, do you sense yourself coming in contact with an old, lost, fading resource?

Explore White authenticity listening by studying Charles Kuralt's interview of Lomax in 1991.⁸ Lomax's White listening orientation is neither innocent nor merely academic; it is an ideological position that rationalizes the economic and carceral exploitation of Black people. Explore the White bad faith of Lomax's comment that he "was giving these people an avenue to tell their side of the story."⁹ The incarcerated musicians he recorded remained incarcerated while Lomax became a famous public figure and a prominent academic.

WHITE COLORBLIND LISTENING EXERCISE

Identity White colorblind listening by entering the imaginative space of a listener who purportedly "does not hear color." Explore the difference between the intention and effect of the White colorblind listener. When Leonard Feather made his bet with Roy Eldridge about being able to hear color, he styled himself as a progressive anti-racist. Was he? Why was Feather offended that Eldridge vowed to play with only Black musicians? Feather's bet focused on the racial identity of musicians and not the qualities of the sounds they were performing. In other words, when Eldridge was challenged to listen for Blackness in the needle drop test, Feather was only concerned with whether the musicians on the recording self-identified as Black, not whether they were playing in a Black style, that is, a style of music originated by Black people and rooted in Black cultures. Upon reflection, isn't it quite strange to think that from a musician's sound the listener would be able to determine how that person self-identifies? Select any music you like, play it for a friend, and ask them if the musician "sounds Black." Have them do the same for you.

WHITE ECSTATIC LISTENING EXERCISE

White ecstatic listening separates music from noise and fetishizes the listening practices associated with Western classical music. If you have the opportunity, attend a classical music performance in a concert hall. Notice the elements of crowd control—especially the seating arrangement, the ushers, and the reaction of audience members to the slightest noise from the crowd. If you are brave, cough loudly, or open a cough drop wrapped in cellophane and see how those around you react. If you are really brave, start dancing, talking, clapping, and singing. Time how long it takes you to get kicked out. By comparison, listen to the same piece of music, but at home, alone or with friends, and dance, sing, or clap along. Is the music inherently un-danceable? Compare how you experience the same piece of music with your eyes closed and with your eyes open.

The upgraded ecstatic listening orientation sharply separates the material, physical, vibrational experience of music from the conscious experience of intuiting sound. Don Ihde writes that for him, the ecstatic experience is ruined by the "slightest scratch" in a record, or the squeak of a violin bow. Is the sharp separation of music and noise plausible? Why do many modern digital recordings include the simulated sounds of LP records popping and crackling under a turntable needle? Classical musicians manipulate their instruments in many ways to get a variety of timbres. Try to listen to these physical manipulations as different forms of noise. The pianist Keith Jarret, like many musicians, vocalizes as he plays the keyboard. Are his vocalizations music or noise? The pianist Glen Gould, well-known for his interpretation of Bach's "Goldberg Variations," also vocalized. Are his vocalizations music or noise?

Chapter 3

Listening to Difference
Creole Critiques of White Listening

Figure 3.1 Sidney Bechet in New York in 1947, alongside Bob Wilber, Freddie Moore and Lloyd Phillips.

Most White people outside the South first heard jazz as performed by the Original Creole Band and other New Orleans musicians, including King Oliver, Kid Ory, Lizzie Miles, Louis Armstrong, Baby Dodds, Sidney Bechet, Jelly Roll Morton, and Jimmy Palao. These listening exchanges were crucibles for White identity. Whites Americans became White by learning how to listen to Creole jazz.

As Creole musicians shaped White identity by performing for Whites, they also reflected critically about Whiteness. Most jazz writers treat Creole jazz innovators as craftspeople but not intellectuals. But why not seek a philosophy of jazz from within the music? The philosophy of music contained in Sidney Bechet's autobiography, *Treat It Gentle*, can be summarized by the injunction: listen to difference. Bechet is a philosopher of music and a philosopher of Whiteness who argued that listening orientations constitute jazz music. *Treat It Gentle* offers an extended critique of White folk revivalist listening and other bad faith modes of White listening.

Similarly, Kid Ory's philosophy is expressed in his music and in his first-person autobiographical reflections. Songs like Ory's version of the Creole folk tune "Eh La Bas" speak to the plantation origins of jazz. Ory's White father wanted nothing to do with him or his music. His mixed-race, Creole-speaking mother taught him folk songs as a child. His mature tailgate style creatively blended blues sounds, folk traditions, and brass band elements. In his autobiography, Ory argues that White listening began on the plantation as a sadistic technique of surveillance and masculine control. Not unlike Frederick Douglass, Ory escaped the plantation by dropping a bag of bricks on the head of his abusive White master. Fleeing to New Orleans, he worked as a musician in taverns. His philosophy of music attunes contemporary listeners to the plantation origins of the blended, creolized sounds of jazz, and the interactive call-and-response among musicians and audiences.

In this chapter, I examine phenomenological portraits of White listening in Creole print and sound culture. Bechet and Ory left substantial archives of recorded music, and both wrote autobiographies. It is also important to examine what newspapers were writing about jazz and jazz audiences. I consider the Francophone press in New Orleans and its relationship to jazz listening. The chapter ends with a reading of Édouard Glissant's travel narrative *Faulkner/Mississippi*. Glissant criticizes White American listening habits because they are decreolizing.

THE CREOLIZING PHENOMENOLOGY OF SIDNEY BECHET

Sidney Bechet (1897–1959) is a phenomenologist of listening who writes poignantly about the experience of the White sonic gaze. Bechet's autobiography, *Treat It Gentle*, contains a phenomenology of listening that is attuned to racial and gender embodiment. Following Bechet's phenomenological insight that music gives you its own understanding of itself, I also treat the recorded sounds of Creole musicians as philosophical texts.

Bechet brings to light how White listening is a phenomenological orientation in space and time. My reading of Bechet is based on Sara Ahmed's proposal to treat listening orientations as devices. The orientational approach to listening examines the habits of communities as well as the material conditions that facilitate listening. The architecture of the American plantation system is a crucial space for understanding the genealogy of the White sonic gaze. The plantation system is a space where creolizing contact took place between Europeans and Africans. Americans first learned how to listen Whitely on the plantation. Historically and ontologically, listening on plantations is the starting point for understanding the structures of the White sonic gaze that persisted through the Jazz Age.

In what follows, I restate Bechet's critique of clogged White ears. Bechet is critical of the listening habits that dominated the American and British Folk Revivals, and he is critical of White listening habits that emerged on plantations.

Reading Bechet's autobiography while studying and listening to his music can be a powerful philosophical experience. When Bechet writes, "The music gives you its own understanding of itself," he can be understood as criticizing the tendency of American and European music writers to think about jazz as a case study of a broad philosophical principle.[1] We need not separate out those who produce the sound and those who theorize it. My purpose in reading Bechet as a phenomenologist is to bring together the insights of a Creole musician and insights of theorists who study music. If we can speak of a Creole phenomenology, then such an approach must be open-ended in its selection of texts, sounds, and source materials.

Within Bechet we find both a Creole phenomenology and a creolizing phenomenology. By "Creole phenomenology," I mean a style of first-person philosophy that has emerged from people who self-identify as Creole. By "creolizing phenomenology," I mean a style of first-person philosophy that explores the cultural and conceptual hybridity needed to understand what it means to be human, given Eurocentrism, colonialism, and the legacies of slavery in the Americas.

Why Bechet? One reason is the availability of sound recordings as well as written traces of this performer's life. Many Creole musicians active during the Jazz Age were either too early to be recorded or they did not have access to or interest with the commercial music scene. Bechet lived a reasonably long life, and he watched the American and European craze for early jazz come and go and then come back again. The most exciting reason to study Bechet is because his music is so good. Bechet was pivotal in defining a New Orleans jazz sound with the two cardinal features of syncopation and improvisation. But listening backward to how Bechet was influential misses the phenomenological importance of his music. We should also listen forward, treating music as motion.

An example of a forward-listening approach to Bechet can be found in the liner notes that NEA Jazz master David Liebman wrote to his 2018 record, *Petite Fleur: The Music of Sidney Bechet*. Liebman, a contemporary, avantgarde musician who spent his twenties touring with Miles Davis, writes: "I think most listeners and writers would agree that when it comes to the soprano saxophone Sidney Bechet rules.""[2]

A pioneer of syncopated music, Bechet was a master improviser and master listener. Famously, he was an ear musician; he never took to reading music. His sound was a creative remix of the brass band palate and the parade traditions of Creole New Orleans, as well as the world of the French Opera, so popular in Louisiana. His tone, his timbre, and his trademark vibrato were borrowed from the classical world. He formed this sound in part by listening to Italian opera singer Enrico Caruso.

After a life in and out of the public eye, at age sixty-two, Bechet dictated his autobiography, *Treat It Gentle*. It was 1959, the year of Miles Davis's *Kind of Blue*. The heyday of New Orleans jazz was long over, as listening publics in Europe and the Americas turned to big band, swing, bebop, postbop, and modal jazz. Bechet was living in France, where he felt less racism and found a large audience for his music.

The main audience for Bechet's autobiography would have been American Whites who began listening to early jazz and blues during the American and British Folk Revivals. *Treat it Gentle* is a critique of its White readers. The Folk Revivals were moments of national nostalgia in musical culture, attempts to look back at the long-lost greats, and to archive them before they became "lost sounds," as Tim Brooks has named them.[3] My portrait of the revivalist listener in the previous chapter is based on Bechet's work.

Before offering details about *Treat It Gentle*, I note the phenomenological importance of the book's narrative structure. The frame story opens with a chapter describing one of Bechet's live musical performances before an appreciative, nostalgic White audience in Paris. The longer, second portion of the book is an allegorical response to the questions raised by the White listener. My analysis of this second part of *Treat It Gentle* shows how creolizing phenomenology keeps an ear toward the colonial realities of racial terror.

The frame story is a good phenomenological tool for indicating the importance of the time and space of listening. Bechet's framing highlights Whiteness on different levels: The Whiteness of the nostalgic listener of the 1950s is a double for the Whiteness of today's White readers. As we (Whites) read about the nostalgic White listener in Paris, we realize that in the twenty-first century, we still occupy a listening position dominated by White nostalgic practices. Bechet also holds that Whiteness is a deep structure of listening that can be noticed only through a historical, allegorical analysis of slavery and the space of the plantation.

While Bechet may not have intended *Treat It Gentle* to be treated as aesthetic theory, there is no reason we cannot do so. Bechet's contributions to sound culture are magnified by the fact that his autobiographical reflections offer philosophically important first-person insights into musical listening. It makes sense to learn as much as we can about how to listen from a master listener. I will return often to Bechet's creolizing concept of active listening, so crucial in jazz music: "[W]hen you get so you really hear it, when you can listen to the music being itself—then you don't have to ask that question. The music gives you its own understanding of itself."[4]

Creole phenomenology prioritizes active listening. Bechet expresses this insight with an innovative reply to the deceptively simple question "Is Jazz Black music?" Answering a White listener's query, Bechet remarks: "If I could give them a straight answer, just in one sentence-like, I wouldn't have to say all this I'm saying."[5] Bechet suggests that listening orientations determine the substance of what we hear, not the other way around. "That doesn't really say what Negro music is. . . . It is a way of feeling. It's a way of listening too, and that complicates it because there's so much difference that can be listened to."[6]

WHITE REVIVALIST LISTENING: NOSTALGIA, AUTHENTICITY, AND DISCOVERY

Treat It Gentle opens with an existential encounter between Bechet and a nostalgic White listener who gazes sonically. The setting is a Paris nightclub in the 1940s. After he performs a set of live, improvised tunes, the enthusiastic audience member approaches Bechet, eager to share his listening experience. The man expresses his love for Bechet's playing, which transports him to "old New Orleans."[7] He praises Bechet, who, he says, "invented jazz." And he worries aloud that that "the music stopped in New Orleans" and "all we have now are legends." The listener tells Bechet that during the set, "he'd had an experience."[8]

Drawing out ideas that are implicit in Bechet, I suggest that White revivalist listening has three elements. White revivalist listening is nostalgic, in its orientation toward music, memory, and time. White revivalist listening is also a loving orientation toward an exotic other. The loving sonic gaze implicitly states, "I hear you as authentic." Lastly, revivalist listening positions White audiences as discoverers of jazz. White revivalists are in bad faith about the relative social importance of mainstream, White audiences who listen to live and recorded jazz; they believe that without White listeners, jazz would die. White listening is an orientation that implicitly states, You, the non-White other, invented jazz, but we Whites discovered it.

Combined, these elements make for unphenomenological, uncritical listening. Bechet writes: "This man, he'd heard me, and I was still playing this old music, I was still playing New Orleans. That's what he told me. 'This music is your music,' he said. They get to think in a memory kind of way about all this Jazz; but these people don't seem to know it's more than a memory thing. They don't seem to know it's happening right there where they're listening to it, just as much as it ever did in memory."[9]

In stating that jazz "isn't a memory thing," Bechet calls the listener on his nostalgic listening. Nostalgic listening turns sound into an echo of the past. The nostalgic listener hopes to hear something in a live set that will remind him of a record that he's heard. For Bechet, playing jazz is not a matter of pedigree or connection to an era, a geography, or a physical body. Jazz is about improvisation. Jazz is "happening right there, where they're listening to it."

Bechet continues: "I told him I played like I always play. That's really all I can say."[10] Here we find an understated refusal of the White gaze. Bechet faces his audience and states to them: *I am not a memory thing*. As a performer of live music, Bechet insists on the historical present and the future. Nostalgic listening is not suited to hearing improvisatory music. Jazz improvisation requires a balance between the familiar and the unfamiliar; structure and freedom; the past and the future. Jazz musicians may be steeped in the history of the music, but they also must find a way to articulate their own commentary on the past. Improvised music works through a tension between past (retention) and the future (protention). So, treating improvisatory music as a memory thing misses much of the phenomenology of the music.

Bechet contrasts musical memory with musical motion. His assertion that music is motion comes in the context of musically navigating the White sonic gaze. Echoing existentialist theory, Bechet insists on his freedom. White listening freezes, objectifies, and others. Nostalgic listening is a poor phenomenological stance from which to hear improvisatory music, since this music is motion. "There's a mood about the music, a kind of need to be moving. You just can't set it down and hold it. Those Dixieland musicianers, they tried to do that; they tried to write the music down and kind of freeze it."[11]

The claim that "music is motion" is a phenomenological point about creating and listening to improvised music. The music "has to be moving" because jazz is a "versioning" or "remixing" style of music. Bechet's critique of White listening practices singles out Dixieland musicians, whom he says have "frozen" jazz. He is referring to musicians who, in the Folk Revival period, sought to play in the style of 1920s New Orleans. The very term "revival" suggests that something has died and now must be resuscitated. Bechet reminds the White listener that he is not dead; like Fanon, he says "no" to the terms of the White gaze. The White listener misses the basic point that New Orleans jazz is improvisational and insists on the future. By contrasting his style from that of Dixieland musicians, Bechet is hearing Dixieland music as nonimprovisatory. Dixieland musicians listen to the past and try to repeat it. They buy in to the myth that jazz styles progress from one era to another, replacing each other. If music is motion, every improvisational performance by Bechet is a new act of creation that can only be understood by thinking about the future. For Bechet, who was performing throughout the 1940s and 1950s, his style was (and is) a valid contemporary form of music. Bechet's style was based around a two-beat feeling, a strong horn line, and perhaps most importantly, collective and individual improvisation. Bechet's style is bouncy, heavily syncopated, improvisatory, and versioning, so each live performance is unique. Listening to the difference of versions is the phenomenological orientation that will allow one to get the most out of the music.

A second feature of White revivalist listening is lovingly orienting one's ears toward an exotic, static other. The revivalist listener practices a form of racialized "love" that has also been brilliantly criticized by Frantz Fanon and bell hooks.[12] Bechet criticizes White listening because it desires to hear the first, the best, or the most representative sounds of some particular genre. White listening freezes sound and also freezes the identity of the musical performer. White revivalist ears are clogged by their insistence on hearing jazz as the music of a racialized other who is held at a distance. Because the listener thinks jazz music stopped in New Orleans, he listens for evidence that the performer in front of him is a genuine representative of a lost sound that he can categorize as jazz based on a small number of aural cues.

The White listener wants to identify a static quality in the music that he can latch on to as definitive of how that music will sound in the future. The revivalist listener's aural orientation is an auditory modification of the racial eyeball test. It listens for a few simplistic markers that can satisfy the question, What are you really? Revivalist ears accord authenticity to a performer to the extent that his or her sounds are echoes of the past. Rejecting this logic of firsts, Bechet points to the stylistic attitude that characterizes his music: improvisation.

> Jazz isn't just me. It isn't just any one person who plays it. There'll always be Jazz. It doesn't stop anywhere. You take a melody . . . people can feel a melody . . . as long as there's melody there's Jazz, there's rhythm.[13]

To grasp Bechet's musical style, the listener must be attuned to how improvised sound references, remixes, and versions past sounds without repeating them. Improvisational listening requires imagination.

Bechet's improvisational approach to music does not posit a line of progress from early to late, from primitive to developed. The idea of musical progress paints a small number of musicians as firsts and then celebrates them as the most authentic, or celebrates firsts as leading to present greatness. Bechet prefers a nonlinear, digenetic understanding of jazz. Musicians can play improvised music and draw on a wealth of old and supposedly outdated styles. Ragtime, swing, and bebop approaches, for instance, need not be considered exclusionary of one another. Bechet has big ears, and he listens to the musicians around him and the emerging styles of improvised music. Bechet's long life meant that he lived through huge changes in listening practices, demographics of listening, and patterns of music reproduction and distribution.

Bechet articulates an improvisational approach to listening when he writes that "music is motion." White listening misses this motion by exoticizing and freezing musicians. White listeners do not consider themselves bad listeners since they profess their love and appreciation of jazz.

The third element of revivalist listening is that White listeners imagine that they have discovered jazz music. This third element is the dialectical parallel of the second. The revivalist thinks non-White people created jazz and Whites discovered it. This places the two into an imaginary social compact. White audiences inflate their importance by assuming that if they didn't exist, then neither would jazz.

The fact that Whites orient themselves as discoverers of non-White culture is hardly news. Where do we begin with the problematic assumption of White discovery? American schoolchildren for generations have been taught to sing, "In 1492, Columbus sailed the ocean blue." The phrase "Columbus discovered America" has been burned into the American psyche, setting the stage for and reflecting colonial forms of listening. In the United States, jazz has frequently been theorized as a musical conversation that takes place for the benefit of Whites.

Bechet writes that the White revivalist listener thinks that "if people like him don't hear" the music, then it would die out.[14] In writing "people like him," Bechet names the Whiteness of his audience. Bechet criticizes both the phenomenological attitude and the discourse of the White discoverer. "Jazz, that's a name the White people have given to the music. What does Jazz mean to you when I come up behind you: 'Jazz,' I say, 'what does that do to you?' That doesn't explain the music."[15]

Pursuing Bechet's genealogical analysis of the term "jazz," we could point out how the word began life as a verb, and it slowly became a noun. As Amiri Barka has argued, "to jazz" used to mean to adopt a playful, improvised approach to melody and rhythm.[16] The terms "rag" and "swing" also started life as verbs. "To rag" was said to consist in "putting pep into the music."

Bechet and other early jazz musicians would "rag" a tune by taking a popular melody and recasting it rhythmically and harmonically.

The revivalist listener turns "to jazz" into "jazz." He listens not for motion, but for repetition. He listens for static qualities in the music that fit a laundry list. Listening practices should, as Bechet says, explain the music. White revivalist listening does not explain the music: It gets the history of jazz wrong as well as the phenomenology of listening to live and recorded sound.

With this last feature of revivalist listening, we are getting to the heart of what makes a form of listening specifically revivalist. To revive is to "restore to life or consciousness," which is precisely how the listener conceives of his act of listening. The assumption is that without the recognition of mainstream, White audiences, the recorded and live sounds of early jazz musicians would die. Digging into this assumption, we notice that White audiences posit a specific social role for themselves that they believe cannot be or has not been fulfilled by non-White audiences.

Revivalist listening is tied to a conception of the "folk." As Robin D.G. Kelley has noted,

> terms like "folk," "authentic," and "traditional" are socially constructed categories that have something to do with the reproduction of race, class, and gender hierarchies and the policing of the boundaries of modernism . . . "folks" either signifies what people imagine to be preindustrial survivals or . . . the cultural practices of the Other.[17]

Kelley describes folk listening as an act of the collective White imagination. White audiences imagine themselves adding value to the music they think has only been heard by a small group of people, in a local setting. Kelley shows the arrogance behind thinking that the value of a musical performance will be enhanced if that performance is archived by and for White ears.

In Bechet's language, White audiences who imagine themselves as jazz discoverers are failing to hear difference. The White imaginary inflates one context of listening and excludes modes of hearing that are outside of its limited experience. White listening patterns have tended to hear jazz sounds as for them.

The three elements of White folk revivalist listening I have identified are nostalgia, authenticity, and discovery. These elements make for toxic listening situations, like the one described by Bechet at the beginning of *Treat It Gentle*. Having stated some phenomenological implications of the revivalist listener, I interpret the lengthy second section of Bechet's autobiography, which gives an allegorical account of listening during the period of American slavery. His creolizing theory places listening within the context of racial terror.

PLANTATION LISTENING: GEOGRAPHY AND GENDER

Two elements of Bechet's discussion of listening during slavery stand out: his understanding of the geography and gender of listening. To understand how White audiences listen to jazz, it is crucial to examine White listening orientations on plantations. On plantations, White sonic gazing was a gendered phenomenon. Feminine and masculine White listening were separate experiences. Bechet places feminine listening within the walls of the big house and masculine listening outdoors, as a form of desire and surveillance.

Bechet's critique of White listening does not end with his analysis of revivalist listening in Europe and America in the 1940s. He makes good on his promise that he cannot give a simple answer as to what is wrong with the revivalist's orientation. The complex answer takes White hearing back one hundred years to the architecture of the American plantation system. As a corrective to the White imaginary, Bechet traces 1940s listening habits to those of the 1840s.

I consider Bechet's work phenomenologically rich in part because it shows that listening is an orientation in space. Bechet attends to the geography of the plantation and the memory of racial terror. Let's begin with Bechet's portrayal of listening in the big house.

Listening in the Big House

The main characters in the allegorical portion of *Treat It Gentle* are Bechet's grandfather Omar, his grandmother Marie, and the White master and mistress. The plot turns when an extravagant ball inside the big house goes wrong. The master sneaks out of the party to sexually pursue Marie, his slave. Finding Marie and Omar being intimate, the master lynches Omar. Complicating things is the master's announcement to his White guests that "Our girl has been raped." The White audience hears "our girl" as a reference to the master's White daughter, whom they believe has been raped by Omar. The master exhibits a classic case of racist bad faith, as discussed by Lewis R. Gordon in *Anti-Black Racism and Bad Faith*.[18] The mistress, on the other hand, hears everything and knows her husband is in bad faith; she hears everything, but is not listened to.

In interpreting this story for its phenomenological importance, I attend to how White listening is tied to White space, following Ahmed's advice that "We 'become' racialized in how we occupy space, just as space is, as it were, already occupied as an effect of racialization."[19] In Bechet, White spaces are filled with music, while non-White spaces are filled with noise. "There was music inside and a whole lot of noise outside—the dogs barking, the carriages drawing up, a lot of voices talking and calling out."[20] If we listen for difference, we notice non-White spaces and the listening habits of non-White people who live in them. The noise of people calling out, turns into conversations, in particular humor and gossip. "All the slaves . . . were outside talking to themselves and carrying on as much as they could, making jokes, gossiping."[21] Bechet attends to sounds of at least three types: noise, speech, and music. The music being played in the big house for the ball is described as "the kind of music that could fit indoors."[22] "Fitting indoors" is linked with domestication, and the sonic difference between White interiors and the noise they shut out.

Bechet's phenomenology of the master's White lust is consistent with Ahmed's claim that listening orientations are desire-forming.

> Orientation is a powerful technology insofar as it constructs desire as a magnetic field: it can imply that we were drawn to certain objects and others *as if* by a force of nature: so women are women insofar as they are oriented towards men and children.[23]

The master's Whiteness is performative. He is White to the degree that he listens to, looks at, and lusts for a young Black female whom he legally owns, but whom he cannot force into having reciprocal desires.

The master's sexual desire for Marie is bound up with listening as an act of surveillance. He is drawn to Marie after voyeuristically watching her dance with Omar in Congo Square. The setting of the master's listening is pivotal. Martin Munro has described Congo Square (*place des nègres*) as the "most important public site for performances of African or Afro-creole dance."[24] In 1817, New Orleans politicians made Congo Square the official site of Sunday slave dances. The 1817 rule consolidating dances in the center of town allowed for a new form of White gazing. Munro reminds us that jazz scholars who invoke Congo Square as the "originating locus of American jazz," often fail to acknowledge the difference between the origin of jazz and the origin of jazz's visibility and audibility to Whites.[25] Bechet and Munro asseverate that White gazing is the dominant orientation through which jazz history has been told.

In short, the master's sexual desire is treated as a blockage that prevents him from experiencing the happiness of the ballroom. He no longer has access to the pleasantness of White sounds inside the big house. White sounds become distracting background noise to desire. The master's White listening is a form of surveillance and desire. He listens in bad faith, estranged, unable to access the happiness of White sounds, unable to satisfy his desire to control sexually a non-White woman who is legally his property.

White Women's Listening

In *Treat It Gentle*, the character of the mistress speaks to how the White sonic gaze is gendered. Unlike her husband, she listens acutely and hears everything. She is a musician, a pianist to be specific, and she listens like one. She hears everything, but is not heard. The existential moment that reveals White feminine listening is solipsistic as the mistress is seated at the piano in a White bad faith attempt to "play back the dark."

Feminine listening is set in a specific physical location: the deep interior of the big house on the plantation. The mistress wants to feel the happiness of a White space, but this desire is blocked. Her desire for happiness is a phenomenological orientation to the space of the plantation. Ahmed reminds us of the connection between desire, disappointment, and space:

> The very expectation of happiness gives us a specific image of the future. This is why happiness provides the emotional setting for disappointment, even if happiness is not given. We just have to expect happiness from "this or that" for "this or that" to be experienced as objects of disappointment.[26]

The mistress expects to find happiness in the walls of the parlor, the folds of the furniture, and most of all in the White, ivory keys of the piano. She is a musician and listens with a sensitivity and subtlety unmatched by her husband. The listening position of the mistress is solitary. She produces sound, but is unable to hear this sound as happy. After hearing about the rape of "our girl," she goes to the piano, alone, inside. She foresees the tragic unfolding of her husband's sexual desire, but feels disempowered. The mistress knows the claim of rape is false, and knows that her husband's sexual jealousy will have tragic consequences. Her keen hearing is her tragic flaw.

In the crucial scene of White feminine listening, Bechet describes the mistress alone at the piano, wanting to play a "ballad she learned as a girl."[27] She touches the piano but is denied the pleasure she hopes to feel in the instrument. All alone, with no audience save herself, she longs for happiness, feeling none. She wants her music to function innocently, as happiness-producing. "She touched the piano and she was thinking how pleasant the room wanted to be, how it wanted to put back all that dark that gathered to it. She sat there touching the piano with her fingers and let the piece play itself out, but in her mind she was thinking about the girl."[28] As devices, listening orientations are complex interplays of machines and human consciousness.

The mistress listens as a way "to put back all that dark that gathered." Bechet theorizes White listening as an attempt at White order, clarity, and happiness. The "dark that gathered" refers to the memory of racial terror, specifically her husband's lie about the "rape" of their daughter and his murder of Omar. She tries to put her piano at the foreground, but she does not succeed. The failed attempt to play back the dark suggests that White listening is the ongoing attempt to place White happiness outside of racial terror. Bechet notices that White feminine innocence is feigned. The mistress feels looked at and listened to, declaring herself an object of Marie's eyes: "that girl's eyes, Marie, look at her."[29] The mistress's experience of being gazed at for the first time is visual and aural. Her White shame is triggered by the "noise" of "Negroes pounding on the door almost before morning."[30]

In *Treat It Gentle*, the dynamics of feminine and masculine White listening are part of a bad faith attempt to "play back" the dark racial terror of the plantation. The White wife suffers from her Whiteness—from the lust and lie of her White husband and her complicity in Omar's lynching. She hears everything, but when she goes to the piano to speak through music, nobody hears her. She cannot even hear herself. "She sat there touching the piano with her fingers and let the piece play itself out, but in her mind, she was thinking about the girl. Marie, her daughter's maid."[31]

Bechet's phenomenology of the sonic gaze highlights gender and geography. White masculine listening is an orientation of surveillance accompanied by sexual desire, exemplified by the jealous master who spies on Black and Creole people at Congo Square. Bechet reminds us that jazz history has been told from the position of White surveillance. The story of jazz is often narrated by White male onlookers and on-listeners who peer in without participating. In *Treat It Gentle*, feminine White listening is depicted as a solipsistic orientation toward interior spaces. Feminine listening orientations are acutely sensitive, but that very sensitivity becomes tragic.

Bechet's creolizing approach to jazz instructs us to listen to difference. Difference listening, unlike sonic gazing, prioritizes improvisation and musical motion. Difference listening is a possible corrective to revivalist listening, the feigned innocence of White feminine listening, and the masculine orientation of surveillance and voyeuristic heterosexual desire. By placing these gendered forms of listening on the plantation, Bechet demonstrates that Whiteness is an orientation that directs us away from the memory of the racial terrors of slavery.

THE CREOLIZING JAZZ OF EDWARD "KID" ORY

Known as the "Creole trombonist," Edward "Kid" Ory was a prominent Creole musician of the Jazz Age. He and his bandmates were among the first artists to bring syncopated, improvised music to the nation. Ory's career is simultaneous with the birth of jazz music and the birth of the vinyl record. Like Bechet, Ory lived a long life (1886–1973) and was a musical pioneer who cultivated diverse audiences for early jazz, first in New Orleans, then in Los Angeles and Chicago, and finally all across America.

Ory is on many seminal jazz records beginning with "Ory's Creole Trombone" (1922), his first recording, which, with only five thousand pressings, was played on the radio and fueled an emerging demand for jazz among White and non-White audiences.[32] Ory was on Vocalion's first race record, "Too Bad," recorded in Chicago in 1926 with King Oliver. During his Chicago period (1925–1933), Ory was a member of the Louis Armstrong Hot Five, along with fellow New Orleans musicians Jelly Roll Morton and King Oliver, recording "Muskrat Ramble" (1926) and other popular records. With Armstrong's Hot Five Ory, he rerecorded "Ory's Creole Trombone" in 1927. Ory played with the best New Orleans musicians of the teens and twenties and was among a handful of musicians on the leading edge of jazz, making what would become classic recordings and pioneering syncopated, improvised music.

Because Ory was one of the first Creole performers whom Whites outside of Louisiana heard or saw, his career is a window into the birth and evolution of early jazz audiences. He played for a huge variety of audiences from live to recorded, from all-White to mixed. He played in vaudeville theaters, and in Black-and-tan clubs. Ory and other New Orleans musicians were performing the music that would become known as jazz, but in this early period the music was known simply as ragtime, and it was deeply connected to vaudeville and minstrel performances.

Ory's unpublished autobiography, reproduced in part in John McCusker's *Creole Trombone*,[33] is a testament to how Creole musicians negotiated the White sonic gaze. As Whites began tuning in to jazz music, musicians like Ory faced White minstrel listeners. Ory's generation, unlike the previous one, played mostly for White audiences. Ory cultivated cabaret audiences in Black-and-tan clubs in Los Angeles and later in Chicago. The music he played for these White audiences challenged them to listen for difference rather than listening minstrely.

Ory's first audiences were on the plantation. He taught himself harmony while playing for the enjoyment of other Creole, Black, and mixed-race people. French-Creole was Ory's first language. Ozeme, his White father, owned the plantation where Ory grew up. His White grandfather had been born in Alsace, France. His mother, Octavie, was listed in the 1880 census as mulatto, and she was Ozeme's *placée* (common law wife). In his autobiography, Ory emphasizes the profound influence of his mother's singing. She and other women chanted Creole folk songs at night in the dark after work. Years later, Ory reworked the Creole tune "Vous Conne Tit La Maison" (Our Little Home) into "Eh La Bas," recorded in 1946, and this remains one of his best recordings. Ory writes that "up to between the ages of seven and eight, I led the normal life of any plantation child."[34] Part of the "normal" life of a mixed-race child on the plantation was that there were two branches of the Ory family—one White and wealthy, the other racially mixed and poor. While Ory's mother was central to his musical education, his White father showed little interest in him or his music, and he was forced to labor on the plantation in near slave-like conditions.

In Ory's early teenage years, his musical skills grew as did his dissatisfaction with what he called the "normal" life of forced labor on a sugar plantation. He moved plantations but found life even more intolerable. Once his musical talents became known, he was forced to play for a drunk, abusive White overseer. In his teens, Ory began slipping off the plantation to hear, and eventually make, music in New Orleans. Ory's chops were good enough that he could earn more money in one night playing at a sex saloon in New Orleans than three months as a brick hauler. Unlike Buddy Bolden of ten years earlier, who played almost exclusively for Black audiences, Ory cultivated a White audience in the city.[35] Following in the footsteps of the Original Creole Band, which toured the nation from 1914 to 1917, Ory moved to Los Angeles, where he performed for mixed audiences in Black-and-tan clubs. The police raided these clubs and shut them down. In northern vaudeville theaters in the Midwest, the floor level was usually all-White, with separate balconies for Black patrons, and sometimes separate entrances.[36] Leaving Los Angeles for Chicago, Ory made records and played once more in Black-and-tans. During Ory's time in Chicago, from 1925 to 1933, he was at the center of the jazz community. He enjoyed high wages and record deals, and he played to full clubs.

As we saw in chapter 2, the White press of the teens and twenties responded to Creole musicians and music by warning of the jazz problem. Regional White newspapers like the Los Angeles *Record* and the Indianapolis *Sunday Star*[37] reacted to Creole performers with a mixture of excitement, exoticism, fascination, and contempt. A typical write-up describes Creole musicians as "wild wailing darkies" performing musical acts that "show the southern plantation darky as he really is in his sportive hours."[38] The national White public had little contact with Creole culture until the teens. Their pre-jazz contact would have been through traveling vaudeville minstrel shows. The word "minstrel" was used in vaudeville bands of the pre-jazz and jazz period to signal a style of performance and a musical repertoire. White vaudeville audiences would have been accustomed to performances that were quick-paced variety shows that mixed physical comedy, dance music, skits, and opera, popular, classical, and patriotic music. The early jazz of Ory and other Creole bands was marked by its transitional nature—their performances were received as part minstrel show.

Ory and his fellow Creole musicians helped cultivate what we today think of as the jazz club or cabaret audience. In New Orleans, Ory and other Creole musicians like Jelly Roll Morton cut their teeth playing for indoor sex shows in the vice district. Beyond New Orleans, most of their performances were either outdoor shows under the tent, or in large theaters, where audiences stood or sat. The Black-and-tan (mixed-race audience) clubs of Los Angeles and South Side Chicago were a new phenomenon. Part of the allure of New Orleans bands was that they might bring new dances and danceable rhythms to the North and West. The real and imagined association of jazz with sex was a large factor in the White reception of jazz. Black-and-tan clubs derive their name from the fact that Whites and non-Whites were able to dance together. Ory's first steady gig in Los Angeles was at a Black-and-tan, the Cadillac Club in 1922. The gig ended when police raided the club and shut it down for allowing Black men to dance with White women.[39]

Ory's ascendancy to a nationally known musician was simultaneous with the birth of the commercial record. Since jazz records were among the first of any records to be sold in mass numbers, he was at the forefront of the mass distribution of sound and the birth of the record. Chicago was the center of the early jazz scene, as indicated by the weekly wages top musicians could earn: forty dollars a week, compared with only one dollar a week in New Orleans.[40] Ory recorded for the *Okey* label, the pioneer of race records. He recalled that in the studio with Louis Armstrong, the "*Okey* people were amazed . . . most of the other bands took all day to make a couple of sides."[41] Ory's keen ear skills—his ability to hear a tune once and improvise over it—enabled him to cut as many as eight sides a session, when other bands were lucky to get two.

The records Ory made changed how American audiences listened, both White and Black. In his autobiography, Ory describes how he came to his mature sound by reflecting on his early experience on the plantation. By asserting that the plantation was a site of racial terror, Ory cut through the White bad faith of minstrel listeners who were trained to think of plantations as humorous backdrops to vaudeville performances of plantation melodies.

Ory was raised on the Woodland sugar plantation, near New Orleans. Unlike Bechet, Morton, and most other Creole musicians of the period, Ory grew up outside New Orleans on a plantation owned by the White side of his family. Although slavery officially ended in 1865, twenty-one years before Ory's birth, his "employment" on the sugar plantation his White French grandfather had founded was forced. The style of syncopated, improvised jazz he helped pioneer has many influences, none deeper than the music he heard and made on the plantation.

Ory's autobiography is a rich source for understanding how creolized musical styles that emerged on plantations were translated for White audiences. The White minstrel listening of vaudeville audiences was preceded by

White plantation listening. In Ory's case, plantation listening took the form of a drunk White master demanding that he play blues while he was sexually assaulting a female cook. The existential refusal of Ory, like that of Frederick Douglass, was a matter of life and death. Ory chose to stand up to the White listener as a matter of physical self-defense and flight. It was not merely the physical drudgery that led Ory to flee the plantation, but the intolerable oppression of how the White master listened.

Ory describes a musical education that began on the plantation and led him to the city. His first instrument was his voice. As a young man working with mules, he would whistle. "I just kept whistling and working and finally, there he was . . . all ready to have the hitching finished."[42] Whistling was a way for Ory to cope with the drudgery of manual labor and teach himself music. Ory recounts listening to background sounds of the plantation, like the rustle of the wagons, hearing musical rhythms.[43] He eventually formed an acapella group, singing with other boys at night to entertain other people of color forced to work at the Woodland plantation. The boys would improvise harmonies over the Creole folk melodies they had learned from mothers and aunts.

> We would stand on a bridge at night and hum different tunes with different harmonies. People could hear us singing and they'd bring us a few ginger cakes and some water. We hummed and when we knowned the tune itself, the melody, the others would put a three or four part harmony to it. It was good ear training.[44]

Ory taught himself to improvise harmonically by singing modifications of Creole folk tunes with other boys.

Ory's ear training on the plantation is tied directly to his mature tailgate musical style. Tailgate-style playing is when a horn player weaves a melody in between the melodic lines of other horn players. Tailgate playing requires collective improvisation and a keen sensitivity to the musical space that is available given the primary melody and countermelodies. Tailgate-style playing is essential to the parade and second-line traditions in New Orleans. Ory's ear training in the acapella group sensitized him to finding space. He would become known for his musical phrasing, and his ability to play a prominent countermelody without stepping on other musicians' melodies. Even before he was familiar with the parade tradition in the city of New Orleans, Ory had heard professional brass bands passing through the Woodland plantation.

By the age of ten, Ory was sneaking off the plantation to go to local dances where he heard professional brass bands. Standing outside White venues like St. John's Euchre Club, Ory studied the rhythms and melodies of professional bands performing dance music. As a pre-teen, Ory already had a diverse musical education, learning by ear French-Creole folk songs, listening to brass band dance rhythms, and experimenting with his own whistling and singing.

In addition to singing acapella for people of color on the plantation, he organized musical parties for the entertainment of workers afterhours. With the goal of purchasing professional instruments, Ory and his young bandmates coordinated fish fries in an abandoned house on Woodland, charging a small amount of money. "We kept every dollar we made with me acting as treasurer and put it aside to buy real instruments."[45] At this time, around 1901, when Ory would be fourteen, he still had never owned a professional instrument and was playing on a homemade cigar-box banjo. When his White father was sick and dying, he bought Ory a professional banjo, though otherwise he had shown no interest in Ory or his music.

From the White side of his family, Ory did not have an audience or support for his music. Being mixed race, he was considered an employee of his father rather than an heir or plantation owner. He notes in his autobiography that he had hoped his father would be supportive of his music. On that score, Ory was disappointed. His Creole-speaking, mixed-race mother, on the other hand, was the center of his early musical education. For her and others on the plantation, Ory improvised acapella songs and put together a band to play at fish fries, large community gatherings where people could eat, dance, sing, and relax. He learned at a young age that his music could be a source of joy and income when performed for the right audience.

As Ory grew older and his musical skills advanced, he sought opportunities outside of the Woodland plantation. While his father had been indifferent to his music, the next powerful White man to employ Ory was not benign, but abusive and controlling. Ory had left the sugar plantation for one farther downriver, where he was employed as a brick carrier. There he was forced to perform music by a cruel White overseer. Ory was repeatedly awakened at two or three in the morning by "old man Tureau."[46] Tureau would be drunk, belligerent, and abusive, yelling that Ory should "Come on and play me some blues."[47] Ory's plea that he was tired from work and had to rise in a few hours to carry bricks was met with disdain from Tureau. Tureau's abuse included repeatedly sexually assaulting a female cook while Ory played the blues. Before long, Ory had enough of this abuse and risked his life to run away from Tureau. While lifting a load of bricks, Ory let it fall onto Tureau's head. As the stunned overseer came back to his senses, Ory had fled, seeking a life as a musician in the city. From 1910 to 1916, Ory made a living playing music in the red-light district, working for Madame LuLu White, the most famous brothel madam in Storyville. Ory's band included other seminal Creole musicians like Johnny St. Cyr, Emile Bigard, and the clarinetist Johnny Dodds.

The dramatic story of Ory and old man Tureau illustrates one mode of White, masculine plantation listening. The White overseer listened to Ory's music to prove he was in control and to satisfy his boredom. Like the White master Bechet describes, Ory's overseer listens as a form of surveillance. Ory's music was the background to the overseer's abusive sexual desires. The overseer's desire to control Ory and the female cook can be understood existentially: The master has a metastable belief that Ory's music and the cook's sexuality were for him. He imagines in bad faith that Ory's music is freely given, and that Ory produces music naturally, the way a tree produces sap. The rape of the female cook also displays a bad faith dynamic of White racist control. The overseer believes that despite her protests, the cook consents.

Ory's escape from Tureau might be theorized in Hegelian terms as the effort of the slave to achieve self-consciousness through willingness to die. An alternative analytical framework is provided by Neil Roberts in *Freedom as Marronage*.[48] Ory fled the plantation to make a living as a musician in the city of New Orleans. Music was an escape; he found work through improvised sound. In flight he sought a different type of labor, a different type of boss, and a different life. As a musician, he would be able to travel widely, making money with nothing more than his banjo or horn and a suitcase. In New Orleans, Ory said he could make four dollars a night, more income than two months as a brick carrier. Like Bechet, Ory's jazz sound was born on the plantation, amid the Glissantian silence imposed by racist oppression. Ory chose a musician's life to flee the surveillance of a White master.

It is important to remember the plantation roots of the White sonic gaze. Ory's creativity in navigating White listening habits should not be romanticized. Cultural mixture in jazz has been a reaction to coercion and control. The blended, creolized sound Ory developed was a way to negotiate racial terror and the White overseer's "love" of blues. Improvised music flourished on the plantation in part because there was a lack of resources. Unable to purchase professional instruments, Ory fashioned his own, as did thousands of others. Lacking access to a professional music teacher, Ory improvised a way to teach himself, first through his mother's tutelage, and also by risking his life sneaking around and standing outside White clubs to study.

I conclude my discussion of Kid Ory by briefly illustrating the methods of "listening to difference" and "creolizing listening" outlined above. Ory's 1946 recording of "Eh, las Bas" is his variation on a Creole folk song he heard as a child growing up on the Woodland sugar plantation in St. John the Baptist Parish, Louisiana.[49]

Ory's "Eh, la Bas" makes for a good case study of creolizing listening. Available on YouTube, the recording was made in the 1940s, when technology was much superior to the 1920s, so each instrument can be heard clearly, including the bass and the drums, which were hard to record in the 1920s and heavily distorted. Ory sings the song in Louisiana French-Creole, and the lyrics of the song signal the space and context. Most importantly, Ory's tone, timbre, and overall sound on the trombone are a hybrid. Ory's sound is creolizing, which is connected to, but also separable from his self-identity as a Louisiana Creole. A self-taught musician, Ory creolized the brass band tradition and the folk music tradition of the plantation. His improvised sounds are a form of motion that orients us toward the future.

To listen forward we must position ourselves in time and space, acknowledging the geography of the White listening stance. The phenomenology of difference instructs us to improvise and create as we listen. A host of important questions can be asked to help orient the listener in time and space. Where, why, and how are we listening? Entertainment, education, and edification—these are all distinct positions that can be occupied by the listening subject. Do I listen alone or with others? Am I listening in my headphones or through speakers? Am I in a sterile classroom with fluorescent lights, a nightclub smelling of alcohol, or on my couch? Do I listen seated at the piano, or with guitar or horn in hand? Am I imitating Ory's melody lines as I listen? Do I stop the recording, over and over, trying to get just one detail right?

Preliminary questions like these help the listener become conscious of whether she or he is listening Whitely. Listening Whitely is not only a historical phenomenon, but it also indicates a performance that can be adopted by different subjects, including those of us alive today, independent of how we identify racially. Listening Whitely in the current phenomenological sense need not be tied to the visual identity of the subject doing the listening, though it may be. White listening is coded by those in the dominant culture as "just" listening. To creolize our listening habits, we begin by noticing that when we listen, we do so as racially embodied and situated in time and space.

In the next few paragraphs, I walk the reader through a possible listening orientation toward the song "Eh La Bas." As Ory sings in Louisiana Creole, "Mo chè kouzen, mo chè kouzin, mo lenme la kizin," we can count along and divide the song into bars. The first four bars match with the lyrics above. If we are not used to counting measures, then it may take a bit of assistance to start hearing "the one," or the downbeat, which refers to the first beat of a measure. We can repeat the first few seconds of the song over and over until the first four measures come into shape, and then count along with the next four measures, corresponding to Ory's melody, "Mo manje plen, mo bwa diven, e sa pa kout ariyen." The first eight measures of the songs can be grasped as a whole, corresponding to the lyrical refrain. It is not necessary to understand the lyrics at this point, but to hear the phrasing of the singing. Phrasing refers to when the singer takes a breath and how his voice rhythmically punctuates certain syllables or rolls over others.

Starting the recording again from the top, we can listen for the second eight bars, where Ory sings the chorus and the hook of the whole song "Eh La Bas" ("Hey you, over there"). Ory is performing a call-and-response with the rest of the band. The call-and-response is a rhythmic echo that provides variety, interaction, and a sense of audience participation. We can first sing along with the leader, then relisten and sing along with the echo. In any live listening setting, the echo will take on a much greater significance, as audiences feel invited to sing along. By singing along, the listener is attuned differently to the sound. I am suggesting that the recorded sound not be treated as a stable object, which always sounds the same, but one that can sound different according to how interactive our listening becomes.

It may be difficulty to find the "one" (downbeat) as Ory sings "Eh La Bas." There is something subtle going on: the "eh la" comes earlier than we expect, and the "bas" lands on the downbeat. Beat two is a rest, and then the echo from the band begins on beat three, and ends on beat one of the next measure. The phrase "eh la bas" is three beats long, but it is not distributed across beats one, two, and three. It is distributed across the last two beats of the measure, and the first beat of the next. This rhythmic displacement gives the song a specific feel. The term "feel" is used by musicians when they are trying to nail down what makes one rhythm sound different from another. The "feel" of a song sometimes lies just beyond our ability to state in words what we mean, as when one performer says to another, "you'll hear it . . . you'll feel it."

The listening orientation just described is "creolizing" because it suggests that recordings are not stable, self-contained objects, but rather relationships. The geography and gender of our listening stance will in part determine the existence of the "time feel" and the meaning of the music. If, as Bechet says, what makes music "Black" or "Creole" is *how we listen*, we will be forced to explore the set of cultural assumptions we bring to the listening situation: Are we willing to take part in a call-and-response that requires us to move, to be noisy, and to interact with a recording, or will we position ourselves as "discovering" something objective in the sounds we hear?

One of the enduring lessons of Creolizing phenomenological thought is the importance of intense self-reflection and autobiographical honesty when listening. Listening seriously to Creole jazz helps us to develop the all-important "time feel" for Creole music and Creole philosophy. The notion of a rhythmical feel is phenomenological: It refers to how listeners attune themselves to sound by performing along with a record or live musician. The music teaches us that if we are trying to *hear* improvisation, we need to *listen* improvisationally. If we want to understand the time feel of jazz, we must listen jazzily. The connection between jazzy listening and creolizing listening is strong. In "Eh Las Bas," Ory takes a folk song and versions it into a two-beat ragtime jazz tune. Through call-and-response, he teaches his audience the rhythm, melody, and lyrics of the tune. The music is philosophy. And the jazz rhythms Ory teaches us in "Eh Las Bas" are philosophical critiques of Whiteness.

JAZ IS A VERB: THE ORIGINAL CREOLE BAND

What can we learn from Creole bands that have no sound recordings? How does one create a phenomenological archive of sound when those sounds were produced, heard, and distributed prior to the era of mechanical recording? With Bechet and Ory, we have autobiographical writings and dozens of commercial recordings. But the seminal Creole band of the early jazz era, the Original Creole Band, did not record. To recognize their contributions to jazz listening, we must rely on period descriptions of their sound as well as scholarly reconstructions. The band was philosophically important because it challenged White minstrel orientations and transforming the minstrel show into a jazz show.

Despite a lack of material from which we might directly understand how the Original Creole Band navigated the White minstrel gaze, thanks to the work of the musicologist Lawrence Gushee, we know where they performed and the style of their shows, including what types of music, dance, and comedy they utilized. We know who was in the band and have a rough sense of their biographies. I draw on Gushee's work, published in his magnificent *Pioneers of Jazz: The Story of The Creole Band*, and offer some original analysis of the period sources utilized by Gushee. The *Lawrence Gushee Papers*[50] at the University of Illinois contain a further wealth of unpublished research about the Original Creole Band, with an entire box devoted to "Vaudeville Performers and the Creole Band." There remains a significant amount of work to be done on this topic in the future.

When the Original Creole Band toured nationally from 1914 to 1917, they brought the sounds of early jazz to audiences outside Louisiana and the American South. Being "Creole" onstage was a style of performance more than a description of the biographies of the musicians. As their performances drove an emerging national White thirst for novel, Creole variations of minstrel tunes, each member of the band navigated what it meant to be a professional musician whose job was to perform racial burlesque for Whites and mixed audiences.

The band consisted of five core members with a diversity of cultural backgrounds. Jimmy Palao, a violinist, led the band. He and George Baquet, the clarinetist, descended from the *gens de couleur libres*, free people of color, in New Orleans. They were multilingual, had formal musical education on professional instruments, and were from middle-class families where skilled trades, including professional musicianship, were the norm. Freddie Keppard, cornetist, was from the Algiers neighborhood of New Orleans, but his parents came from Virginia and North Carolina. Keppard spoke Creole.[51] The band's bass player, Bill Johnson, was musically self-taught, came out of the blues tradition, was first-generation New Orleanian, and did not speak Creole. In the 1880 census, his mother was listed as mulatto, and his father might have been White.[52] Henry Prince Morgan specialized in dancing and comedy. He was an expert buck-and-wing dancer. He was the only member of the group to regularly black up for audiences.[53]

White minstrel listeners aggressively conflated personal biography with stage presence. Palao, Baquet, Keppard, Johnson, and Morgan could be "Creoles" onstage, in the eyes and ears of Whites, regardless of their personal background. Whites practiced minstrel listening by fetishizing the authenticity of band members. Driven by a sense of hokum and humbug, Whites expected not only to be entertained but also to be quizzed. They asked themselves if these were "real" or "fake" Creoles. White vaudeville audiences did not have the same aesthetic framework as cabaret listeners who emerged later. As Neil Harris has shown, these early listeners did not draw a sharp line between entertainment, edification, and scientific inquiry. Early jazz music was part of the circus sideshow tradition, initiated in large part by the Kansas-born, Boston Conservatory–educated band leader Percy George Lowery (1869–1942).

The Creole Band refigured the sounds and devices of the minstrel show, challenging the White imaginary that reduced them to their onstage roles. From the 1840s to the 1880s, roles like "Old Black Joe" were played by White actors who blacked up. By the late nineteenth century, Black vaudevillians were more sought after than White actors, though they often played the same stock roles from the plantation routines of forty years earlier. The stock dramatic device for the plantation act was to depict the South before the war, and to portray slaves as happy and ex-slaves as nostalgic for their old masters. The Creole Band challenged White audiences to hear the Creole sounds as related to but different from Black sounds. Jimmy Palao used the term "Jaz" on his promotional cards in 1916. Three years later, he added "Creole" before his name. Palao's advertisement of himself as both a "Creole" and a "Jaz" musician shows that he wanted audiences to listen to him as a Creole-identifying musician from New Orleans who was playing a new style of ragtime called "Jaz."

If the members of the Creole Band read the White press, they might not have recognized themselves in the reviews. "A noisy Creole band gives a ragtime repertoire, interspersed with fun and jokes. The bandmen are Creoles, but there is a very funny, burned-cork comedian at the head of the troupe who hits off the hoary traditions of ni****-land amusingly."[54] For members of the Creole Band, the "hoary traditions" were a job opportunity. They were professionals who played stylized, racialized roles. The Creole Band was at the same time playing avant-garde syncopated, improvised music, and performing throwback acts from an earlier tradition. The band is a window into one of the most important cultural moments in American musical history. The music that would come to be labeled and heard as jazz was birthed through a creative transformation of the burned-cork tradition.

Members of the Creole Band portrayed Creole-ness onstage as a way to carve out a living as professionals in a crowded entertainment industry. The term "Creole" in the band's name had less to do with the personal identity of the musicians and more to do with a style of performance. The band was one of the first to regularly use the word "Creole" in its advertising and self-description. In the teens, there was not yet a solidified meaning for the term among White listeners. Creole was closely associated with the term "minstrel" and was sometimes used interchangeably in band names. Traveling vaudeville troupes that toured on the same circuit as the Original Creole Band included the Sunny Dixie Minstrels, Lowery's Minstrels, the Georgia Minstrels, and Hugo's Minstrels. In a band's name, the word "Creole" signaled that they were from New Orleans, and that they played ragged, syncopated music.

When Kid Ory and Sidney Bechet wrote autobiographical reflections about their lives as professional musicians, they emphasized the plantation roots of their blended, syncopated, improvised sound. It is hard to think of a greater clash of worldviews than that between White audiences who imagined the plantation as a space of hokum humor, and the Creole, Black, and mixed-race performers for whom plantations were all-too-real spaces of racial terror. What we know from the phenomenological record is that these performers never once thought of themselves as dancing clowns. Take Henry Prince Morgan, who played the role of "Old Black Joe." Though he played a stylized, racist role onstage, Morgan was a consummate professional. He was an expert dancer. He was college-educated, having studied music and math under W. C. Handy at Alabama A&M. He read music expertly, performed on multiple instruments, and had been taught music by the father of the blues.

Alain Locke's *The Negro and His Music* (1936) was one of the first comprehensive studies of the minstrel tradition. The history of minstrelsy is now being studied seriously among White theorists. There are various reactions to the fact that early jazz was part minstrel show, including the defensiveness and evasion of Ted Gracyk, who argues that popular music in the United States is *not* indebted to the minstrel tradition. Such evasive White approaches differ significantly from the analysis of Eric Lott in *Love and Theft,* and *Black Mirror: The Cultural Contradictions of American Racism*.[55] Lott has demonstrated how minstrel listening is a foundational orientation device of American popular culture.

The cultural, existential exchanges between the Original Creole Band and their White audiences were decisive moments in the formation of the White sonic gaze in America. The band taught White Americans that "to jazz" was a verb. Jazzing was a way of listening that turned tradition on its head. Most

White listeners didn't get it. When they paid to consume the sights, sounds, and spectacle of Palao, Baquet, Keppard, Johnson, and Morgan, they were humbugged.

FRANCOPHONE NEWSPAPERS IN NEW ORLEANS

Print culture in the Jazz Age was a powerful orientation device. Prior to the era of recorded sound, newspapers were the main source of information about how musicians sounded and where they could be heard. The mainstream White press wrote extensively about the Creole Band, but the Black Anglophone press and the Francophone newspapers of New Orleans did not.

In the Jazz Age, Anglophone Black newspapers flourished, including the *Defender*, *Crisis*, *Opportunity*, and the *Freeman*. Surprisingly, as Gushee notes, the Original Creole Band was barely mentioned in Black newspapers.[56] I have examined the archives of the Indianapolis *Freeman* and the Chicago *Defender*, and my conclusions are consistent with Gushee's. My research shows that between 1905 and 1920, in the *Defender*, for example, one finds no more than seventy-five mentions of the word "Creole," and most of those are references to other touring companies using "Creole" in their name. Billy E. Jones's music column in the *Defender*, "New York Notes," began mentioning the band's whereabouts in late 1916. Jones usually devoted a simple one line for each band he thought worth covering, stating what theater they'd be playing. The November 18, 1916, "New York Notes" states simply but effectively: "The Creole Band is at the Pentages Theater. Ogden, Utah." Jones did not, as far as I can tell, write reviews of the band's performances, though he let readers know where they could find the company as it toured the Midwest.

In New Orleans, there were two Francophone print traditions. One appealed to the White-identifying Creole population, the other to the Black-identifying Creole population. "These two Creole literary communities have most often diverged to the point of not recognizing the other."[57] For different reasons, neither of these print traditions covered early jazz music.

New Orleans had a thriving Francophone press beginning in the nineteenth century. The journals run by and for Black-identifying Creole readers peaked in the nineteenth century and covered politics, not aesthetics. The political newspaper *L'Union* ran from 1862 to 1864, and the journal *La Tribune de la Nouvelle-Orléans*, the *New Orleans Tribune*, a bilingual political journal, was published in the 1870s. These newspapers were too early to cover the emergence of jazz music, and they were mostly concerned with politics. Thus, the Francophone press read by Black-identifying Creoles did not directly shape aural orientations to jazz music.

The Francophone press serving White-identifying French speakers was dominated by *L'Abeille de la Nouvelle-Orléans*, the *New Orleans Bee*. The archives of *L'Abeille* are available digitally through the Jefferson Parish Library.[58] These archives, as well as a small amount of secondary literature, show that *L'Abeille* oriented itself to a Europhilic readership. Founded in 1827 and staying in publication until 1925,[59] *L'Abeille* primarily covered business and politics. The theater section was overseen by Louis Placide Canonge (1822–1893), a prominent White-identifying Creole playwright and journalist. Canonge was active in the early 1870s, directing the French Opera House in New Orleans, composing operas, and writing music criticism. Canonge's theater section in *L'Abeille* examined opera music, not vaudeville. As the archives of *L'Abeille* reveal, in the twentieth century and long after Canonge was dead, the theater section continued to cover French Opera to the exclusion of other music. Why was *L'Abeille* unconcerned with jazz music, given that the newspaper was in print at the height of the Jazz Age?

I posit that *L'Abeille* did not cover jazz because its White-identifying Creole readers were invested in "becoming White." *L'Abeille* helped forge White listening orientations by encouraging the White-identifying Francophone public to enjoy "classical" rather than popular, lowbrow, and commercial music. Early jazz was the music of vaudeville, brass bands, parades, dances, fish fries, and blues joints. Bechet's and Ory's music grew from the plantation and drew upon plantation sounds and influences. For White-identifying Francophones, jazz was too Black. Readers of *L'Abeille* chose to read a French language paper that covered opera music to distance themselves from both Anglos and Black-identifying Creoles. *L'Abeille* helped establish a public aesthetic taste that aligned classical music with purportedly French, European, and White values.

In 1929, Ruby Caulfeild published *The French Literature of Louisiana*,[60] in which she explained the divide between White-identifying and Black-identifying Creole writers of the late nineteenth and early twentieth centuries in New Orleans. The White-identifying Creole authors were "proud of their French ancestry and the term 'creole' is dear to them. This name they use in its original sense, not always remembered: 'colonial', of 'pure European stock', not mixed with Indian blood."[61] White-identifying Creoles like Canonge used Creole to mean "of pure European stock," a meaning nearly opposite to that used by the Original Creole Band.

Unlike the mainstream Anglophone press of the Jazz Age, which developed a love/hate relationship with jazz music, the Francophone press in New Orleans largely ignored jazz. Canonge advocated classical listening in the French Opera as a way to shore up European identity.

THE CREOLIZING LISTENING OF ÉDOUARD GLISSANT

In his travel memoir, *Faulkner/Mississippi*, Édouard Glissant (1928–2011) recounts coming to the United States and speaking with Whites about the similarities between the American South and the Caribbean. Arguing that New Orleans is "the land of Creolization," where Antillean cultural traces are found in Creole languages, cooking, and music, he was met with clogged ears. "You cite a whole list for a skeptical audience that does not wish to know that its history travels with the seas."[62] Glissant has a name for the decreolizing listening orientation of these American Whites: They listen "genetically" rather than "digenetically." Americans who listen genetically are concerned with tracing their culture back to a single origin. Genetic listening is like the revivalist impulse to search for the first, best, and most representative sounds of jazz. From Glissant, and building on the insights of Bechet and Ory, I develop the idea of digenetic, creolizing listening, which is an alternative to the decreolizing practices of White sonic gazing.

In *Faulkner/Mississippi*, Glissant brings together an analysis of the American South and the Global South that challenges American exceptionalist thinking. From Glissant we learn that a creolizing approach requires cultural and conceptual hybridity, and must speak to the project of being human given the variety of colonial situations. Jazz in particular exemplifies just how deeply the United States is a "crossroads for the other souths," in the words of J. Michael Dash. Drawing on Glissant as well as Paul Gilroy, Dash offers a Black Atlantic corrective to White listening in his "Relating Islands: The South of the South in American."[63] The enormous body of thinking about creolization that has emerged from late-twentieth-century Caribbean writers, including Glissant, is a palliative to American exceptionalism. American exceptionalism—the idea that the United States is fundamentally different from other nation states—makes for bad listening by drawing an artificial boundary between the United States and the Caribbean. The exceptionalist jazz narrative distances jazz music from the improvised, syncopated, creolized, musical forms found in Haiti, Cuba, Jamaica, Trinidad, Puerto Rico, Martinique, the Dominican Republic, and so many other parts of the Caribbean, as well as Central and South America. The exceptionalist listener asserts that jazz could not have happened anywhere else.

The difference between the terms "creolizing" and "Creole," as I'm using them, is the difference between the name of a constellation of cultures and the name of a philosophical strategy. Creolizing listening is an activity, and "to creolize" should be understood as an intellectual project. This is the sense in which one can engage in "creolizing the canon," as Neil Roberts and Jane Anna Gordon conceive of it. It is also kindred to the spirit of Michael Monahan's *The Creolizing Subject: Race, Reason and the Politics of Purity*.[64]

Creolizing listening could also be considered jazzing listening. Before jazz named a genre of music, it described a style of playing time. Jazzing meant rhythmic variation. Here the similarity between the action of creolizing and jazzing is important. Creolizing is philosophical orientation in time and space. Jazzing and creolizing can be considered imaginative, improvisatory reorientations toward Whiteness.

Faulkner/Mississippi is a useful text for mapping White American culture. Glissant's creolizing approach to the fiction of William Faulkner begins with the importance of colonial geography. "Algeria at the beginning of this century is certainly not Mississippi in the middle of the last century, but we find the same question: What must be renounced, and what must be accepted."[65] Glissant's reading of Faulkner suggests strategies for theorizing and creolizing American jazz. He reads Faulkner with special attention to what he names the problem of genesis. In the United States, genetic thinking shows up as a national myth about racial purity. White thinking is genetic because it seeks a unitary origin for White identity. Genetic thinking is similar to existential bad faith. White Americans try to convince themselves that they are racially pure, not mixed. The conviction "I am White" is "metastable" in Gordon's and Sartre's sense, meaning that a White consciousness may both believe and not believe itself to be White. Put differently, the assertion of racial purity by American Whites is marked by a constant anxiety about mixture.

Glissant's creolizing reading of Faulkner brings Americans face-to-face with the existential question of what it means to be White. Once Whiteness is described as a problem, Whites can begin asking themselves the basic question of creolization: "Is cultural interaction or 'interchange' a harbinger of intermingling, miscegenation, and finally Creolization?"[66] Glissant indicates how Whiteness is laden with a basic contradiction: Whites in the United States must continually assert and perform their Whiteness to mask the reality that they are culturally, ethnically, racially, and sonically mixed. Monahan calls this contradiction "the politics of purity."[67]

Glissant interprets Faulkner's writing as containing both creolizing and decreolizing moments. Faulkner orients his readers to a supposedly pure American past, which is at odds with two creolizing strategies found in his writing: orality and repetition. The "oral techniques of accumulation, repetition, and circularity . . . combine to undo the vision of reality and truth as singular, introducing the multiple, the uncertain, and the relative instead."[68] Glissant reads Faulkner against himself: His narrative strategies are less White, less pure than he thinks.

Glissant implicates Faulkner in the project of White nation building, while at the same time revealing how Faulkner's narrative techniques disrupt this project. Faulkner's fiction demonstrates an American fear of racial mixture. The United States is a post-slavery society with a fundamental anxiety about miscegenation. The need to define and protect Whiteness is reflected in the literary figure who fears finding out they are a racial "half-breed."[69] The desire for purity is contradicted by the genealogical fact of mixture. "Black-and-White is already outmoded; it neither accepts nor resolves the racist contradiction in the United States, where there are Latinos, West Indians, Asians, immigrants from Eastern Europe, all differing from each other in some respect, and different from both Blacks and Whites."[70]

Glissant's distinction between genetic and digenetic thinking helps us understand why the White sonic gaze is so instant upon not only racial purity, but a protectionist notion of culture. Digenetic thinking problematizes Whiteness by noticing how it shows up as a desire for purity, a fear of mixture, and an amnesia about colonialism. While "Whites from Louisiana generally refuse to admit any such connections . . . between Louisiana and the Caribbean," it is clear that "the cooking—the spices, the hearty vegetable soups (Lafcadio Hern's gombo zheb), red beans, and pork—and the music are principally the same in the culture of this whole area. The African trace was kept alive."[71]

The digenetic approach interprets the White desire for purity as a willed ignorance of the geography of the plantation. This leads to an inability to hear the repetition of the slave system across the Americas. Genetic White listeners believe that American slavery was long ago, and fundamentally different from slavery in the Caribbean and Latin America. Genetic thinking is manifest in the desire for a sharp conceptual and imaginary Southern border. In terms of music, genetic thinking has led to the narrative that jazz "could only have been born in the United States," a sentiment that ignores, as I've said, the deep similarities between jazz and other creolized, improvised music across the Caribbean and Americas.

The digenetic thinking modeled by Glissant is found in a variety of his works, including *Caribbean Discourse*[72] and *Poetics of Relation*.[73] In *Caribbean Discourse*, he clarifies that digenetic thinking is not a celebration of conglomeration, but a reorientation toward cultural mixture that has been both imposed from above and created from below. "Creolization as an idea is not primarily the glorification of the composite nature of a people. . . . The idea of creolization demonstrates that henceforth it is no longer valid to glorify 'unique' origins that the race safeguard and prolongs."[74] As Monahan's reading of Glissant emphasizes, creolization is not carving out a middle between two racial extremes, or establishing a third racial category to be set alongside White and Black in the United States. "To assert people are creolized, that creolization has value, is to deconstructs in this way the category of 'creolized' that is considered as halfway between two 'pure' extremes."[75]

In *Poetics of Relation*, Glissant connects the dots between his digenetic framing of Whiteness and his theory of listening. Like Bechet and Ory, Glissant analyzes White listening on the plantation. Glissant's study of plantation listening demonstrates how to listen for difference. The emergence of listening habits on plantations was a negotiation between "the dialectics [of] the oral and the written."[76] Glissant calls orality "an act of survival" for colonized people.[77] The plantation was a dominant system that organized sound, expression, and listening for enslaved people, as well as those who enslaved them. "In the silent universe of the Plantation, oral expression, the only form possible for the slaves, was discontinuously organized. As tales, proverbs, sayings, songs appeared—as much in the Creole-speaking world as elsewhere—they bore the stamp of this discontinuity."[78] In her discussion of Glissant, Guillermina De Ferrari calls plantations the "social and linguistic laboratories" where "collective stories converge in violent and yet creative ways."[79]

It is here, in the context of orality on the plantation, that we find in Glissant's thought a connection between Creole languages and creolizing as an intellectual and normative posture. "Creole" is the generic name for the linguistic forms that emerged from the violent confrontation between European, new world Indigenous, and African languages. Glissant imagines creolization as a form of "renewal" and "forgetting" that can only be understood from the perspective of movement.[80] Glissant, like Bechet, treats language, sound, and music as motion.

There is a good reason why creolizing thought treats music and language as forms of motion: For African-diasporic peoples, making music and speaking are sometimes survival strategies—strategies that should not be reduced to, but that are conditioned by White listening. In *Poetics of Relation*, Glissant makes this case, linking jazz music to the material conditions of plantations and to the linguistic transformations necessary to communication under colonialism. Glissant explores "how speech functions in this Plantation realm," marking three types of creolized speech, and arguing that this speech became jazz: "the rudimentary language necessary to get work done," "stifled speech," and "disguised speech, in which men and women who are gagged keep their words close. The Creole language integrated these three modes and made them jazz."[81]

Glissant describes plantations as "spaces of silence" from which music comes.[82] White American ears have mainly attuned themselves to blues and jazz, to the exclusion of "salsas and reggaes," "biguines and calypso."[83] But the music born of silence includes the national and transnational forms that emerged from the Black diaspora. Naming "jazz, biguines and calypso" in the same breath, Glissant reminds us that syncopated music of different kinds emerged from the repeating plantation structure, where the three-against-two and two-against-three polyrhythms that survived the middle passage were violently creolized with European and Indigenous rhythms. Glissantian listening requires the flexibility to note the transnational similarities of the music born of silence, while also noting the different spaces where music is heard. A creolizing perspective relates the blues to "towns and growing cities" and "jazz, biguines, and calypsos" to "barrios and shantytowns." The geography of listening matters. Glissant's creolizing perspective places rhythms (orientations in time) in relation to places (orientations in space).

Glissant's philosophy, like that of Ory and Bechet, invites White listeners to confront their bad faith desire for purity and genesis. *Today's White American listeners should accept that their listening habits were born on plantations where Whites silenced Black people they held in bondage.* As with Ory's overseer, old man Tureau, White boredom and male sexual desire have persisted as motivations for letting "subalterns" sing the blues for the benefit of the colonizer. Glissant elucidates how White listening practices on plantations are Faulknerian: White listeners struggle with repetition, orality, and the call-and-response that comes to them from non-Whites. Good listening is a cultural interchange that transforms all participants. White listening is a response to and a dance with otherness. If Glissant is correct, White American listening, like Faulkner's prose, has creolizing and decreolizing elements. White listening is not just White, it is creolized. In a sense then, American listening is not just American, it is also Caribbean, African, Indigenous, European, and Latin American. The genetic listener insists that jazz could only have happened in the United States, but it would make just as much sense to assert that jazz could only have happened in the Caribbean. Creolizing listening is antagonistic to the American exceptionalist practices of listening that reduce unstable racial identities to categories of authenticity.

The critiques of White listening offered by Sidney Bechet, Kid Ory, and the Original Creole Band are instructive. Anticipating a claim that would emerge later in mainstream philosophy, they argued that Whites in the United States were not born White, but have become White through praxis—the praxis of listening. Navigating gummed-up White ears was a fact of life for Creole musicians. These Creole musicians were philosophers in the sense that they studied listening as a craft and taught Americans how to hear. For Whites, the syncopation of tunes like "Eh Las Bas" was new, different, exciting, and exotic. Through call-and-response, Creole musicians taught White audiences philosophical lessons about time and space, in the form of finding the one, hearing rhythmic displacement, and ultimately, hearing how to swing.

Listening Exercises for Chapter 3
Listening to Difference

Sidney Bechet has a phenomenological approach to music that instructs us to *listen for difference*. Listening for difference prioritizes the listener's perceptions of sound. In response to the question "What is Black music?" Bechet remarked that it depends on how we listen. Bechet's insight challenges the A/V litany, which treats music as a substance. Bechet's critique of White listening provides a phenomenology of listening that can be used in the classroom as part of a Jazz Pedagogy.

What is the contemporary significance of Bechet's idea that "music contains its own explanation of itself"? One implication is that philosophical ideas can be taught through music. While the hip-hop-based education of Marc Lamont Hill (and others) has paved the way for analyzing lyrics, Bechet's creolizing phenomenology of listening is attuned to sounds, especially rhythms, which are vehicles for expressing theoretical truths, social critiques, and notions of freedom and liberation. Creolizing listening orientations also allow us to hear mixture without appealing to romantic ideas of cultural development or apolitical mutual borrowing. Colorblind White listeners point to White jazz masters as evidence that jazz is a music where everyone borrows from each other. A creolizing listening orientation listens for the difference between a dominant culture borrowing from those cultures it dominates, and the other way around.

LISTENING FOR VERSIONING

Dick Hebdige coined the term "versioning" to describe how Caribbean musicians transformed and remixed songs.[1] Versioning is similar to covering, except that it requires a more complete reinterpretation of a song. The spirit of versioning is captured in Bechet's comment to the White revivalist listener that he never played the same song twice, even though throughout his career he versioned many tunes. Listen comparatively to three versions of "Petit Fleur," one of Bechet's most well-loved songs.

Begin with Bechet's 1952 rendition of "Petit Fleur." Take some time with the recording to identify the instrumentation, tempo, rhythmic feel, and the main notes of the melody. Write down five words that describe Bechet's timbre (tone quality) and style on the soprano saxophone. His sound is highly unique, especially the heavy vibrato. Bechet learned to play by imitating the classical singers of the French Opera in New Orleans. He was a master ear musician. Listen to the horns that complement the melody by playing in the open space around Bechet's lead.

Compare Bob Wilber's version of "Petite Fleur." Wilber spent much of his career imitating the sounds of Bechet, although in this recording we can hear some differences. Most notably, Wilber has a different tone and he uses less vibrato. What similarities and differences do you hear? Do you hear Wilber as imitating or versioning Bechet's sound?

The third version of "Petite Fleur" comes from the contemporary avantgarde musician David Liebman and can be found on his record *Petite Fleur: The Music of Sydney Bechet* recorded in 2017. Liebman deconstructs the tune. He is not imitating Bechet's tone or his vibrato, and he takes liberties with phrasing and rhythms, while the guitar accompaniment offers modern harmonies. Given Liebman's background, these liberties are not surprising. He was Miles Davis's tenor player from 1970 to 1974, worked extensively with John Coltrane's drummer Elvin Jones after Coltrane died, and went on to lead dozens of his own projects, all in the vein of contemporary, post-1960s jazz.

LISTEN FOR CALL-AND-RESPONSE IN COLLECTIVE IMPROVISATION

Check out a video of Sidney Bechet performing "Sweet Georgia Brown" in 1958, available on YouTube.[2] Watching the video will help you hear the interaction between the lead instrument (Bechet's soprano saxophone) and the trumpet and trombone accompaniment. Early New Orleans jazz was marked by collective rather than individual improvisation. The opening forty-five seconds of the video demonstrate collective improvisation. Bechet states the melody and the other horns play around the lead. While in some cases the brass might have been arranged in the statement of the melody ("the head"), more than likely, they were taking liberties. This performance was made in 1958 and clearly reflects the bebop influences, especially the practice of each musician taking a whole solo chorus of improvisation. Write down the order of the solos. The piano goes first. Which instruments follow? As the soloists improvise, what do the other instrumentalists do? During the piano solo, what other instruments do you hear? The musicians who are playing in the background during the solos are "comping," a jazz phrase that likely comes from the word "to compliment." When the bass solo comes, what other instruments do you hear? In the middle of the trombone solo, can you hear the trumpet and saxophone come in? This is a moment of collective improvisation. Notice how the crowd claps, cheers, and screams. How would you characterize the call-and-response among the musicians? Between the musicians and the crowd? How does the crowd react to the drummer's solo? This recording is a fine example of how Bechet's style developed in later years as he creolized early jazz (collective improvisation) with modern concepts (individual improvisation). The modern style can also be heard in the piano harmony, in the drum style, and in the brass solos.

LISTENING TO A REGRESSIVE REMIX

The musician Kenny G has been criticized for his remix of Louis Armstrong's version of the pop song "What a Wonderful World." Armstrong recorded the song in 1967, decades after his initial success and at the end of his long career. Nevertheless, the song topped the charts in the United Kingdom, and later, in 1988, rose to the top forty in the United States. Does this song strike you as "jazz"? Why or why not? Is the rhythm syncopated? Does the label "jazz" affect how you hear the song? Adopting Bechet's principle that music is mostly in the listening, try listening to the song as jazz and then listening as not-jazz. Does it make any difference? The notion of a "regressive remix," which I borrow from Eduardo Navas, is that a version of a song may lack such integrity and basic musicality that the original sonic material has been destroyed, and not in a good way.[3] Assess the guitarist Pat Metheny's opinion that Kenny G's version is a regressive remix of Armstrong's material.[4] Is Metheny appealing to a decreolizing notion of jazz purity? Here is an excerpt from Metheny: "Not long ago, Kenny G put out a recording where he overdubbed himself on top of a thirty-plus-year-old Louis Armstrong record. With this single move, Kenny G became one of the few people on earth I can say that I really can't use at all—as a man, for his incredible arrogance to even consider such a thing, and as a musician, for presuming to share the stage with the single most important figure in our music."[5]

HEARING AND PLAYING BECHET'S MELODIES

Using a piano (or online piano app), play along with Beceht's recording of "I Found a New Baby" (1958).[6] Use the settings function on YouTube to adjust the playback speed to 0.75 or 0.50. This function will slow down the recording without pitch alteration. Listening to the recording slowly will give you time to hear pitches and rhythms. The melody begins at around the 0:50 second mark. Listen to the short phrase from 0:50 seconds to 1:00 repeatedly until you can copy it. At first, listen without trying to play along. Repeat as many times as necessary to find the first phrase of the melody. This may take twenty or thirty times or more. Don't be discouraged by slow progress, especially if you do not have previous musical experience. The opening melody is a descending minor triad plus a tritone: A♭, A, F, and D. Compare Ethel Waters's 1925 version of "I Found a New Baby." You'll hear how the musical phrase you just learned maps onto the lyrics. Play the melody on the keyboard while singing. Each word maps onto the six-note phrase. The lyrics will help you remember the melody and rhythm.

VISUAL TIE-IN

Reflect on the difference between listening to sound with and without visual cues. In the examples above, did it help or hinder your listening to watch a video recording? The Library of Congress has wonderful black-and-white photographs of Bechet taken by William Gottlieb (see figure 3.1). As you view these high-quality images, zoom in and look for details that tell a story. Examine the subtle particulars like hairstyles, how everyone is dressed, how Bechet holds his instrument, and the facial expression of Bechet.[7] Break down the composition of the photographs and ask: What stories do they tell? Photos from live performances of Bechet's in New York clubs speak powerfully to the moment. The recordings of Bechet you've studied are all low quality compared to today's recording abilities. Based on the images from the period, *imagine what it would have sounded like to hear Bechet while sitting in a tiny club only a few feet away.* Imagine how loud the music would have been. Do you think the audience is mostly dancing or mostly sitting down? Does Bechet's music inspire you to dance? Why or why not?

Chapter 4

The Ears of a Guilty People
Africana Critiques of White Listening

Critiques of the White sonic gaze abound in Africana sound and print culture. Black philosophers of existence, including W.E.B. Du Bois, Frantz Fanon, Angela Davis, bell hooks, and Lewis Gordon, have articulated variations on the problem of White listening. Harlem Renaissance philosophers Alain Locke, Zora Neale Hurston, and Alice Dunbar-Nelson intensely debated the White problem. Black sound culture, especially spirituals, the blues, jazz, and vaudeville, is a rich archive of existential, phenomenological critiques of Whiteness. If we keep in mind that the Jazz Age was also the Harlem Renaissance period, the Great Migration period, and the time of the international Negritude movement, it makes sense that Black existential philosophers, blues and jazz musicians, and Harlem Renaissance thinkers converged in the belief that White listening is a problem. Black thinkers have commented extensively on how White Americans have become White through their ears.

The fundamental criticism emerging from these existential debates is that Whites consume sounds and images of Black people in music, theater, and the White press, while ignoring critiques of the White consumption of Black culture. Ironically, critiques of Whiteness are found not only in the Black literature and press that the White public ignored but also within the blues, jazz, and spirituals that Whites listened to, loved, collected, and archived.

THE PROBLEM OF WHITE LISTENING IN BLACK EXISTENTIAL THOUGHT

The six patterns of White bad faith listening named earlier were drawn from formulations of the White problem in Black and Creole existential thought. In this chapter, I consider the problem of White listening as articulated in Black existential thought, Harlem Renaissance thought, and Black journalism.

I have an inclusive definition of Black existential thought. In their preface to *Not Only the Master's Tools: African American Studies in Theory and Practice*, Jane Anna Gordon and Lewis Gordon argue that existential philosophy can be expressed in a wide range of print and sound cultures, perhaps none more significant than blues and jazz music. "The first, most influential wave of Black existential reflection was in music and then literature. The quintessential Black existential response in music is the blues. The blues focuses on life's difficulties and brings reality to the world of *feeling* or Black suffering and joy."[1] Blues and jazz are existential cultural forms in the sense that they "welcome improvisation" and "defy predictability and human closure."[2] "Jazz, rhythm and blues, soul, funk, reggae, samba, salsa and hip hop—[are] exemplars of the existential credo of existence preceding essence and its connection to the question of freedom."[3] Against the cliché that blues is a music of sadness, they argue, "The blues . . . is life affirming."[4] Indeed, the blues is "an important adversary of anti-black racism."[5]

The terms "existentialist" and "phenomenologist" in the traditional sense name European philosophers such as Husserl, Heidegger, Beauvoir, Sartre, and Merleau-Ponty. A growing body of scholarship shows how Africana thinkers anticipated the themes and methods of European existential thought. In *Being Apart: Theoretical and Existential Resistance in Africana Literature*, LaRose T. Parris notes that "Due to their peoples' history of enslavement, oppression, and marginalization in the West, Africana thinkers engaged with the existentialist issues of Being and Freedom in the late nineteenth and early twentieth centuries well before their European counterparts."[6] In "Africana Phenomenology: Its Philosophical Implications," Paget Henry argues that Du Bois was the first to offer a "comprehensive phenomenology of Africana self-consciousness."[7] Henry roots Africana phenomenology in the slave narratives of Frederick Douglass and Harriet Jacobs, while including the work of "Edward Blyden, Antenor Firmin, Marcus Garvey, Ida B. Wells, W. E. B. Du Bois, Alain Locke, Frantz Fanon, Wilson Harris, Sylvia Wynter, and Lewis Gordon."[8] In *Fanon and the Crisis of European Man*, Lewis Gordon distinguishes the European tradition of existentialism from the Africana tradition that preceded it, which he calls "the philosophy of existence."[9] Boiling the philosophy of existence down to three ideas—a conception of the lived body; a sense of the self-other relationship as the source of values; and an account of anguish and liberation—Gordon writes, "One need only find Black philosophers who hold these theses and one will encounter, regardless of their self-ascription, existential philosophers."[10]

Among Black philosophers of existence, the White problem is formulated as a problem of reality, knowledge, and value. Whiteness allows Whites to invert reality, evade knowledge of themselves and others, and flee from moral responsibility for White violence. In *Darkwater*, Du Bois asks White readers, "But what on earth is Whiteness that one should so desire it?"[11] In Gordon's variation, "The White problem . . . is that there doesn't seem to be any salvation for Whites in a racist world once racism is admitted to be oppressive."[12] Fanon admonishes, "Let us have the courage to say it: *It is the racist who creates the inferiorized.*"[13] In all of these formulations, Whiteness is understood as death. As Gordon maintains, "To be Black may mean to suffer, literally and figuratively, on an everyday basis, but to be White may ultimately mean—at least when moral reflection is permitted to enter—to be condemned."[14]

Formulations of the White problem appear in the work of Sartre, Beauvoir, Richard Wright, James Baldwin, Steve Biko,[15] and others.[16] In a popular piece for *Ebony* magazine in 1965, historian Lerone Bennett Jr. put it this way: "There is no Negro problem in America. The problem of race in America, insofar as that problem is related to packets of melanin in men's skins, is a White problem. And in order to solve that problem we must seek its source, not in the Negro but in White America."[17] In *Biko: Philosophy, Identity and Liberation*, Mabogo More reveals how Steve Biko treated the White problem as a "critique of white liberals' view that South Africa's problem is a 'black problem.'"[18] In Biko's words, "There is nothing the matter with blacks. The problem is WHITE RACISM."[19] As More emphasizes, Africana critiques of Whiteness have an international dimension given the fact of "worldwide antiblack racism."[20]

The White problem is often understood as a problem of vision. Visibility, hyper-visibility, and invisibility are major concepts in Black existential literature. Among Black existential thinkers one also finds frequent discussions of sound, music, orality, language, and listening. In the Black existential tradition, spirituals, the blues, and jazz are studied as theoretical contributions to the study of human existence.

Cast as an issue of sound, the White problem is that White listeners dehumanize themselves and others by listening from a position of power. White listeners are socialized to think listening is a quiet, passive, neutral, unembodied, nongendered, nonracialized practice. White listeners often claim that they are the ones who "discovered" the music of Black performers, whom they cast in the role of the primitive. White listeners often ignore Black critiques of White listening in sound and print culture. When White listeners do pay attention, they tend to listen selectively, especially to Black women, whose voices they appropriate. White ears, as Du Bois ciphers, are the "ears of a guilty people."[21] Ignoring Africana critiques of Whiteness is part of a larger cultural pattern that Parris has named "being apart," which is "the historical, ontological and epistemological peripheralization of African people and Africana knowledge production in the West."²² The habitual failure of White people to listen to non-White people is a failure of human recognition.

Lewis Gordon analyzes White listening as a form of White bad faith. In *Bad Faith and Anti-Black Racism,* he argues that White bad faith is a pervasive feature of White experience that allows White people to think that racial differences are natural and that race is something others have. White bad faith is generally a rationalization of White mediocrity. For instance, White listeners minimize the musicianship of Black performers by coding them as "naturally" good at music, unlike White and European musicians who are praised for their skill.²³ Like all people experiencing existential bad faith, the White listener in the United States has an implicit knowledge of the truths that she or he holds at a distance. Anxiety is just beneath the surface of White self-confidence. Whites know they are racially embodied, but they evade this knowledge when they deny that being White means having power over non-Whites.²⁴ In his discussion of racial embodiment and the White problem, Mabogo P. More insists on the important difference between "being-a-black-philosopher-in-the-world" and "being-a-white-philosopher-in-the-world."²⁵ *Being-White-in-the-world* is an embodied, existential reality that "absolve[s] white philosophers from taking racism as a philosophical problem seriously, but also effectively keeps racism easily and expediently on the margins and out of sight for them."²⁶

Gordon argues that White jazz audiences habitually miss the phenomenological dynamic that makes for good jazz listening: the call-and-response.²⁷ In "Sketches of Jazz," he describes the interaction among performer and listener when there is existential reciprocity: "Have you ever watched the audience? They synchronize themselves with the song, they participate, they give and take from the musicians, they contribute to the music"²⁸ Gordon confirms that the "give and take" between audience and performer is a relationship, not a substance. Jazz is "dialectical."²⁹ But when jazz first found "a path into *White* and therefore mainstream popular culture," audiences dismissed it as too noisy, too bodily, and too Black.³⁰ White listeners reduced jazz music to "ni**** music."³¹ Like Bechet, Gordon challenges the label "jazz," substituting "African American Classical music" to remind White readers that what makes music "classical" is not a European pedigree. Criticizing the way mainstream White Americans listened primarily to other Whites play jazz, Gordon writes: "The all-White Original Dixieland Jazz Band. *Original?/* Benny Goodman, 'king of swing.'/ *King* of swing? So while Black musicians were being stereotyped for their rhythm, White musicians could still claim the highest accomplishments over it."³²

In his recent philosophical memoir, *Looking Through Philosophy in Black,* the existential thinker Mabogo More devotes a wonderful chapter to "Philosophy and Jazz," observing that "Jazz's only *telos* is to discover, create, and attempt to define what it means to be human. . . . *In this sense jazz is an existential art.*"[33] More finds existential inspiration in jazz, especially Miles Davis's unflinching opposition to American racism. Analyzing a comment once made to Lewis Gordon—"Jazz? Naaa, that's White people's music!"—More notices that not only have Black jazz musicians faced institutional racism, they have faced White audiences who try to appropriate jazz by turning it into their music—music they've "discovered," "saved," and "rediscovered."[34]

The auditory White problem in a central concern in Africana existential thought. If Whiteness is a kind of death, then White listening is a deadening of the eardrums. I turn now to Du Bois and Fanon, who offered foundational critiques of the White sonic gaze.

W.E.B. DU BOIS

Du Bois, the paramount theorist of the White problem, was a vigilant listener. His phenomenology of listening in *The Souls of White Folk* and *Darkwater* portrays bad faith White listening as well as what I will call, following Veronica Watson,[35] "estranged" White listening. For Du Bois, bad faith White listening is, like the category of "Whiteness" itself, a tool for "ownership of the earth."[36] Du Bois's phenomenology of the White experience is grounded in a political economy of Whiteness, which is to say that he understands being White as both a personal identity and a social force that distributes wealth unevenly and unjustly. More specifically, White listening is a mechanism to control social spaces such as theaters, churches, schools, homes, neighborhoods, and communities. Foreshadowing Sartre's concept of bad faith as a God-complex, Du Bois notes that Whites in the United States have used listening to deify themselves: "These super-men and world-mastering demi-gods listened, however, to no low tongues of ours, even when we pointed silently to their feet of clay."[37] Estranged Whites are tragic figures in the classic sense: Their anxieties, discomforts, and misfortunes are of their own doing; they cling to myths of merit and beauty that are rationalizations of White violence and theft. White estrangement is a process by which Whites become aware that *they are the problem*, and begin to reject the psychological, material wages of Whiteness.

It is noteworthy that in both *Souls* and *Darkwater*, an imaginary interracial conversation is the literary device that drives the analysis of White listening. Du Bois addresses his White readers in the first person, inviting them to begin the process of White estrangement or White double consciousness. I examine two portraits of White estrangement in Du Bois's work. The first is the figure of the "Gentle reader," of *Souls* and *Darkwater*. Du Bois directly names and challenges the listening habits of this gentle, White reader. The second portrait of estranged White listening is the character "White John" and his White father, the Judge, in *Souls*. Drawing on Watson, I treat White John and the Judge as estranged from Whiteness in the sense that their personal anxieties, unhappiness, and failures are caused by their racism, although they are only dimly aware of this.

In *Darkwater*, Du Bois portrays a sympathetic White reader whose belief system is circumscribed by the unstated supremacist premise of White culture that "Whiteness alone is inherently and obviously better than brownness."[38] This unanalyzed premise of White thinking "leads to curious acts."[39] When sympathetic Whites are asked about the White problem, they respond evasively, with coded speech. The beliefs of the White speaker "are continually playing above their actual words an obligato of tune and tone, saying: 'My poor, un-White thing! Weep not nor rage. I know, too well, that the curse of God lies heavy on you.'"[40] In this imagery dialogue, the White interlocutor does not listen well when asked to talk about Whiteness because they become embarrassed, angry, defensive, and ashamed. Instead of hearing evidence, the White listener reduces critiques of Whiteness voiced by Black people to expressions of jealousy. Heard through the filter of pity, the Black interlocutor is no longer an equal partner in a speech situation, but a "poor, un-White thing," whose wish to be White has led them to question the value of Whiteness. The sympathetic White consciousness uses the listening orientation of pity to distort reality.

In *Darkwater*, Du Bois not only refuses to be problematized by the White questioner but he also reverses the situation by asking the White reader to comment on the White problem: "I do not laugh. I am quite straight-faced as I ask soberly 'But what on earth is Whiteness that one should so desire it?' Then always, somehow, some way, silently but clearly, I am given to understand that Whiteness is the ownership of the earth forever and ever, Amen!"[41] Du Bois demonstrates that Whiteness is the existential, psychological, economic reality that turns being White into being rich, to paraphrase Fanon. The estranged White listener admits through silence that they know White identity is a "faulty" "title to the universe."[42] The evasive White listener hides from the fact that "right here in America," there is "orgy, cruelty, barbarism, and murder done to men and women of Negro descent."[43]

Du Bois summons the White reader to experience Whiteness as strange: "The discovery of personal Whiteness among the world's peoples is a very modern thing—a nineteenth and twentieth century matter, indeed."[44] By situating the White discovery of Whiteness in a dialogue between a sympathetic White person and a Black person, Du Bois pioneered what would become an important trope in existential literature. These face-to-face encounters, going back to Hegel's master/slave chapter in the *Phenomenology of Spirit*, are used to personalize complex social processes. Coming to terms with the foreignness of Whiteness involves a number of considerations, personal and political. Whiteness would be treated as a social role that Whites inhabit, often unconsciously; Whiteness would be understood as a modern force that enabled European colonial violence and chattel slavery; and on the personal level, Whiteness would be treated as something most of us Whites are still "discovering," in the sense that we are contending with what it means to have cultural and economic power simply by virtue of being White.

In *Souls*, DuBois calls his sympathetic, estranged White listener "gentle," the same term Bechet used when addressing revivalist Whites. Like the frame story in Bechet's *Treat It Gentle,* the entire narrative arc of *Souls* is a dialogue between Du Bois and the estranged White reader. If White readers have traveled the distance from the Forethought to the Afterthought—with its bitter indictment of "guilty ears"—their hearing should be "tingling with the truth."[45] Du Bois uses the existential first person to press his reader into a conversation about the White problem. "I who speak here am bone of the bone and flesh of the flesh of them that live within the Veil."[46] He identifies himself as Black, and his audiences as White: "This meaning is not without interest to you, Gender Reader; for the problem of the Twentieth Century is the problem of the color-line."[47] Du Bois depicts the reader of *Souls* as going through White estrangement, which is a process of "awakening," that may come "in a sudden whirl of passion" or "more likely in a gradual dawning sense of things he had at not first noticed."[48] Whites may begin with the "vague, uncomfortable feeling of the stranger."[49]

White people who experience moments of lucidity about how their everyday, mundane actions bolster and express White power would indeed feel strange. It is strange that Whites are harmed psychologically by White supremacy, even as they benefit immensely materially. "The White man, as well as the Negro, is bound and barred by the color-line"[50] Du Bois's estranged White reader is invited to consider several implications of the White problem. Estranged Whites would need to renegotiate their relationship to White supremacist violence in the United States, and across the globe. Du Bois names the White economic consolidation, which harms the "darker nations" of the earth. Estranged Whites would need to explore solutions to poverty, crime, and inequality that are rooted in theories of White, not Black, behavior. The burden of confronting, explaining, and dismantling White violence would be placed on Whites. The sociological study of race, ethnicity, and culture would treat Whites as a "folk," that is, a social group with racial characteristics. White Americans would ask how White selfhood is connected to narratives about racialized others. Finally, estranged Whites would begin to challenge the psychological wages of Whiteness, through which Whites position themselves as noiseless listeners. Du Bois affirms that White estrangement can be motivated by opening one's eyes and ears to European colonialism, "a chapter in human action not pleasant to look back upon."[51] Estranged Whites would begin to feel "War, murder, slavery, extermination, and debauchery" as White problems. [52]

Du Bois's insight that "being a problem is a strange experience" can be taken as a phenomenological lesson for White listening.[53] Whites in the United States are socialized to evade the strangeness of being White when they participate in a "conspiracy of silence" about "the question of questions—the Negro problem."[54] When the White press does mention race, it is only in a "farfetched and academic way."[55] White silence is a collective refusal to speak about White violence, and a collective refusal to listen to those who speak out. White silence is an auditory means that allows Whites to feign ignorance about racism, and evade moral responsibility for anti-Black racism and the ongoing effects of chattel slavery and European colonization of the African, Asian, and American continents.

From the phenomenology of Whiteness in *Souls* and *Darkwater*, we learn that even sympathetic Whites habitually listen evasively to Black thinkers who articulate the White problem. When asked directly to break the conspiracy of White silence, Whites listen through emotions of fear, embarrassment, anger, and pity.

Souls, like Bechet's *Treat It Gentle*, uses the frame narrative of a conversation with a White reader as well as allegory. The allegory of the character White John treats the White sonic gaze as an unstable and mostly irredeemable instrument of White violence. The White sonic gaze exerts itself as crowd control in music theaters, White homes, and Black educational spaces. Du Bois depicts the listening orientation of the character White John as a violent attempt to control who is in the listening audience of a musical theater. White John shows an unease with his own racism, however, when it is revealed that the Black man he wants removed from the theater is his childhood friend. White John is unsettled by the presence of a Black male in the audience and feels he cannot really *hear* the music in the presence of this racial other. He threatens to lynch the Black male and demands that the usher remove this space invader[56] from the theater. In the final moments of the encounter, White John realizes the man he's been harassing is his childhood friend from Georgia. "Frozen into his chair," he starts to offer a handshake, but then refuses as John is removed.[57] The performance of Lohengrin's "Swan" continues with an all-White audience, but White John is shaken and begins, dimly, to face his White hypocrisy.

We learn that the characters John and "White John" grew up as childhood friends in Georgia. Du Bois uses the racial adjective only with White John, never with John. This naming practice centers Black experience, similar to the contemporary naming practice of calling majority White colleges

"Predominately White Institutions," or "PWIs." Both Johns are sent North for college and return to their hometowns dissatisfied. Du Bois analyzes White duplicity through the character of "the Judge," White John's father. He is a symbol of White, Southern aristocratic racism. When John goes to the front door of the Judge's home, he refuses to hear. John is directed to the kitchen door, and reaching the parlor, he is not allowed to sit. The Judge listens Whitely by refusing to listen on terms of equality and by controlling space. The Judge wants to speak and be heard; he doesn't want to listen. From the allegory of White John, we learn that White, masculine listening is crowd control over public and private spaces for listening. White John is an anxious, unhappy White listener whose duplicity is reflected back to him through an encounter with a Black childhood friend.

In *Souls* and *Darkwater*, Du Bois addresses himself phenomenologically to what he calls *the ears of a guilty people*. He speaks to a "gentle," White reader who is invited to experience estrangement from Whiteness by taking seriously the critique in *Souls*. The White reader is given listening instructions as they progress through the book. Estranged White listening would mean breaking the "White silence" about racism and listening to non-Whites on terms of equality and mutual recognition. The political benefit of estranged White listening would be felt only if Whites relinquished White "ownership"—that is, control over segregated listening spaces.

FRANTZ FANON

In a footnote in *Black Skin, White Masks*, Fanon illustrates how White listeners in the United States have expressed a toxic "love" of Black people: "So it is not surprising to see him identify with the Black man: White hot jazz bands and the blues, and spiritual singers, White authors writing novels where the Black hero airs his grievances, and Whites in Black face."[58] From the minstrel listener to the White savior, the revivalist, and the hipster, Whites mishear. In *Wretched of the Earth*, Fanon describes White American folk revivalist listeners as "colonial specialists" who filter their jazz experience through clogged senses: "In their eyes jazz should only be the despairing, broken-down nostalgia of an old Negro who is trapped between five glasses of whiskey, the curse of his race, and the racial hatred of the white men."[59] For Fanon, the White jazz fan's love of Black people is an illness that harms both the White person and those they "love." Inspired by Fanon, I have shown in earlier chapters how this toxic White love plays out in the history of jazz listening in the United States.

Fanon's critique of the White sonic gaze moves in several directions, including toward White, European existentialism. My earlier discussion of

Beauvoir's *Day by Day* as a slum narrative is based on Fanon's writings. And I treat Fanon's critique of Sartre as an argument that Sartre should listen better and be wary of benevolently appropriating the voices of Black people. Sartre was an anti-racist, anti-colonial thinker, and critical Whiteness theorist who ruthlessly called out White behaviors—especially those of the French antisemite, the French White liberal, and the sexual sadist who "loved" non-White people. Yet "Jean-Paul Sartre forgets that the Black man suffers in his body quite differently from the White man."[60] Given my earlier analysis of Beauvoir's relationship with Wright, we can ask: Did Sartre also feel that his engagement with Black philosophers "absolved" him of his Whiteness?

The relationship between Fanon and Sartre was one of mutual respect and negotiation, like that of Beauvoir and Wright. As is well known, Fanon pushed back at any mishearing coming from Sartre, asserting that "Seeing only one type of Black man and equating anti-Semitism with negrophobia seem to be the errors of analysis."[61] This type of pushback is a way to say to Whites who become conscious of the White problem: Do not swing from ignoring Black voices to fetishizing them. Fanon diagnoses how White anti-racists disenchanted with White supremacy may seek relationships with non-White people to exorcise feelings of anxiety, guilt, and estrangement. Disillusioned White intellectuals, no less than any other type of White people, may identify toxically with Black culture by professing the depth of their knowledge of Black authors, culture, history, and aesthetics. One might call this intellectual slumming. As a White ally once said to Fanon: "You must understand that I am one of Lyon's biggest fans of Black people."[62]

I've been teaching philosophy in the United States for more than twenty years. In this time, I've noticed a sea change among many of my White colleagues. They have gone from outright hostility and indifference to diversity to becoming diversity "allies." As Whites in academic and popular culture enter a phase of White consciousness, where they earnestly and enthusiastically take on the project of listening to the voices of non-White people, we must be critical. Like Fanon, Ahmed warns that White ally listening can amount to slumming. In Predominantly White Institutions, the politics of White listening can be coupled with degrading hiring practices, where so-called "diversity hires" are expected to be the voices to which institutionalized White ears are oriented. "If diversity becomes something that is added to organizations, like color, then it confirms the Whiteness of what is already in place."[63] As White philosophers confront the White problem, feelings of shame may be replaced with a feeling of pride in being anti-racist. Ahmed writes: "The White response to the Black critique of shame and guilt has enabled here a turn towards pride, which is not then, a turn away from the White subject and towards something else but another way of returning to Whiteness."[64]

One implication of Fanon's and Ahmed's critique is that White existential philosophers need to discuss *White* authenticity rather than attending to the authenticity of the oppressed. For example, too many people read Sartre's discussion of authentic Jewishness as a claim about what it means to be Jewish, which it is not. Such readings replicate the logic of the "Jewish question," a parallel phenomenon to the "Negro problem." If Sartre, a non-Jew, were able to completely elucidate Jewish experience, then there would be no need for Jewish people to write about Jewish experience. If White phenomenologists can write "Black philosophy" and speak as experts about Black experience, there would be no need or space in philosophy for Black people writing about Black experience.

On Fanonian grounds, an existentially authentic White response to the White problem today must acknowledge the demographic and conceptual Whiteness in the field of philosophy. In 2018, the membership of the American Philosophical Association, the biggest philosophy organization in the United States, was 70 percent White, with 127 individuals identifying as "Black/African American," a total of less than 1 percent.[65] We White academics who write books about Whiteness should also work to diminish White power in the academy. We must own the Ahmedian-Fanonian criticism that Critical Whiteness Studies re-centers us White folk. When Whites start talking and writing about the White problem, we are still in a position where Whites are doing the talking. White existentialists of the 1940s made an important leap: Once aware of the White problem, Whites should talk less and listen more. But the White attitude of "I'll just listen" can also go wrong. There is no such thing as *just* listening. In institutionally White situations, Whites participate in Whiteness not by virtue of their desires, but by virtue of material conditions. White philosophers can be driven by a desire to keep their Whiteness untheorized, unseen, and silent. Since most of us White philosophers think of ourselves as creating philosophy, not *White* philosophy, it can be a shock to have one's Whiteness noticed. This is the experience George Yancy describes so brilliantly in *Look, A White! Philosophical Essays on Whiteness*.[66]

For me, a White philosopher studying debates about Whiteness in White, Black, and Creole thought, I must confront the potentially appropriating effect of asserting the views of select Black or Creole voices, while ignoring wider debates. I should not speak sloppily of "the" voice of "the" oppressed. In *The Black Register*, Tendayi Sithole quotes Mabogo More: "Black philosophers, within the contexts of worldwide white supremacy, share a certain Othered experiential reality. . . . In an antiblack world, the racial context or situation may determine to a large extent the kind of philosopher a black philosopher becomes."[67] The existential question raised for us White folks is parallel: *In a White supremacist, anti-Black world, what kind of philosopher does a White philosopher become?* When Beauvoir listened, she drew on the techniques of French primitivism as well as the embodied Black perspective of Wright; when Sartre listened, he also drew on the techniques of primitivism and Negritude, and on the Black-embodied perspective of Wright and Fanon. White listening can be morphed into a practice where Whites feel their Whiteness, including the sting of responsibility.

When Fanon connected nostalgic White jazz listening to the practices of White listening among White European existentialists, including Beauvoir and Sartre, he made an important move. Fanon diagnosed a toxic White love of Blackness that drove different patterns of White listening. Fanon recognized that listening is power. He showed that listening habits are a major dimension of the relationship between Whites and non-Whites globally, and in the United States in particular. His phenomenology of Whiteness provides a framework from which Whites can better understand the nature of our racist and anti-racist habits. From Fanon, we learn to be skeptical of "loving" White listening orientations. We learn to approach with some skepticism the decolonial critiques of Whiteness put forward by White thinkers, which may represent a new phase of the toxic White love of Blackness.

BLACK EXISTENTIAL FEMINIST CRITIQUES OF WHITE LISTENING

Angela Davis's book *Blues Legacies and Black Feminism: Gertrude 'Ma' Rainey, Bessie Smith, and Billie Holiday*[68] is a landmark. In it she voices a Black feminist politics of the blues. Davis shows that Black, female blues musicians of the Jazz Age were some of America's finest existential theorists. Davis argues for the philosophical importance of Black print (and sound) culture in her "First Lecture on Liberation," writing that "The history of Black literature provides, in my opinion, a much more illuminating account of the nature of freedom, its extent and limits, than all the philosophical discourses on the theme in the history of Western society."[69] My interpretation of Sidney Bechet, Kid Ory, and members of the Original Creole Band as philosophers of sound is indebted to Davis. She demonstrates how Black women oriented themselves toward each other through a call-and-response that opposed misogyny and racist violence. *Blues Legacies* is a Black existential feminist critique of the White sonic gaze. It argues that White listeners have ignored and appropriated the voices of Black women. White listening orientations to Black music have placed White listeners outside the call-and-response. Davis—such as Gordon, Du Bois, Fanon, and Ahmed, and like the authors considered below—gives an existential critique of White listening that applies to musical listening as well as listening in conversation and listening through the mediation of written texts. Davis joins these Black existential thinkers in warning against degrading White listening practices in domestic, artistic, and educational spaces. The critique that White listeners ignore, then appropriate the voice of Black women is a broad critique of Whiteness.

Davis shows that in the Jazz Age/Harlem Renaissance period, Black women sang the blues to dramatize the human condition. They were some of the first Black existentialists, and their lyrics are foundational texts of American Black feminism. Their subject was freedom, and just as importantly, the vehicle through which they expressed these existential truths was existential. Blues musicians freely *appeal* to their audiences, who may respond or not.[70] Black blues musicians of the 1920s used the call-and-response in their lyrics on records, as well as in live performances, to create dynamic relationships among performers and listeners, collapsing the distinction between blues listening and blues performance. Women who listened to blues records gave a collective reply to the records of Bessie Smith and others, articulating their existence, desires, and personal freedoms. Blues lyrics about sex, travel, and drinking spoke to the freedom of Black woman to control their choices and sexuality.

If we think of how the White American market ignored Black blues musicians when they were alive, and then claimed to "rediscover" them years later, we can describe the White sonic gaze as a listening orientation that involves refusing to listen to the other, and then taking credit for the other's voice through the narrative of "discovery." In chapter 2, I discussed how this contradictory White orientation played out among White blues listeners in the American Folk Revival. While Davis does not discuss the White listeners of the folk revival, her work is well-suited to the case.

Davis studies blues lyrics and how Black women listened to other Black women through mechanical recordings. Mechanical recordings facilitated mediated reciprocity. Rather than face-to-face exchanges between musician and audience, possible in live listening situations, the mediated listening orientations of Black women created anti-patriarchal, oppositional stances to the norms of masculinity and Whiteness that could be expressed in living rooms and listening parties. Davis notes that Black people in the South were the biggest consumers of 1920s blues records.[71] We also know that Black women were the first to record the blues.[72] Davis's existentialist perspective helps us understand that blues music is a creolizing Black cultural form that has fundamentally shaped how Americans hear. Because the call-and-response is central to blues and jazz music, good listeners must be active participants in the musical dialogue.

Davis's insights into White listening are an outgrowth of her phenomenology of Black women's experiences. Davis's account of blues listening is phenomenological in that she analyzes "Quotidian expressions of feminist consciousness" found in the lyrics, melodies, and rhythms of early blues recordings.[73] Ma Rainey and Bessie Smith spoke to thousands. The records they made were the first American commercial records of any kind. Their race records transformed how Americans listened.

White people were mostly uninterested in buying blues records in the 1920s. Record companies, beginning with Okey, marketed blues recordings as "race records" to demarcate them from the White mainstream. As we know, the White interest in blues records was a late development. During the Folk Revival, White hipsters, and later, mainstream White audiences, collected race records, consuming what they thought were the "lost sounds" of an American folk culture. As large folk festivals became popular, record companies and promoters searched for aging folk and blues musicians who could be "rediscovered" and celebrated. Race records became valuable commodities among White collectors.

Davis argues that Whiteness is a set of implicit instructions for listening. "The racially segregationist distribution of the recording industry implicitly *instructed White ears* to feel repulsed by the blues and moreover, to assume that this sense of revulsion was instinctive."[74] While Davis's primary focus is describing how the blues works among Black female listeners, I'll use her claim about implicit instructions of Whiteness to illuminate how White approaches to the blues have missed the call-and-response dynamic.

Davis uses phenomenology to name Whiteness. Naming is an important phenomenological strategy because White institutions use anonymity as power. One of the luxuries of Whiteness is that Whites within White institutions feel little resistance to their way of listening. White listening is felt as natural, neutral, and passive. White music consumers in the 1920s would have felt uncomfortable if record companies marketed specifically "White" records to them. Majority Whites could remain indifferent to the existence of new race records because they heard the term "race" as a euphemism for Black. The way Whites experienced race records in the 1920s illustrates the power of leaving Whiteness anonymous.

White blues listeners have felt "repulsed" by the blues, Davis writes. Her existentialist analysis of racial hearing points out that Whites naturalized emotions of disgust. The evidence that White listeners experienced repulsion when first listening to blues and jazz music is strong. The White discourse of the "jazz problem," detailed in chapter two, is a portrait of White disgust and fear. In the Jazz Age, Whites lived their Whiteness through a fear of Black sexuality and miscegenation.

Davis's notion of implicit instructions speaks to the institutional dimension of the White sonic gaze. White listening orientations in the Folk Revival period placed White people in serial, nonmutual relationships with other Whites. Whites related to other Whites by selective hearing, by making themselves guardians and interpreters of non-White voices, and by organizing themselves toward a non-White "folk," in festivals, listening parties, and amateur collector situations. White folk listeners placed themselves outside of the Black community's struggles with the very issues expressed in blues records of twenty years earlier that they collected and consumed: sexism, anti-Black racism, poverty, and the struggle for personal freedom.

A fundamental way White Americans have related to other Whites is through their consumption of Black culture, sounds, and images. Robin D.G. Kelly writes, "Given the central role of race in the making of American identities, there is no reason why (White) audiences should disrupt, reverse, or challenge narratives of conquest."[75] Du Bois's wages of Whiteness argument applies to how Whites listened to the blues: The economic effect of the American Folk Revival was the directing of White resources to archiving the past, not supporting living Black artists. Folk listening directed White listeners away from the economic demands of the blues. White folk listeners consumed Black culture selectively so they could avoid the critiques of Whiteness and masculinity found in blues lyrics. Whites misheard the blues music, missing the revolutionary, feminist sounds and messages. Paradoxically, White listeners ignored the Black critiques of White listening expressed in the blues records they collected.

Hipster, countercultural Whites were some of the first White Americans to experience a crisis of Whiteness brought on by listening orientations. Their White double-consciousness was inspired by the realization that non-White people had been listening critically to them. They began to experience the blues as speaking to them, addressing issues in White experience. But because White hipsters experienced their Whiteness as a lack, void, and silence, they turned to Black music as a substance they could consume to fill a hole. This resulted in nonreciprocal, one-way hearing. Whites who think that their proximity to Blackness absolves them of Whiteness do not make good listeners.

Davis's feminist phenomenology of listening demonstrates how White listeners have misunderstood the call-and-response of the blues. Whites who collected blues records and attended large folk festivals were not experiencing the call-and-response as a feminist challenge to patriarchy and misogyny. White folk listeners, as Bechet also argued, fetishized Black music from a previous era, distancing themselves from ongoing, contemporary dialogues about feminism, domestic violence, and racism. White listeners heard the blues as expressions of a Black "folk" culture, in Kelley's sense, which allowed them to hear blues lyrics as evidence that Black men and women had static character traits. White orientations also missed the existential significance of first-person storytelling in the blues. Similar to how Eurocentric philosophers believe that Black music should be studied through White philosophers like Adorno or Hegel, the White blues listener figured himself an amateur ethnographer. White blues listening placed Whites in the position of intellectual and theorist and placed non-White others in the position of "folk" to be studied.

The upshot of Davis's critique of the White sonic gaze is that White Americans, especially males, have benefited from a listening orientation that places them outside the call-and-response of Black existential thought. Historically, White listeners have ignored, then appropriated the voices of Black women through the narrative of "discovery." As the White academic and popular investment in Black existential thought grows, the pattern will repeat itself, unless disrupted.

BELL HOOKS

Like Davis, bell hooks offers an insightful variation on the problem of White listening. White listening is, in her unforgettable phrase, a mode of "eating the other." In the classic piece "Eating the Other: Desire and Resistance," hooks argues that Whites consume non-White culture to assuage White anxiety.[76] hooks's phenomenology illustrates how some estranged White people feel their personal Whiteness as an emptiness. This feeling of White emptiness motivates Whites to consume non-White culture, which they perceive as fullness. hooks's critique, like those above, is especially relevant to today's academic and popular situation, as Whites on social media are trading lists of their "top-five Black authors" and White activists at Black Lives Matter marches are holding signs that say "White Silence Is Violence" and "I Get That I Will Never Get It."

Anticipating my thesis in this book as a whole, hooks argues that critiques of Whiteness have been part of Black thought since slavery, although Whites have seldom read, studied, or taken seriously these critiques. "Although there has never been any official body of Black people in the United States who have gathered as anthropologists and/or ethnographers to study Whiteness, Black folks have, from slavery on, shared in conversations with one another 'special' knowledge of Whiteness gleaned from close scrutiny of White people."[77] Veronica Watson agrees, arguing that Black writers have anticipated the themes of Critical Whiteness Studies: "My work seeks to bring an even larger range of voices to the conversation by recovering the writings of African Americans who have pursued this line of analysis since the nineteenth century."[78]

By pointing out that eating the other takes place in mass and academic culture, hooks raises a serious concern about how White, especially male, philosophers "consume" the theories of Black women. Inclusion work, diversity work, and critical Whiteness work may ironically leave Whiteness intact at a conceptual, demographic, and institutional level. hooks points out that White philosophers theorizing race have generally problematized Blackness and normalized Whiteness. White writers have "not focused their critiques on White identity and the way essentialism informs representations of Whiteness."[79] Whiteness got a pass, for instance, in the philosophical debates over strategic essentialism and identity that centered on female and Black identity in the 1980s and 1990s. Now that studies of Whiteness are more common in academia, we are faced with the question of how White theorists will place themselves in dialogue with Black, Creole, Indigenous, and other traditions of analyzing Whiteness. Will we White philosophers today listen to Black philosophers the way White revivalists listened to Bessie Smith records: by ignoring and then appropriating the voices of Black women?

White identity was, and still is, often based on the reductionist belief that White culture is basic, empty, blank, and neutral. Whites who buy in to the thesis that Whiteness is "basic" fail to see how this conception of White identity creates a problematic dynamic toward non-White others. If non-White music, dance, and theory are marked, in hooks's words, as "more exciting, more intense and more threatening" than White culture, it is no wonder that Whites writing about Black culture do so with a "combination of pleasure and danger."[80] hooks confirms that in philosophical and pop cultural listening, Whites have cycled between ignoring Black culture and seizing upon it as a "spice [or] seasoning that can liven up the dull dish that is mainstream White culture."[81]

In "Representations of Whiteness in the Black Imagination," hooks criticizes the tendency of White intellectuals to write about Whiteness while ignoring critiques of Whiteness written by people of color.[82] hooks indicates why the emergence of Critical Whiteness Studies can be met with some skepticism: Only the name is new, not the concept. Thinking with DuBois's comment in *Darkwater* that the discovery of personal Whiteness has been a late development, we can understand the emergence of Critical Whiteness Studies as potentially another iteration of the ignore-then-appropriate listening dynamic. Whites can claim to have been the first to discover both minority cultures as well as the majority, White culture.

hooks gives a psychological and sociological explanation for White listening consistent with what we've learned about American jazz audiences: Many Whites tune in to Black culture out of White boredom and White anxiety. The consumptive desire is driven by a White identity crisis: "One desires 'a bit of the other' to enhance the blank landscape of Whiteness."[83] When Whiteness is experienced as not only emptiness, then non-White culture—especially music, food, fashion, and speech but also theory—are turned into objects of consumption. White slumming "assuages feelings of deprivation and lack that assault the psyches of radical White youth who choose to be disloyal to western civilization."[84]

The Black existential critiques of Whiteness studied above suggest a variety of answers to the question of White existence. Whiteness has been understood as death (Gordon), ownership (Du Bois), toxic love (Fanon), appropriation of women's voices (Davis), and eating the other (hooks). The advice to White people that emerges from these critiques is simple: Listen better. Listen better by treating ear training as a necessary part of confronting the White problem. Listen better by attending to the huge variety of critiques of White listening in the Black and Creole traditions in the United States and the Black Atlantic world. Whites should confront White listening habits across the board, including musical listening, listening in face-to-face dialogues, and listening through mediation of the written word.

The advice to White philosophers is to do philosophy from an embodied, community perspective. Read other people, listen to other people, and speak up about White violence. Read and cite Black, Creole, Indigenous, and non-White authors, especially women, not to take credit, but as an act of solidarity, humility, and humanity. Talk less, listen more. As Frederick Douglass said in an 1888 speech before the International Council of Women: "I do not feel like taking up more than a very small space. . . . Men have very little business here as speakers, anyhow; and if they come here at all they should take back benches and wrap themselves in silence."[85]

HARLEM RENAISSANCE CRITIQUES OF WHITE LISTENING

Should we bother writing for clogged White ears? Do White audiences understand the Black literature and music they consume? Is Black art that is performed for White audiences authentic?

These questions were passionately debated among Harlem Renaissance intellectuals, including W.E.B. Du Bois, Alain Locke, Zora Neale Hurston, and Alice Dunbar-Nelson. I emphasize the term "debated," since the opinions among these Harlem Renaissance thinkers were diverse. For her part, Alice Dunbar-Nelson was unconvinced that White audiences would read or properly understand her self-consciously Black journalism or her regionalist Creole fiction. She cultivated a readership of other Black women and urged other Black writers to do the same. Zora Neale Hurston devoted considerable thought to the dynamic of White and Black audiences who consumed Black folk culture. Her unique, quasi-anthropological approach to folk culture insisted that it was the performance contexts for and listening orientations toward Black performers that determined their folk "authenticity." I study Hurston's insights into the nature of the Black spiritual and her difference of opinion with both Du Bois and Alain Locke. Hurston thought that her peers misunderstood the importance of social context for Black spirituals; she believed that spirituals performed in concert halls for mixed or predominately White audiences were not folk spirituals, but "neo-Spirituals." She emphasized the importance of Black audiences and the call-and-response in Black folk contexts. Du Bois and Locke, by contrast, were famously enthusiastic in their support for the social movement to stage Black spirituals for White audiences. Spirituals were first introduced to mainstream White American audiences when choirs from Historically Black Colleges and Universities (HBCUs) went on tour to raise money to save their universities. Du Bois would accuse Locke of not going far enough in problematizing the White sonic gaze, while, for his part, Locke thought White audiences could be reached and transformed. He was adamant that Whites abandon their minstrel listening orientations in favor of classical, ecstatic listening orientations. Not unlike White savior listeners who thought orchestral jazz was an elevation of the genre, Locke believed that spirituals performed for mixed audiences would transform and creolize the genre of the spiritual into something classical rather than merely folk.

To appreciate these Harlem Renaissance critiques of the White sonic gaze, they should be read intertextually. The Black thinkers of the Renaissance read and commented publicly on each other's work, and commented on the silence of their White colleagues, most of whom ignored the Black press and Black literature. As Locke's *The Negro and His Music* shows, he comprehensively studied the White literature on Black music, writing approvingly of Paul Whiteman and Hughes Panassié, while offering correctives to their White primitivism. Paul Allen Anderson notes, "White jazz critics of the 1930s and 1940s, for the most part, did not put themselves into a dialogue with relevant African American debates on racial identity, the folk inheritance, musical evolution and the social consequences of art."[86] Listening to music was a different story. White Americans were drawn to Black and Creole music like flies to honey; Whites consumed and wrote copiously about Black and Creole culture. Such was the situation among Black writers in the Jazz Age: They studied Black music and wrote about it; they studied White audiences and White jazz discourse, and wrote about it; they debated among each other whether it was futile or useful to respond to White misperceptions. In short, they developed critiques of clogged White ears that fell on clogged White ears.

I consider the theme of the White sonic gaze in the work of Locke, Hurston, and Dunbar-Nelson, beginning with Locke's project of writing for White ears to in an effort to transform White minstrel listeners into classical jazz listeners.

ALAIN LOCKE

Alain Leroy Locke is an important theorist of listening and philosopher of music who believed White minstrel listening was poisonous and should be replaced by classical listening orientations. He rejected vaudeville and was skeptical of Black folk music, such as the blues, jazz, and spirituals, which he thought should be elevated to the concert stage to attain musical maturity. He was criticized by Du Bois, who thought he was too White-facing, and by Hurston, who thought he misunderstood Black folk culture.

In *The Negro and His Music* (1936), Locke hoped to guide the future of Black music toward a style he called "classical jazz," which he thought was emerging in the big band, orchestrated music of Duke Ellington, Fletcher Henderson, Paul Whiteman, and Benny Goodman. Classical jazz would be a cosmopolitan mix of Black and White. He believed many of the best jazz musicians were White, and that conservatory-trained arrangers and composers should compose classical music with jazz themes. He even credited Whiteman with ushering in the "'coming of age' party for jazz."[87] As folk forms, he considered the blues, jazz, and spirituals emotional music that needed elevation. Locke emphasized that White musicians could authentically play and compose jazz music, arguing that the important aesthetic question was that of good or bad jazz music, whether "written by White or Negro musicians."[88] The main danger Locke foresaw in White-created jazz music was not White appropriation, but devitalization. "[I]n many cases the effort to lift jazz to the level and form of the classics has devitalized it."[89]

"For better or worse," Locke wrote in *The Negro and His Music*, "jazz is . . . the spiritual child of this age."[90] While aligning his project for a "New Negro" aesthetics with the Jazz Age, Locke also claimed "the Negro never had a jazz age. . . . He was born that way."[91] In this phrase, there is an ambivalence that runs deep in Locke's thinking about jazz. For him, jazz was sociologically significant because it spoke to the modern dimension of Black identity. Yet Locke thought of jazz as pre-modern folk music that needed uplifting. His notion of Black folk culture echoed the White concepts it challenged.

Locke's skepticisms of early jazz music and vaudeville performance were motivated by his belief that White listeners placed "vaudeville chains" on Black performers.[92] White minstrel listeners conflated actors with their roles, listening with their eyes, not their ears, sensing only "the tawdry American convention" of minstrelsy.[93] For Locke, healthy listening meant listening "with closed eyes."[94] Locke gives the case of White and Black audiences experiencing a performance of dancer Bill "Bojangles" Robinson. "It is excellent vaudeville," but upon listening with eyes closed, "it becomes an almost symphonic composition of sounds."[95]

Locke advocated classical jazz listening because he thought it would challenge minstrel images and transform popular notions of what it meant to be Black. He wanted to shape a new image of Black culture among both Black and White audiences. He placed a high value on White intellectuals and musicians who took an interest in Black folk forms and distanced himself from popular opinions, mass culture, and commercial music of all kinds. The least phenomenological of the thinkers I examine, Locke approached jazz as an object of scientific study, using as his data the writings of mainstream White jazz critics. Hurston would criticize Locke for failing to understand the everyday, quotidian, folk contexts for listening to Black music. Thinking pragmatically, Locke sought to reconcile those he called "detractors and enthusiasts" of jazz[96]

In developing his notion of classical jazz listening, Locke relied on the views of a generation of White critics and classical musicians. The result was a culturally conservative critique of Whiteness. As Leonard Harris shows, Du Bois criticized Locke's conservatism. Du Bois thought Locke's work was "written for the benefit of White people and the behest of White readers and started out primarily from the White point of view."[97] In an effort to synthesize "detractors and enthusiasts" of jazz, Locke treated White primitivist jazz discourse as legitimate but in need of correction. Thus emerged a debate about how White authors used the concept of "primitivism" versus how the concept was understood in Black thought, usually as an antidote to claims that Black people lacked history and culture. Locke separated "original and genuine primitivism" from its "sophisticated substitute."[98] White primitivists turned to African art as no more than a "mine of fresh motifs."[99] Distancing himself from those who "mined" African art, Locke praised French composer Darius Milhaud's use of Black and Indigenous musical motifs.[100] Locke thought Milhaud's primitivism was healthy because it transformed European music. "When a body of folk music is really taken up into musical tradition, it is apt to do more than contribute a few new themes . . . the very foundation of the art are in the process of being influenced."[101] Unhealthy primitivism turned to Black art for "fresh motifs," while leaving European modernism untouched.

Though he challenged White primitivism and White minstrel listening, Locke's argument for the aesthetic superiority of what he called classical jazz over folk jazz is, to me at least, unconvincing. I think it is built on a false distinction between folk and classical music that devalues folk contexts for listening. Locke thinks of folk music as "produced without formal musical training or intention by emotional creation."[102] Though Locke has an ethnic, not biological notion of race, he says there is an "in born" quality of rhythm in "folky Negroes," mentioning Bessie Smith by name.[103] Emotionally powerful but "often wholly illiterate," Smith and other folk musicians "knew nothing about written music or composition."[104] I side with Hurston's critique of Locke's view of folk culture. I think Locke is insufficiently phenomenological and relies too much on experts, not quotidian expressions of life and first-person narratives.

Nonetheless, Locke's challenge to White primitivism is important because it shows how listening orientations can oppose the "cultural distortions of the plantation tradition," getting rid of the "minstrel taint."[105] He argued that classical jazz listeners could listen in such a way to avoid the "decadently neurotic" listening habits of White primitivists.[106] Locke located unhealthy primitivism in American vaudeville minstrel listening. Locke's idea of healthy primitivism was part of the debate in Renaissance thinking about how to theorize Black culture given the long shadow of scientific racism. In "The Legacy of the Ancestral Arts" section of *The New Negro*, Locke rejects the simplistic connection between Black art and African art found in mainstream White discourse. There are connections between African and new world Black rhythms, but otherwise "there is little evidence of any direct connection of the American Negro with his ancestral arts."[107] Healthy primitivism rejects the idea of biological racial traits, especially the assumption that Black people are naturally rhythmic and White people are naturally arrhythmic.

Lockean "healthy primitivism," viewed from a Du Boisian perspective, might be understood as suffering from an underdeveloped political economy of Whiteness. Locke's belief that "jazz, in spite of its racial origin, became one great interracial collaboration" is optimistic.[108] When Locke remarks, "it has been White musicians and critics who for the most part have capitalized jazz, both commercially and artistically," it is clearly tongue-in-cheek.[109] White jazz musicians indeed *capitalized* on their Whiteness in the 1920s, a period of intense racial segregation, lynchings, and violence against Black people generally, and a time when White owners, managers, label executives, and writers dominated the music industry. James Weldon Johnson called the summer of 1919 the Red Summer because there were so many White-on-Black race riots across the country, including the Chicago race riot of 1919. The Tulsa race massacre occurred in 1921. The second Ku Klux Klan was founded in 1915 and saw its highest numbers in 1924. Few Black musicians of the Jazz Age were admitted to schools like the New England Conservatory of Music, one of "the only centers liberal enough to have them."[110] Yet these conservatory-trained musicians were the only "master singers" in the Black community, according to Locke. Anti-Black racial terror—as discussed by Salem Tutt Whitney below—was part of the everyday experience of the commercial Black musician playing for White, Black, and mixed audiences. Saying that Whites "capitalized" commercially on jazz is an understatement.

In *The Negro and His Music*'s chapter on "Negro Musicians Today," we get a partial political economy of Whiteness from Locke, who critiques the

"American ear."[111] Like Bechet and Fanon, Locke imagines a dialogical existential encounter, this time between a classically trained Black musician and a White listener. "It is still possible for a Negro who has mastered the classic repertory of the world's music, or at least the European half of it, to be artistically insulted by the query: 'Why don't you sing spirituals?'"[112] In this imaginary dialogue, the Black artist resists the obnoxious assumption that they ought to play Black folk music. The White "public still expects the Negro to sing and dance principally. In fact, *prejudice* has seriously handicapped the Negro musically."[113] This is one of the few places Locke describes White listeners in terms of racial prejudice. Prejudiced listeners turn all Black musicians into representatives of their race. As Gordon notes, these same questions would not be asked of a White musician. "Do you also play country music? Do you play heavy metal?" George S. Schuyler, in his debate with Langston Hughes over "The Racial Mountain," makes the same point. Hypocritically, White listeners do not treat White folk music as "expressive or characteristic of the Caucasian race."[114]

While Locke calls White listening a "ghettoizing" force, and despite having an account of White listening that acknowledges anti-Black racism, when it comes to the economic dimension of White listening, Locke's position is not as convincing as that of Du Bois.[115] Leonard Harris[116] shows that Locke's most pointed reply to Du Bois came in 1928 in the piece "Art or Propaganda."[117] Locke proffered that propagandistic art "perpetuates the position of group inferiority even in crying out against it."[118] With this brilliant phrase, Locke turned the table, arguing that it was Du Bois who perpetuated minstrel stereotypes in arguing against them. For Harris, the Du Bois-Locke debate boiled down to "how the goal of creating alternative images should be achieved" given that "Black people were nearly always portrayed in literature as inherently inferior."[119] In my view, when Locke writes that a "convinced minority must confront a condescending majority," he places the burden of changing White listening orientation on Black artists more than White audiences. In other words, in the final analysis, Locke's thinking about jazz is still indebted to the "Negro problem" and not the Du Boisian problem of Whiteness.

ZORA NEALE HURSTON

One of Zora Neale Hurston's contributions to the critique of White listening was to show that Black folk music performed in concert halls for classically oriented White listeners was "bleached."[120] It lacked the call-and-response found in folk contexts like Jook joints and churches. Like Bechet, she argued that what makes Black music Black is not how it is performed, but how it is heard. Like Locke, she rejected White primitivism. Unlike Locke, she believed that the blues, jazz, and spirituals needed no uplift. She pursued a phenomenology of listening rooted in place, maintaining that "musically speaking, the Jook is the most important place in America."[121]

In "Characteristics of Negro Expression" and "The Sanctified Church," Hurston argued that White and Black classical listeners reified Black folk music.[122] Hurston's opposition to staging spirituals for White audiences is well known, and the following passage is widely cited: "There has never been a presentation of genuine Negro spirituals to any audience anywhere."[123] A different version of the same sentence, offered in the same work, shows that the inauthenticity of what Hurston called the "neo-spiritual" lay in the listening, not the production: "In spite of the goings up and down on the earth, from the original Fisk Jubilee singers down to the present, there has been no genuine presentation of Negro songs *to White audiences.*"[124]

Hurston criticized White classical listening because it reified Black folk music by removing the music from the improvisatory settings where it functioned. White classical listeners approached the concert hall as a space of order, ownership, and crowd control. According to Hurston, the norms of listening in concert halls were so different from the norms of listening in churches and Jooks that the music became unrecognizable. Hurston argued that the White demand for Black theaters in the North allowed White men to control Black women's bodies, since White audiences craved women who were perceived as light-skinned and skinny.

In "Characteristics of Negro Expression," Hurston offers an original theory of Black folk culture distinct from the Lockean and White primitivist variations. For Huston, Black folk culture "is not a thing of the past. It is still in the making."[125] She distinguishes White imitations of Black culture and Black "imitations" of White culture. Black and White culture do not stand in an equal relationship in the predominantly White American culture industry. Black-White and White-Black cultural exchanges must be understood through economies of power, not idealized, colorless notions of mutual borrowing.

In a section titled "Originality," she tackles the question of whether Paul Whiteman is an original—he isn't, she says. Unlike Locke, Hurston argues that Whiteman plays inauthentic jazz. Her conclusion is complex and reveals a unique idea about cultural contact between Black and White musicians. The fundamental point is that Black and White cultural forms cannot be understood as contacting each other in a relationship of artistic equality in which each tradition borrows from the other. In the United States, Black and White cultures have always been intertwined, and White culture has struggled for dominance. Similar to the view of Glissant discussed earlier, Hurston believes that White culture presents itself as a pure, "original source," thus denying how Whiteness has always been marked by its relationship with non-White cultures. Thinking digenetically, Hurston argues, "What makes for originality is cultural modification, not appeal to 'original sources.'"[126] Whiteman's genetic search for a supposedly pure Black music is doomed for the same reason: There is no "original source," which is itself unmodified, unmixed, or unrelated to Whiteness. Against the common assumption in White aesthetics that "the Negro is lacking in originality," she argues that Black folk culture fluctuates, with musical additions and subtractions happening constantly in the trading of musical ideas between musicians and their listening communities.[127] For Black people, who exist "in the midst of a White civilization," originality has meant modifying White culture. Black cultural forms such as language, food, religion, and music are "reinterpretations" of White culture, which is transformed through Black labor that puts White culture to its own "uses."[128]

Hurston's comments on Whiteman have been read as the colorblind claim that all cultural exchange is blending and trading. In *Primitivist Modernism: Black Culture and the Origins of Transatlantic Modernism*, Lemke Sieglinde suggests that Hurston thinks "cross-cultural appropriations have a catalytic effect on the creation of new art forms—Black or White."[129] I think this reading misses the fact that Hurston situates cultural exchanges "in the midst of a White civilization." Kathy Ogren has a more satisfying reading of Hurston's notion of cultural modification. She hears Hurston offering a "comment on the *White appropriation* of Black performance."[130] Ogren indicates the economic reality of Whiteman's "imitation" of Black culture. "[W]hite audiences created a demand,"[131] for White big band music, "music more accurately described as popular music with jazz influences."[132]

Hurston's notion that neospirituals are inauthentic has mostly to do with audience reception and performance context. Neospirituals are "dressed in tuxedoes" when they are performed in concert hall for White (and Black) audiences.[133] Folk music is folk music by virtue of how, where, and when it is heard. And while Hazel Carby criticizes Hurston for imaging a Black folk culture that is outside of time and space, I think Hurston's analysis of the Jook is sensitive to the flux and context of folk forms.[134] When Hurston writes that "musically speaking, the Jook is the most important place in America," she offers a phenomenology of listening that is situated in space and time.[135] While she romanticizes Jooks, she isn't necessarily committed to thinking Jooks are fading resources of the past that must be archived before they disappear, a sentiment familiar from White folk revivalist listeners who chased "lost sounds." She analyses how the term "Jook" originated as a verb. "The singing and playing in the true Negro style is called 'jooking.'"[136] The music of the Jook is the blues, which laid the basis for jazz. There is a clear parallel here to Baraka's discussion that "to jazz" was a verb that became a noun. Baraka and Hurston demonstrate the importance of the language we use to capture Black cultural forms. To grasp the dynamism of blues and jazz culture, one must appreciate the difference between ragtime and "to rag," jazz and "jazzing," or Jook and "jooking."

The blues music of the Jooks took its shape through oral repetition and cultural exchange among audiences and performers. "The songs grow by incremental repetition as they travel from mouth to mouth and from Jook to Jook for years before they reach outside ears."[137] The phrase "outside ears" marks a distinction between those blues listeners who were part of the Jook culture from which the blues originated and where it mainly lived, and those who were not part of Jook culture. Outside ears can refer to a number of communities: White folk collectors, Black folk collectors, Northerners, religious prudes, hipsters, and others. Paradoxically, as Carby notes, Hurston wanted to assert that folk music was inherently valuable as a cultural practice among oral, rural communities, not because it reached outsiders; yet Hurston became a facilitator for transmitting folk culture to the outside ears of her readers.

Hurston did not conceive of her fiction and folk writing as an inauthentic staging of folk culture for elites. By contrast, the "Negro theater" popular in the North is "only Negro in cast and could just as well have come from pre-soviet Russia."[138] Hurston thought Black theater was inauthentic because it was dominated by White listening orientations that "bleached" the music. "The bleached chorus is the result of a White demand and not the Negros."[139] White listening is a "White demand" for Black culture and Black bodies of a specific type. In Jook culture, Hurston says, there is participation from Black women of different skin tones, with all sorts of body shapes, and types of hair, including natural hair.[140] In Northern theaters, Black female singers and actors who don't fit the White taste have "been banished by the White producer and the Negro who takes his cue from the White."[141] As for "the use of Negro material by White performers," many are trying, but none do it "realistically."[142] Having already dismissed Whiteman as an imitator, she names another White whose "outsider ears" did not situate jazz music within modes of Black folk cultural transmission. "Gershwin and the other 'Negro' rhapsoditsts come under this same axe. Just about as Negro as caviar or Ann Pennington's athletic Black Bottom."[143]

It may have been this passage from Hurston—"And God only knows what the world has suffered from the White damsels who try to sing Blues"[144]—that led Sieglinde to assert that Hurston thought there was something innate that makes one a good blues performer. Sieglinde's motivations aside, White critics have been known to use a similar strawperson argument against Black critics for years; the latter are charged with essentialism about Black identity. We saw this strawperson argument in chapter 1 with Sudhalter, and it was advanced by Lee Brown against Baraka.[145] In arguing that Whites don't sing the blues well, neither Hurston nor Baraka assume anything innate about White people, Black people, or any other cultural group. As Baraka explains: "The idea of a White blues singer seems an even more violent contradiction of terms than the idea of a middle-class blues singer. The materials of blues were not available to the White American, even though some strange circumstance might prompt him to look for them. It was as if these materials were secret and obscure, and blues a kind of ethno-historic rite as basic as blood."[146]

Hurston emphasizes that "If one listens closely," to spirituals performed in churches rather than recital halls, they will detect a central difference.[147] "Each singing of the piece is a new creation. The congregation is bound by no rules. No two times singing is alike, so that we must consider the rendition of a song not as a final thing, but as mood. It won't be the same thing next Sunday."[148] A folk spiritual is an act of creation that takes place through the reciprocity of performer and audience, singers, and hearers. In concert halls, where audiences are trained to sit still, tap a foot quietly, and not cough, there is little of the call-and-response that makes Black folk music work. Hurston does not think it requires sophisticated anthropological training to know the difference between the call-and-response of Black churches and Jook joints and the muted, modified call-and-response of audiences in classical theaters. "Let him step into some unfashionable Negro church and hear for himself."[149]

For Hurston, as part of folk culture, spirituals are being made constantly and forgotten.[150] Spirituals are dynamic, and even when archived to print, they don't remain the same long; they are "variations on a theme" and "moods," not things.[151] Hebdige calls this versioning. A neospiritual may sound similar to a folk spiritual, but this is a mere "sound effect."[152] Backing off slightly on the romantic language, Hurston concludes that neospirituals are not under "condemnation"; rather, "they are a valuable contribution to the music and literature of the world. But let no one imagine they are the songs of the people, as sung by them."[153] As much as a concert hall version of spiritual might channel the energy of the Black church, it is not a Black church. Nor is the concert hall a Jook. While Hurston's polemic leaves us with the idea that there are only two performance contexts—folk/authentic versus concert hall/inauthentic—the reality is that there are dozens of variations. Her critique was aimed at Locke and Du Bois, aimed at the history of Historically Black Colleges and Universities forming choirs to raise money, and especially aimed at the White culture industry represented by the Whiteman and Gershwin.

I draw my remarks about Hurston to a close by reflecting on the final section of "The Sanctified Church," titled "The White Man's Prayer." After providing a transcript of a sermon of C.C. Lovelace, in Florida, in 1929, in which she archived the call-and-response dynamic of a Black church, she noted that among these parishioners, it was an insult to say that a Black preacher sounded White. Hurston writes in dialect: "Why he don't preach at all. He just lectures. And the way they say the word 'lecture' make it sound like horse-stealing. 'Why, he sound like a White man preaching.'"[154] Here we find a profound statement about race and aural orientations: Preaching like a White man means speaking without listening to the audience.

ALICE DUNBAR-NELSON

The last Harlem Renaissance–era critique of Whiteness I consider comes from Alice Dunbar-Nelson. She anticipated the debate between Locke and Du Bois about the White sonic gaze, concluding that addressing White ears was futile because Whites won't listen to critiques of themselves in Black newspapers, literature, or music. In her thirty-year career, Dunbar-Nelson wrote four separate columns for Blacks and cultivated a national audience of Black women.[155] As Judith Fetterley and Marjorie Pryse argue, in her regionalist fiction, set in New Orleans, she developed a phenomenology of the sounds of New Orleans.[156] I will show how her phenomenology included a critique of White classical listening, surveying her column "Un Femme Dit" and two of her short stories, "Anarchy Valley" and "M'Sieu Fortier's Violin." [157]

Dunbar-Nelson was a prolific, prominent writer of the Jazz Age. As Akasha Gloria Hull has shown, she was one of the few female poets included in *The Book of American Negro Poetry*, edited by James Weldon Johnson in 1921, and *Caroling Dusk: An Anthology of Verse by Negro Poets*, edited by Countee Cullen in 1927. My understanding of Dunbar-Nelson is indebted to Hull, an academic, poet, and critic, whose 1987 *Color, Sex and Poetry: Three Women Writers of the Harlem Renaissance* considers the contributions of Dunbar-Nelson, Angelina Weld Grimké, and Georgia Douglas Johnson.

"Une Femme Dit," Dunbar-Nelson's column for Pittsburgh's Black newspaper, the *Courier*, debuted on January 2, 1926. "Une Femme Dit" offered a first-person, phenomenological take on White listening. In the Black press of the time, women's columns were mostly about beauty and fashion.[158] In "Une Femme Dit," Dunbar-Nelson theorized about social issues, including women's rights, sexual violence against women, the Rhinelander case, mixed race identity, labor exploitation, and Black masculinity.[159] She composed from a self-consciously Black female perspective and wrote for other Black women. "From a Woman's Point of View" was the first name of her column, but she changed it to the French "Une Femme Dit" (a woman says) to emphasize the diversity of ideas and backgrounds among the women of color for whom she wrote. Her title emphasized her embodied experience of gender as well as that of her audience. Katherine Adams, Sandra Zagarell, and Caroline Gebhard argue that Dunbar-Nelson's column, with its feminist listening orientation, prefigured the "radical feminist gender critique" in Kimberlé Crenshaw and Patricia Hill Collins.[160]

Dunbar-Nelson used her column to argue that Black journalists should not engage with the White print media's misrepresentations of Black experience. On February 27, 1926, she wrote a response to a White journalist: "But—why should all of us or any of us waste perfectly good time, type, paper, or energy frothing at the pen over what our White contemporaries think or write of us? We will rush into print and assert, deny, asseverate, fulminate, vociferate, and use up the dictionary, the thesaurus, and the encyclopedia with masses of statistics to prove that these statements made by the Nordics are all wrong. And to whom do we prove them? To our own dear selves. For said Nordic never sees our answers, or our papers or our statements. Wouldn't read them if he did."[161] Dunbar-Nelson wrote this injunction not to waste perfectly good paper on Whites two years before the propaganda debate between Locke and Du Bois. Adams, Zagarell, and Gebhard reveal that DuBois was aware of Dunbar-Nelson's work and drew upon it. He requested that he be able to use her article "People of Color in Louisiana" for his own writing.[162]

According to Dunbar-Nelson, the problem with White listening was that Whites wouldn't read Black newspapers or literature, making it fruitless to try to "get our answers over to the other side of the racial stream."[163] Even if the White public did read critiques of Whiteness found in Black newspapers, she says, they would misunderstand. Like the blues women of her time, Dunbar-Nelson chose to speak to other Black women.

Why was Dunbar-Nelson pessimistic about the "Nordic" ears that misrepresented Black experience? One answer is found in her fiction. As Judith Fetterley and Marjorie Pryse argue, in her writing, Dunbar-Nelson's queered White male spaces with the phenomenological strategy of foregrounding the ordinary.[164] In the short story "Anarchy Valley,"[165] she describes New Orleans saloons as "great, gorgeous, gaudy places" filled with "a sound of mens' voices in a heated discussion."[166] Dunbar-Nelson hears "pianos and swift-footed waiters, tables and cards, and men, men, men."[167] She takes our eyes across the saloon, following the "sunlight from the bar-room." Our noses follow the "long whiff of pipe-smoke."[168] But it is her ears that are most awake: "the clink of glasses, the chink of silver, and the high treble of a woman's voice scolding a refractory child, mingle in incongruous melody."[169] In her phenomenology of the sonic architecture of the French Quarter, she argues that the saloon is a masculine soundscape where men argue loudly, listening to music, drowning out the sounds of women and children.

Dunbar-Nelson's short story "M'Sieu Fortier's Violin" (1899) is a phenomenological critique of White classical listening.[170] She argues that White classical listening is Eurocentric and excludes Creole classical listening. The protagonist of the story, M'Sieu Fortier, is a Creole classical musician who is pushed out of his place as first-chair violinist in the French Opera in New Orleans by a White boss. Dunbar-Nelson depicts White listening as crowd control over who belongs in classical theaters, as would Du Bois. In the story, Fortier is a man with "New Orleans Creole blood" who plays first chair at the French Opera house in New Orleans until he is fired by an unmusical, Anglophone "American" who takes over the theater.[171] Having lost his income and profession as a classical musician, and not making enough money as a cigar-roller in the day, Fortier is too poor to afford tickets for the opera house where he once played center stage. Not able to afford the cheapest seat in the back of the house, Fortier must sell his violin so he can eat. A wealthy White fan of the opera who has slummed in the French district for years prevails, giving Fortier fifty dollars for his instrument.

With these lush images, Dunbar-Nelson moors White listening habits to the architecture of the French Opera house in New Orleans. When Fortier is fired by a White listener, he loses his seat as a first violinist. White listening pushes him from center stage to offstage. Like Du Bois's character John, Fortier is removed from the theater for being too Black. Though Creole, Fortier is too Black for the White Anglophones and the White-identifying Creoles of the French Opera. These White classical listeners are struck by a Europhilic desire for the music of France, Germany, and Italy, performed by White Europeans and White Americans. Like John Sullivan Dwight, they demand silence in the symphony.

"M'Sieu Fortier's Violin" is a comment on the clogged White ears of the theater owner as well as the White and White-identifying Creole audiences for the French Opera. Dunbar-Nelson renders the Anglophone American a philistine for preferring European versions of music to those of the creolized American South. In a wonderful twist ending, the wealthy White slummer who buys Fortier's violin is haunted by violent nightmares. He cannot sleep until he gives the violin back to Fortier. His sleeplessness and nightmares are an expression of White anxiety, White discomfort, and White shame. The White slummer's love of Creole music is toxic and poisons him. Like all revivalist listeners, he wants to add to his collection, in this case literally, by taking Fortier's violin from him, supposedly persevering it. The White bad faith of the collector is obvious: His desire to preserve Creole music is at the expense of the Creole musician he claims to love.

Alice Dunbar-Nelson was the least interested in addressing White audiences among the Jazz Age writers discussed above. Locke wrote for all audiences, including White ones, while criticizing Whites for their unhealthy primitivism. Hurston wrote for Black and White audiences, challenging Whites to refigure their idea of Black folk culture. Du Bois wrote stinging indictments of "guilty White ears" and demonstrated that White estrangement is a process of awakening to the bankruptcy of Whiteness. Neither Locke nor Du Bois took the Black existentialist feminist step of disengaging from the conversation with Whites about their mis-hearing of Black existence. Like blues women, and like Davis and hooks, Dunbar-Nelson wrote especially for the ears of Black women, becoming a killjoy whose journalism was a resonator for anti-sexist, anti-patriarchal complaints.

SALEM TUTT WHITNEY: A VOICE FROM BLACK VAUDEVILLE

I give the last word in this chapter to a voice from the pre-jazz world of Black vaudeville. White minstrel listening has rightfully been one of the main targets of Creole, Black, and White criticism of the sonic gaze. I have shown that white minstrel listening is damaging since it conflates actors with roles, projecting stock characters like "Old Black Joe" onto Black people. A problem with many treatments of Blackface minstrelsy, though, is that they are unphenomenological; they do not include first-person accounts of those minstrel musicians and actors who performed for White audiences. In *The Negro and His Music*, Locke offered a genealogy of the minstrel tradition, but he theorized from the top down and dismissed "vaudeville chains." Du Bois was similarly uninterested in the perspective of Black vaudeville actors, and even Hurston, who explored the Jooks and churches, thought that vaudeville was inauthentic. Even Lott's groundbreaking *Love and Theft* sheds light on first-person voices from Black vaudeville.

The Black entertainment press of the turn of the century is an important archive of Black existential critiques of White listening. The Indianapolis *Freeman* (1888–1926) provides a glimpse into the lifeworld of musicians and actors who performed for vaudeville audiences. These musicians implored the White press and White audiences not to conflate Black actors with their roles. In the *Freeman*, the first illustrated nationally circulating Black newspaper, actors were shown out of costume, as professionals. In the pages of the *Freeman*, they debated how best to respond to and subvert clogged White ears.

The *Freeman* is one of the most important and least-studied texts of the Jazz Age. It provides ample testimony from Black actors who performed for White minstrel listeners. As theorists across disciplines become more willing to deal directly with the implications of Blackface minstrelsy, they will benefit from consulting first-person narratives of Black performers, especially those found in the *Freeman*.

I highlight the writings of Salem Tutt Whitney (1869–1934), a playwright, performer, producer, comedian, and journalist. His column, "Seen and Heard in Passing," anchored the *Freeman*'s theater section. Whitney was in demand as a Blackface comedian and leader of the national Black theater troupe *The Smart Set*.[172] He helped set the stage for the emergence of jazz. Tutt's composition *Silas Green from New Orleans* was the second-longest-running show in the United States written by a Black composer, while his show *George Washington Bullion* ran for twenty years.[173] In the pages of the *Freeman*, Whitney defended himself and his actors against the racism of the White press. He gave phenomenological descriptions of White and non-White listening practices, describing the space and the sound of theaters across the country where his troupe performed. In the prerecorded sound era, the print reviews in the *Freeman* functioned as early records of performances and the interaction of audiences. In the *Freeman*, many Black and non-White actors describe their experiences performing for White audiences on the vaudeville circuit.

The *Freeman* was the principal communication network among Black vaudeville actors and musicians and the first illustrated national Black newspaper in the United States. Black vaudeville was a popular American entertainment form of the late nineteenth and early twentieth centuries. As the central mode of disseminating popular songs in the United States between 1900 and 1930, vaudeville shaped White listening.[174] The traveling minstrel troupes of the late nineteenth century were America's first mass culture. As we learned early from the discussion of the Original Creole Band, vaudeville performances were eclectic variety shows with shifts in tone, repertoire, and style. Audiences might expect comedy, opera, sentimental music, juggling, animals, and Blackface minstrelsy, a vaudeville staple. The archives of the *Freeman* are a wealth of information about the performance styles of Black musicians and actors at a time before recorded sound. They reveal how non-White musicians navigated the listening habits of White audiences across the United States.

The *Freeman* was an orientation device mainly for Black, Creole, mixed race, and non-White vaudeville performers. In the *Freeman*, a general newspaper and trade journal, intellectuals discussed working conditions,[175] the racial wage gap,[176] the gender wage gap,[177] and how to navigate White audiences. Most of all, the periodical described the importance of being a true artist, dedicated to technique and the highest standards of performance. The *Freeman* connected performers from across the country who read the paper to find employment, build their brand, gossip, debate aesthetics, and learn about the styles and sounds of rivals and friends.[178] Members of the Black entertainment community communicated with each other in the pages of the *Freeman* through photos, illustrated advertisements, and columns.

As an illustrated paper, the *Freeman* was a new technology for distributing images. It ran photos and drawings of non-White performers at a time when the White press used only cartoon caricatures. The editors of the *Freeman* declared it would "portray the colored race as it is, and not as it is misinterpreted by many of our White contemporaries."[179] The *Freeman* was a self-consciously Black newspaper, which tracked "the rapid strides of progress being made by the Black portion of the American populace—the Negro."[180] The *Freeman* took on the White press, which, it said, propagated stereotypes such as "the 'shiftless Negro.'"[181] The paper provided a first person, autobiographical space for performers to challenge how they were listened to by Whites. It billed itself as a "medium that will inject into your veins race pride."[182] The *Freeman* also addressed itself to "White managers," who would scour the paper for new talent.[183]

The most important difference between the *Freeman* and White papers of the time was that its photos showed actors as actors, distinct from their roles. Actors' names would appear, as well as the styles or roles that the performer had at his or her disposal. An ad from 1914 asked for "comedians, strong ballahoo man, and tenor singers."[184] An ad from 1910 reads, "Wanted! Wanted! Wanted! Good colored teams, man and wife. Sketch teams that can work in stock musical acts, novelty acts, and all other singles and doubles. . . . State salary in first letter and send photos." This ad, like others, asked performers to send in photographs.[185]

The audience for these images was other Black performers, professionals, critics, and agents. Matt Sakakeeny[186] and Aleen J. Ratzlaff have argued that the images published in the *Freeman* "provided an avenue through which Blacks, overlooked by the mainstream press, conveyed their viewpoints and life experiences. Visual images provided multiple layers of messages in which understanding was not limited to words or a specific place or time."[187]

The other basic difference between the *Freeman* and White newspapers is that the authors of the *Freeman* read and critiqued the White press, but the opposite was not true. The *Freeman*'s primary critique of the White press was that it conflated Black actors with their roles. While the White press used primitivist language to claim that Black performers were naturally better actors, singers, dancers, and comedians than White people, a major accomplishment of the *Freeman* was to detail the importance of craft. Dozens of articles relayed the importance of study, lessons, music school (if available), and control over one's instrument. The *Freeman* contained insider language that emphasized commercial success, musical technique, mastery of craft, ethnic pride, intimacy among actors, and political-economic critiques of Whiteness. The editors knew that White theater managers read the *Freeman* as a way to search for new talent, but they implored White critics and the White public to listen more critically and to abandon the assumption that Black actors were playing themselves onstage. A substantial discourse about how to listen emerged. It asserted that good listening required separating actors from roles. The *Freeman* rejected minstrel listening and demonstrated that Black and mixed-race performers in vaudeville listened to each other differently than how Whites listened to them. These performers listened to each other as musicians, actors, and professionals.

Salem Tutt Whitney has a special place as a theorist of American listening. As a playwright, performer, producer, comedian, poet, and journalist, he was at the forefront of everything vaudeville.[188] In his eclectic column, "Seen and Heard in Passing," Whitney offered reviews of performances, gave advice on professional success, related stories from the road, including encounters with White audiences, ranked performers, and offered general comments on aesthetics, politics, economics, and history.

Whitney criticized the White press and White listeners for their racist listening orientations. He argued that reviews of Black vaudeville performances conflated the actors with their roles. The White press "referred to the performers as 'darkies,' 'mokes,' 'ni****,' etc. The merit of the show was given slight mention, and nearly always there was some sarcastic reference to the Negroes making a vain attempt to imitate White folks."[189] The White press also commented negatively on Black audiences. "Considerable space was given to a ludicrous description of the occupants of 'ni**** heaven' meaning the gallery."[190]

Whitney's study of how White vaudeville audiences laughed is a complex portrait of the interaction between Black vaudeville performers and White and Black spectators. In his column of October 30, 1915, Whitney gives a phenomenology of a mixed audience reacting to a joke. Whitney studied how the same joke would be heard by Whites and non-Whites in the audience. Black audience members, often relegated to the balcony or a separate space cleared by a rope, laughed at the racism of Whites, while Whites laughed ignorantly at caricatures of Black life. Whitney explains how his comedy sketch "We'uns ain't got no country" was a critique of White American racism and imperialism that was lost on White listeners in the audience. "Straight—Hear that bugle? That is a call to arms; follow the flag and be ready to fight, bleed and die for your country./ Comedian—Whose country?/ Straight—Why your country!/ My country! Our country!/ Comedian—Hast thou ever stopped to consider that we'uns ain't got no country (Loud applause)."[191] Whitney argues that White audiences laughed because they held the racist view being mocked by the joke.[192] Whites were ignorant to the political critique in the joke, which was to point out the "unholy and pernicious system of discrimination, segregation and disenfranchisement, practiced against the colored people by most of the Whites of this country."[193]

Whitney also describes the experience of performing with the Smart Set Company for White audiences in White towns. He focused on how Black performers could navigate White terroristic violence inside and outside the theater.[194] His column offered practical, first-person advice for how Black musicians could avoid White violence. Whitney wrote frequently about the physical space of the theaters where the *Smart Set* performed. From the *Freeman* we learn that in the teens, there were varied ways Black audiences were segregated inside the theaters, from Black-only balconies to separating audiences only symbolically by a piece of rope. "The Southern Whites refuse to sit in theaters or other public spaces on terms of equality with Blacks, but stretch a rope or flimsy piece of cloth between the two and the problem is solved."[195] Whitney, like Du Bois, maintained that White listening is crowd control. Navigating White spaces outside the theater was dominated by one concern: physical safety. The threat of being lynched was real and constant.[196] Being a well-dressed Black professional in the South was perceived as an insult to local Whites, who called Whitney "an insolent 'ni****" and threatened him "with annihilation for not doffing my hat in a White restaurant where there were only White men, all of them wearing hats."[197] Within the walls of the theater, in costume, and sometimes in Blackface, Whitney was not perceived by his White audiences as a threat, but in local restaurants, hotels, or other public spaces outside the theater, he and his troupe were treated as space invaders. Whitney wrote: "ny exigency that places the Negro in a position of equality to or superiority over the Whites is intolerable to the Whites."[198]

The *Freeman* ran a number of pieces related to the question of why there was an increase in White attendance at Black vaudeville performances in the 1915 season.[199] Whitney writes about performing for these growing White audiences,[200] while the composer James Reese Europe quipped that finally White people had caught on to the fact that Black bands could play syncopated music better than the White bands that imitated them.[201] Whitney remarked that White audiences should prefer his Blackface comedy to that offered by White comedians in Blackface.[202] Europe noted of his composition, *Darkydom,* "there was a number containing a peculiarly syncopated passage which not a single White orchestra ever succeeded in playing correctly, while colored orchestras played it without effort, unconscious of its intricacies."[203] Europe attributed the ability of Black orchestras to swing, not to natural ability but to the fact that these orchestras were "the originators of the highly syncopated melody so much in favor to-day."[204] Europe describes how his compositions used syncopated, swung rhythms, which Black musicians played better than White musicians: Early jazz "takes the form of a highly syncopated melody, which in the early period of its development was known as 'rag-time' music. Since the dance is born of music, it is quite apparent that the modern dance is a creature of the syncopated melody."[205] When Europe wrote that Black orchestras had a "superior sense of rhythm," he was using language that could be understood as primitivist, specifically in the sense of attributing an ability to play swing rhythms because of an innate racial trait. But over and again Europe attributes the ability to swing to "training in his arts."[206] Black musicians were good at playing syncopated music because "he is the originator of the highly syncopated melody so much in favor to-day. It is therefore only natural that the Negro musician should interpret the music best."[207] Other writers in the *Freeman*, such as Carl Ditton[208] and E. Azalia Hackley,[209] also argued for the importance of craft, recommending professional lessons, study, learning to read music, and instrumental technique. The *Freeman* was a venue for pedagogical and professional advice for Black musicians and actors—all of which was lost on White audiences.

Whitney's critique of White minstrel listening in the *Freeman* is an important supplement to the more widely known Black existential critiques of Whiteness. Whitney shows that Whites consumed the sights and sounds of the minstrel show and read White newspapers, while ignoring the extensive discussion in the Black press about White violence, White racism, and White misperceptions of Black people. I contend that Black vaudeville, one of the crucial settings for the emergence of early jazz listening orientations, has been misunderstood because it has not been sufficiently studied phenomenologically from the perspective of the actors, musicians, composers, and producers who built it. Like Du Bois and Locke, Whitney and his peers implored Whites to read critiques of themselves in the Black press. Whitney knew this was unlikely. His column "Seen and Heard in Passing," like Dunbar-Nelson's "Un Femme Dit," was a forceful way of reclaiming space from White ears.

The existential critiques of White listening considered in this chapter span from Whitney's turn-of-the-century invectives against White minstrel listeners to Harlem Renaissance debates over folk and classical listening to Fanon's warnings about White existentialism to contemporary Black feminist concerns that White philosophers are appropriating Black thought and occupying White space. My phenomenological portrait of six types of bad faith White listening, drawn from Black and Creole philosophy, is not a relic. The minstrel listener, the savior, the revivalist, the hipster, the colorblind, and the ecstatic listener—they are very much with us today. I consider these categories of White listening to be part of what Alcoff calls the "analytic of Whiteness."[210] It will only take a bit of imagination and humility for White people today to see and hear themselves somewhere in this analytic of White listening.

Minstrel listening continues today when White audiences tune in to hip-hop culture and think it represents "the" Black experience. A Black colleague recently told me that when she went to her dean's office for an academic meeting, he put on soul music to, as he said, "put her at ease." White savior listeners are everywhere; the last one I ran into was a White CEO of a nonprofit who was leading a diversity retreat to "help" low-income people of color "learn fiscal responsibility." A revivalist listener I met at a recent philosophy conference was upset when I suggested that some forms of hip hop are contemporary examples of jazz. He clung to the idea that jazz peaked in the music of Coltrane and Davis, and that it's been downhill ever since. As for the hipster listener, I confess that my students accuse me of being one. Having been raised and deeply influenced by my jazz hipster, beatnik father, *I would call myself a White hipster in recovery*. Before the Trump era, colorblindness was the dominant rhetoric of most American politicians since it was introduced by Lee Atwater as part of the Southern strategy. Republicans and Democrats alike used coded, colorblind rhetoric to harm Black people and non-Whites. And I am reminded of the White ecstatic listener when I turn on the radio to a classical radio station and hear the intonation, inflection, and air of the announcer. Using what people used to call the Hollywood accent, today's classical announcers sound like the voice I heard as a kid in an old TV ad for soap: "Calgon . . . take me away."

Listening Exercises for Chapter 4
The Ears of a Guilty People

Race records are primary sources of Africana existential thought and practice. The stories these records tell are cocreated by the listening orientations we adopt toward them. Their meaning is not static, as revealed by the genealogy of listening presented in *The Sonic Gaze*. Race records are living texts with a saturated history of interpretation. Race records *invite* a listening orientation of freedom, but they do not demand it.

As Angela Davis has shown, the records of blues women express a Black existentialist feminism politics of liberation. The blues is an existential art. As you listen, study the lyrics as well as the form of blues and early jazz recordings. It is no surprise that existential thinkers such as Angela Davis, Jean-Paul Sartre, Simone de Beauvoir, Lewis R. Gordon, Robin Kelley, La Rose T. Parris, Mabogo P. More, Tendayi Sithole, and so many others have been drawn to blues and jazz. *Jazz and blues music expresses a theory of freedom in sound.* The philosophy of freedom is not inherent in blues and jazz records, but is coconstituted by the listener's participation, especially in how we hear and feel the rhythmic pulse. To reciprocate the appeal of blues and jazz rhythms, we must learn how to hear accents and offbeats through noisy participation. In attuning our imagination, we can become aware of the construction of time and space. Understanding rhythm through participatory listening is a phenomenological exercise. As we "listen for difference," our imagination produces multiple interpretations and orientations. Each new listening act can become a "versioning" of a recording. Just as drummers learn to hear a quarter-note click and "swing the metronome," active listeners can learn how to *swing their imagination* in relationship to what they hear.

The playlist below comprises race records from my personal collection, which I inherited from my father. Of the more than five thousand records in his collection (mostly jazz 33s from the 1940s, 1950s, and 1960s, but also many 78s), only a few records remain in playable condition; the rest were stored improperly and succumbed to water, mold, and insects. When my father passed away in the summer of 2017, in a fog of grief I selected a few gems from the collection. These records sat in a box for three years, until December 2020, after most of the current manuscript was completed. When I cataloged these records, I was in for a shock. Though I did not know it at the time, the records I had rescued mapped almost precisely onto my arguments in chapter 4. Among these records is the first recording ever made by Bessie Smith ("Down Hearted Blues"), as well as my father's personal favorite, "Backwater Blues," which I've sung and played hundreds of times with him and dozens of Kansas musicians, many of them cousins, uncles, and aunts. My father was a Beatnik hipster—and a wonderful blues pianist, guitarist, and vocalist. His sound was deeply rooted in two traditions. The first was the Kansas City blues tradition. He studied the vocals of Joe Turner, and the minimalism of Count Basie, and he emulated the stride piano style of Midwestern and Southern pianists, especially Kansas-City–born Pete Johnson, whose left hand he worshiped. His second influence was the music of the Baptist church, especially the hymnody represented in *The Baptist Hymn and Praise Book*. He was raised in the Baptist church, sent to a Baptist boarding school in rural Arkansas as a teenager, and attended Moody Bible Academy in Chicago, where he trained to become a Baptist minister. An apostate by age twenty-five, his new religion became blues music. Like Mezz Mezzrow, my father tried to turn against his Whiteness. Fascinated with the Black culture of the segregated city where he was raised, he slummed in Black clubs and neighborhoods, and he eventually moved our family into a cold-water loft on the Black side of town. Our loft, in a bar district where all-night music didn't cause anyone to call the police, became a hotspot for local musicians to jam, party, and listen to records until dawn.

The records in this listening list all tell a story. For me, the story is very personal, as I've just shared. As you listen, ask yourself what story these records tell *you*. If you are able, try to get your hands on one of these race records, literally. Embrace the physicality of these hundred-year-old antiques once sold at furniture stores, Black barbershops, and shoeshine stands. Imagine their journey from the record players of Black consumers to the trash bin to the hands of White hipsters. The hundred-year path of these records expresses the entire thesis of *The Sonic Gaze*.

PLAYLIST PART ONE: THE KANSAS CITY SOUND

Listen for the continuity between swing rhythms and shuffle rhythms. Listen digenetically and comparatively to four recordings from Kansas City bands from 1927 to 1954, from the early big band era to the birth of rhythm and blues.

The first time listening to each recording, listen for the basic rhythmic pulse and think about the story each rhythm tells you. Use your imagination to formulate a response to the call of the rhythms. Try the following exercises as warm-ups. Using a metronome, note the tempo and time feels. In a group, have everybody clap on the one; then the one and three; then on the two and four. Try having half the group clap on the one and three, and half the group clap on the two and four. Where is the pulse stronger? What story do you hear in each song and rhythmic style? As you listen to each rhythm, write down the first three words you think of.

Benny Moten's Kansas City Orchestra,"Moten Stomp," 1927, Victor 209596.[1]

Listen for the syncopated two-beat feel of the bass line, played by Vernon Page on tuba. The tempo is a quick 240 bpm. Slow the recording down to 0.75 at first. Clap along with the tuba on beats one and three. Listen for the jittery, staccato sound of the bass. Then listen for (and clap with) the banjo playing on the off beats (two and four). The Moten band had a horn-driven sound; identify the instrumentation. There is no piano in the rhythm section, and the drum is inaudible. Imagine how the tune would sound live in the presence of an extremely large bass drum on every quarter note. Visualize the sound by looking at images of period drum kits. In 1927, before electrical recording techniques, bass drums had to be minimized because they interfered with the needles used to etch recordings. Kansas City bands were known for their "riff"-based approach to swing music. A riff is a short, repeated phrase. Listen for riffs and sing them, even if they are only a few notes or beats long. Kansas City jazz composers often wrote big band charts by beginning with a riff and elaborating it.[2]

Pete Johnson and His Boogie Woogie Boys, "Baby Look at You," 1939, Vocalion 4997.

This recording features Kansas City blues singer Joe Turner on vocals and the boogie-woogie piano master, Pete Johnson. Listen for the driving rhythm coming from Johnson's piano (announced with his powerful, pounding piano intro) and the bass playing of Abe Bolar, who performs on an upright string bass. Contrast the legato (smooth) feel of the upright bass to the jittery two-beat feel of the tuba in "Moten Stomp." The tempo is still fast but, slightly slower, at 220bpm. Note how musicians take solos, improvising melodies over the main melody. The form of this song is a twelve-bar blues. Identify the lead trumpet sound of Orin "Hot Lips" Page. Identify the alto saxophone soloist, Buster Smith, and visualize his alto saxophone.

Count Basie and His Orchestra, "Me and the Blues," 1949, RCA Victor 20-2127-B.

Bill "Count" Basie was an unrivaled composer, arranger, band leader, and pianist. He was an architect of the blues-based Kansas City sound, having worked under Benny Moten before leading his own band. "Me and the Blues" represents the subtle, laid-back, sparsely arranged big band style that Basie pioneered. Listen for the powerful eight-bar opening with a two-beat feel, strong trumpet line, and reed section swell. Note how the band backs off as Ann Moore's blues vocals take over. Listen for the orchestral arrangement style of Basie, which uses the band to support and frame the vocals. The arrangement is a beautiful example of how Basie left musical space for each voice in the band. Note how the horns play in the spaces around the vocal melody. Underneath it all, you can hear the rhythm section swinging hard, with a minimal number of notes. Visualize a large crowd dancing to the music. At its peak in the 1930s, Kansas City's jazz district had more than fifty jazz clubs within a few-block radius.

Joe Turner and His Blues Kings, "Well All Right," 1954, Atlantic A-1212.

The standout feature of this recording is the shuffle rhythm, which is the basis of rhythm and blues and early rock music. Joe Turner's blues vocals are delivered in his classic "shout" fashion, and there is a call-and-response with the other members of the band. The musical form is a classic twelve-bar blues in the key of C. Sing along with the chorus when Turner shouts "yes, yes," and "all right then." Listen for the similarities and differences between this record and "Baby Look at You" from fifteen years earlier. Pay attention to the subtle changes in the rhythm section: The piano plays in boogie-woogie fashion, the bass has a quarter-note pulse, but the drums are much louder, and there is a heavy backbeat. You can hear the drummer hitting the snare drum loudly on beats two and four (the backbeat). The tempo is much slower, at 160 bpm, compared to 220 bpm. The slower shuffle with a heavy backbeat is what defines R&B and rock music.

PLAYLIST PART TWO: THE EXISTENTIAL SOUNDS OF BLACK BLUES WOMEN

As Angela Davis has shown, the 1920s race records boom was driven by blues women Mamie Smith, Ethel Waters, Ma Rainey, and others. Listen for the feminist politics of resistance, liberation, and community in the lyrics of these recordings. They tell stories of Black women fighting back against abusive, cheating lovers. These romantically betrayed and physically abused Black women are not victims, but agents who embrace erotic desire, the Jook joint lifestyle of drugs and drinking, and the freedom of being professional musicians. These women drink, sing in barrelhouses, enjoy sex, and carry knifes to cut up the men who mistreat them. The listening exercises below emphasize the sounds of blues women—especially rhythms, melodies, timbres, antiphony, and instrumentation. Most of the recordings feature boogie-woogie or stride piano accompaniment. Listen for the subtle differences among four of the greatest jazz pianists in the American canon—Clarence Williams, Pete Johnson, James P. Johnson, and a young Fletcher Henderson. Listen for the diversity of styles incorporated in these early jazz records, spanning the country blues tradition, New Orleans tailgate-style playing, vaudeville, French Opera, ragtime, and classical inflections. Taken as a whole, the sounds of these blues women contrast with the Kansas City style that emerged from the territory bands and the ragtime piano feel of Missouri musicians Scott Joplin and James Scott.

Agnes Lynn, "Jazz Baby," 1919, Columbia A2745.

Although "jazz" is in this title of this tune, the rhythm is straight, not syncopated. There is no two-beat feel typical of early jazz, but a steady, unaccented quarter-note pulse. The lyrics allude to the singer's ragtime-playing father and mother, who meet at a cabaret, marry, and have a daughter, who is the "jazz baby." This record has a Tin Pan Alley, commercial sound, not a blues-based or brass band sound. Recorded in 1919, before the birth of the race record, this is a commercial attempt to capitalize on the term "jazz" without much of a jazz or blues feel. Look up the Columbia ad for this record in *The Music Trader*, July 12, 1919. Contrast the image of White couples dancing with the Blackface minstrel image accompanying Al Jolson's record "I'll Say She Does."

Bessie Smith, "Down Hearted Blues," Clarence Williams Piano, 1923, Columbia A3844.

This is the first record Bessie Smith ever made. Selling two million copies, it "went platinum" in today's lexicon. Along with Mamie Smith's "Crazy Blues" of three years earlier, the success of this record launched a wave of public interest among Black Americans for blues records that lasted until the Depression. Davis gave the definitive analysis of the lyrics of this song in her *Blues Legacies and Black Feminism*.[3] "'Down Hearted Blues' ends with an address to men in general—a bold, feminist contestation of patriarchal rule: 'I got the world in a jug, the stoppers in my hand. I'm gonna hold it until you men come under my command.'"[4] Study the piano feel of Clarence Williams. Listen to what his left hand is doing. Can you hear the "stride" (or jump) between the notes in the bass?

Bessie Smith, "Jail House Blues," 1923, Columbia A4001.

The syncopated rhythm of this record contrasts dramatically with "Jazz Baby." Listen to the pulse of the piano player's left hand. Irvin Johns's stride-style piano has the left hand syncopating and the right hand playing accompaniment. Compare the Moten band's use of a tuba bass on the one and three, and the banjo playing the upbeats. The tempo is slow (70 bmp) and you can imagine couples dancing and swaying to Smith's commanding vocals. Contrast Smith's vocal phrasing with that of Lynn on "Jazz Baby." Smith uses call-and-response to create drama and interaction. The lyrics tell the story of a blues woman forced to spend thirty days in jail for playing an illegal house party. Why does the protagonist ask the jailkeeper to put her in a cell with a woman and not a man?

Bessie Smith, "Mistreatin' Daddy," 1923, Columbia 14000-D.

In addition to Smith, this record is special because it features two towering figures of early jazz: Don Redman on clarinet and Fletcher Henderson on piano. Both were composers, arrangers, and band leaders. Between 1921 and 1923, Henderson played piano on an astounding 150 race records, often backing Ethel Waters.[5] He would go on to become one of the most important big band composers, arrangers, and band leaders in America. Henderson's left hand is not as driving rhythmically as that of Clarence Williams, Irvin Johns, and other stride pianists; in fact, when he toured with Waters in the early 1920s, she complained that he "wouldn't give me what I call the 'damn-it-to-hell bass,' that chump-chump stuff that real jazz needs."[6] Waters told Henderson to study the earthy, rough, stride piano of James P. Johnson. A perfectionist, Henderson practiced to the piano rolls of Johnson until he could play the music "perfectly," in Waters's opinion. See if you can hear the rhythmic difference of the piano versus Williams in "Down Hearted Blues," and Johns in "Jailhouse Blues." Redman's clarinet adds a rhythmic and harmonic contrast to the voice and piano. Listen for the call-and-response between the singer and the clarinet. Henderson and Redman are locked into each other rhythmically and melodically and offer a swinging counterpoint to Smith's vocals. The contrast between Smith's growling vocals and Henderson's polished touch speaks to the diversity of playing styles in early jazz, which drew on blues and classical playing. The lyrics for "Mistreatin' Daddy" should be read with Davis in mind. Smith was a feminist pioneer who broke the silence about domestic abuse of women. Smith does more than complain about being beaten; she takes back control by threatening to dismember the man who "used to knock your mama down." What do you think of when she sings these lines? Do you think this story transcends the moment in which it was written? "If you see me sitting on another daddy's knee. Don't bother me, I'm as mean as can be. I'm like the butcher right down the street. I can cut you all a-pieces like I would a piece of meat." How do these lyrics fit with your conception of women's roles in the 1920s?

Sara Martin and Clarence Williams's Harmonizing Four, "Graveyard Blues," 1923, Okey 8099-B.

This recording is notable for the diversity of styles it brings together into one song. Early jazz creolized many strains of music. Sara Martin's funky, crackling voice blends with the stride piano of Williams, the New Orleans sound of Sidney Bechet on soprano saxophone, and the New York, pre-Armstrong brass sound of Thomas Morris on cornet. Identify the saxophone and the cornet and listen for the call-and-response and tailgate playing. Martin's voice is hornlike, and Bechet's saxophone sound, with its tremendous vibrato, is vocal-like. Bechet learned to play his horn by imitating the sounds of the classical singers of the French Opera in New Orleans. Imagine the musicians having a dialogue with each other. Imagine what the horns are "saying" in response to the vocals.

Luciellle Hegamin and Her Blue Flame Syncopators, "Syncopatin' Mama," 1923, Cameo 317/365.

Hegamin's vocal style is very different from Smith's and Martin's. She was a popular recording artist for the Cameo label and was the second Black blues singer to record after Mamie Smith. Her vocal style is more straight than swung, compared to the other blues singers above, although the title of this song is "Syncopatin' Mama." Her sound is indebted to the popular, classical, and vaudeville styles, though a clear two-beat bounce pulse moves through the entire rhythm section and her vocals. What adjectives come to mind to describe her vocal timbre? Often this vocal timbre is called "clean" or "pure," as compared to the "dirty" timbre of blues singers. Do you agree with these descriptions? Consider how the terms "pure" and "dirty" are racialized. In American classical music—especially outside of the French Opera tradition in New Orleans—Black, Creole, and mixed-race singers faced tremendous discrimination based on the myth that their voices were not suitable for the European classical music of the German and Italian traditions. At the same time, in vaudeville, non-Whites performed opera numbers often, which they interspersed with popular, ragtime, and jazz numbers. Do you think Hegamin "sounds Black"? Explore your assumptions about what makes a person's voice "sound White." Go back and listen to Anges Lynn and explore whether she "sounds White."

Bessie Smith, "Backwater Blues," 1927, Columbia 14195-D.

This astounding record shows the pianist James P. Johnson at his finest. A pioneer of stride playing, Johnson lays down a heavily syncopated rhythm with his grumbling left hand. His right hand beautifully illustrates the call-and-response between vocalist and pianist. Listen for what Ethel Waters described as the "'damn-it-to-hell bass,' that chump-chump stuff." Sing the words "chump-chump" along with Johnson's bass line. Compare this record to Fletcher Henderson's playing on "Mistreatin' Daddy" and see if you agree with Waters that Henderson had perfected the stride style of Johnson. Visualize Johnson and Henderson at the piano and imagine their "touch" on the keys. Whose style is more percussive? Do you get the sense that Smith and Johnson are locked-in rhythmically? How would you describe the musical conversation happening between them? Can you hear them feeding off each other?

Ethel Waters and the Ebony Four, "Go Back Where You Stayed Last Night," 1925, Columbia 14093-D.

How would you describe Waters's vocal style—her timbre, her rhythm, her phrasing, her vibrato, and her interactions with instrumentalists? The name of the group, "Ebony Four," signals that the musicians were playing in a self-consciously Black style aimed at Black audiences. Based on the sound, why do you think Columbia made the decision to market this style as "race" music aimed at Black Americans? Write down the instruments you hear. Identify the cornet, tuba, and piano. The pianist is Pearl Wright. Waters described her relationship with Wright as "a sort of telepathy. I never had to tell her what I wanted."[7] Compare Wright—the only female pianist in this listening list—with Henderson and Johnson. As before, think about her touch on the keyboard and her percussive left hand outlining the bass figures. Since there is a tuba playing bass, how does the left hand of the pianist interact with the two-beat feel of the bass player? What story is Waters telling when she sings: "He broke my heart. How I'd love to break his face"?

PLAYLIST PART THREE: BLACK SPIRITUALS

The race record market included recordings of Black spirituals. In 1909, the Fisk University Jubilee Singers released the first of their records, "Swing

Low, Sweet Chariot." The Fisk Singers introduced the White world to the concert-arranged Black spiritual in 1871. In the selection below, "Roll, Jordan, Roll" (1922), we hear a melodic characteristic that ties the spiritual to the blues—the flattened seventh. Flattened thirds and sevenths are used by blues and jazz musicians to give their melodies a somber feeling. Sing along with the record and use a digital piano to identify the pitches. You can hear the Jubilee singers bending and scooping notes. Listen for the drawn-out phrasing of the words "I want," when the lead voice scoops from a sixth up to the octave. The rubato tempo (slowing down and speeding up) also links this recording to the blues. The major differences between this spiritual and the blues include the following: its lyrical content (religious, not secular), its performance context (concert halls, not Jook joints or house parties), and its instrumentation (acapella). As you listen, reflect on the debate among Harlem Renaissance intellectuals about the authenticity of concert-arranged spirituals and their relationship to the Black folk music tradition.

Fisk University Jubilee Singers, "Roll, Jordan, Roll," 1922, Columbia A3657.

Except for "Jazz Baby," this is the oldest record of the bunch. The original Fisk University Jubilee Singers were established in 1871, five years after Fisk was opened. The Historically Black College was facing bankruptcy, and the Jubilee Singers toured to raise money. The eighteen-month singing tour, which included extensive travel in the United States, as well as in England and Germany, raised over forty thousand dollars and introduced White audiences to concert-arranged Black spirituals like "Roll, Jordan, Roll." Why were White audiences so invested in listening to this music? What story did they hear in the lyrics, melodies, and rhythms? What story do *you* hear? W.E.B. DuBois praised the concert-style spiritual as an elevation of Black folk music, while Zora Neale Hurston called the style inauthentic. Hurston believed that concert halls with White listeners "bleached" the music. As you listen to the lyrics, "Roll, Jordan, roll. I want to go to heaven when I die to hear the old Jordan roll," imagine two distinct listening orientations: that of the White concertgoer and that of the Black churchgoer. How did these audiences listen differently? Imagine a third listening orientation: that of enslaved Black people who originated this song. In her definitive work on the subject, Eileen Southern[8] notes several points about the origins of spirituals among enslaved people: Singing was "usually in a minor key or as being plaintive, mournful, or wild"; performances were "inseparable from some form of body movement—if not dancing or working, then hand clapping, foot tapping, or swaying of the body"; and "Performances shaped the song, determined its rhythm, melody, texture, tempo, text and *finally, its effects upon listeners.*

This was largely because of the importance of *improvisation* in the African traditions."[9] Lastly, listen to the song while keeping in mind Southerners' assessment of the White sonic gaze: "Adding to all this complexity was the practice of audience participation—indeed, in the strict sense of the term there was no audience; there were only singers and non-singers. The *white listeners* might sit quietly, showing their appreciation of a performance by facial expression and applause at appropriate times, but the slaves actively participated in the performance."[10]

Afterword
Say Their Names: Breonna Taylor, George Floyd

In 1939, Du Bois responded to an invitation to speak in Chicago with a letter that indicated with clarity how he should be introduced. Rightfully, he insisted that his name be spoken correctly. "My name is pronounced in the clear English fashion: Du, with *u* as in *Sue*; Bois as in *oi* in *voice*. The accent is on the second syllable."[1]

This simple story is a reminder to all of us, but especially us White folks, to listen better. We listen badly when we don't learn how to hear and pronounce the names of non-White people. How many African American and Latinx students—along with Chinese and Chinese American students; Indian and Indian American students; Indigenous students; and many others —have endured their White teachers struggling over their supposedly "difficult" names?

At the Predominately White Institution (PWI) where I teach, 40 percent of the students are non-White, and the faculty is 82 percent White. In my classes on Africana Philosophy; Black Humanism; Race, Gender, and Culture; and the Philosophy of Hip-Hop, I am in the minority as a White person. Because I teach four courses a semester, with class sizes of up to eighty students per section, I find novel ways to learn students' names. In an average semester, I have almost two hundred new names to learn. Between the sheer number of names to memorize and my horror of mispronouncing anyone's name—and no doubt, my own White shame—I feel overwhelmed. The most important teaching technique I've learned in twenty years is that I should know my students' names and pronounce them properly. On the first day of class, I have students write down their name and how it's pronounced phonetically. I've recently included preferred-gender pronouns. I ask students to pair up and explain how they got their name and what it means. It is easy to remember a person's name when they explain its origin and importance. No two stories are the same. A person's name is perhaps the most important part of their identity.

Transgender and nonbinary students at my school have fought hard to have their chosen names and gender identities recognized institutionally. Being correctly named on university IDs, in e-mails, and on class rosters is no small matter. For trans students especially, waiting to hear if the school has changed one's name can be a painful and unjust experience. The least our universities can do is to let trans and nonbinary folks graduate with a diploma that has their real name on it, not their dead name.

Because I ask students to tell me how to pronounce their name, I have an archive. I study in between classes, working on pronunciation. I have students correct me when I get their name wrong. I try to own my White identity by making it a valid subject for classroom discussion. If a White Ph.D. can talk all day about Black identity, he can surely learn to talk about the fact that he is a White person teaching Black studies to mostly Black students.

According to a popular myth that springs from the White sonic gaze, Black names are "hard to pronounce." Key and Peele's skits "Substitute Teacher" and "East/West College Bowl" take on this myth. Key and Peele are biracial comedians whose brand of humor says a lot about White listening. Both "Substitute Teacher" and "College Bowl" reverse the White sonic gaze. Key and Peele's comedy problematizes White listening by challenging us White people to do better when it comes to so-called "Black-sounding" names. In my classes, we also talk about the economic implications of White listening. I show the YouTube clip "José vs. Joe: Who gets a job," in which a Latinx man (José Zamora) changes one letter of his name. He suddenly gets callbacks, though his résumé is the same. We look at data from the National Bureau of Education that demonstrates White employers discriminate against applicants with "Black-sounding" names. I tell the story about my own "weird" White name and explain that I've never been discriminated against because of it. I ask students directly: Do your White professors know your name? Do they pronounce it correctly? Do they act like it's a big deal to have to say it properly? The results are anecdotal, but with two hundred students a semester, I have a good sense of what is happening at my school. "My White teachers don't know my name." "My White teachers can't pronounce my name, I just gave up." "My White coach can't remember my name—it's John—but he calls me a different 'Black' name each time." "Just call me Shay—it's easier." These students are well aware of the White sonic gaze as a personal and institutional force. As a White professor, I hear my students saying to me: "When my White teachers can't pronounce my name . . . what's the point?" "How can I feel included if my White professors can't pronounce my name right?" "Are they going to wait until I'm dead to 'say my name'?"

Three weeks after the murder of George Floyd, the president of my university called an emergency meeting. The president, a White woman, pulled together an ad hoc group of ten people. I looked over the Zoom invite, wondering who was selected and what our purpose was. I assumed I was on the call because of my position on the Campus Equity Committee. By appearances, the president put together a group of mostly Black coworkers—an interesting assemblage, given how White our faculty and senior staff are. The pretense for the meeting was vaguely spelled out in a hurried e-mail, and the time for the meeting changed twice. All this added to a sense that the president was weighing something important. Clicking the Zoom invite, I saw in the taciturn faces of my Black colleagues a skepticism that said, "Why am I here? What are we doing?" I, too, was skeptical, but also morbidly curious: How would our White president frame this meeting about supporting "Black lives"?

I see the White football coach is on. Later the president says she's heard that there "might" be racism in the locker room. Several assistant coaches, mostly Black, are also on. I recognize a Black professor from athletics. A White colleague from English is there. Two newly hired senior administrators are there: One is a Latinx male; another is an African American female.

We waited for the president to tell us why we cleared our schedules. She began by introducing everyone. This went fine until she came to the only two Latinx people on the call. She said with a smile "And this is Christian . . . uhhh . . . wait . . . I can never pronounce your last name . . . what is it again?" Christian (not his real name; all names and titles have been changed) politely corrected her. Christian has worked for the university for years and been in dozens of diversity meetings with the president. He is one of the most visible diversity advocates on campus. Next up was James, who was hired one semester ago under a newly created position for diversity. Once again, without a hint of White shame, our president said, "Oh . . . I always mess up your last name . . . What is it again?" It's irrelevant, but James's last name is hardly difficult to pronounce even by the standards of White mediocrity. He replied with a polite correction, and the meeting moved on. The president said, "I don't need to tell you that we're really experiencing a difficult time on campus with a lot of turmoil and a lot of questions given the deaths of George Floyd, Breonna Taylor, and what's happening with the Black Lives Matter movement. I'm going to turn this meeting over to James . . . He'll explain it."

My university's student population is 40 percent non-White, a result of aggressive recruiting efforts in Black high schools in Philadelphia and Latinx schools in the Lehigh Valley over the past ten years. Having been at the university for eighteen years, I've watched our predominately White campus shift. The shift in student culture has been positive and seismic, while the predominantly White culture of faculty and senior staff has been stagnant and reactionary. Ten years into the university's aggressive recruiting effort targeting Black and Latinx students, only 6 percent of the faculty is Black and 3 percent is Latinx. That's what you call a Whiteness problem.

As James began speaking, I ground my teeth silently. The president called the meeting, why isn't *she* saying why she got us together? Why is she having James explain the situation? Having been a White diversity worker on my campus longer than the current White president's soon-to-expire-term, I knew what was going on. She was calling her "Black friends" to tell her how to respond to the national outcry over the deaths of George Floyd and Breonna Taylor. I knew this because in 2017 she did the same thing in response to the Unite the Right Rally in Charlottesville. Back then, we had no office of diversity, no office for inclusion, and no institutional support for diversity work done by volunteer faculty and staff. Ten days after the eruption of White violence in Charlottesville, no e-mail or social media message came from our president, a prolific Twitter user. In a moment of anger, fueled by my White privilege and the protection of tenure, I wrote her an e-mail, "Dear K----, We are the most diverse campus in our system (as our public-relations office touts constantly); 20 percent of our students are Black, 15 percent are Latinx, we have a small Jewish population, a growing population of Muslims (many of whom are visible minorities), and we have many students from immigrant, queer, and other communities marginalized by White supremacist violence. The events in Charlottesville are terrifying and are going to have a ripple effect. The presidents of many other universities have issued statements. I think you should, too. Sincerely, Storm."

The reply was quick. "Can we meet asap?" I agreed, showing up to a meeting with: myself (a White faculty member); a White male colleague from the Art Department who had never done any diversity work that I know of; the director of public relations—a White woman whose messaging to the campus always included the phrase ". . . as the most diverse campus in our system . . ."; and one person of color, a staff member. I looked around the room, frustrated, but unwilling to back down.

In 2017, the president chose a White male diversity worker—me—to be her diversity conscience. She was listening Whitely. She could only hear the message that Black Lives Matter from a White, Jewish male. My colleague and I exchanged knowing glances that said, "Yup, she's listening to *you* because you're a White dude." I explained that Charlottesville was traumatizing to our community and that to say nothing would be aiding and abetting White supremacist violence. I told her how colleagues at other universities were being doxed and harassed with death threats. I explained that the rise of the alt-right was among White, middle-class college students—exactly the kind of students who were becoming a minority on our rural Pennsylvania campus. I told her that campuses were becoming recruiting grounds for White nationalists and that hate crimes were surging. I explained the psychological effects on my own children when they saw protestors on the news chanting, "You will not replace us. The Jew will not replace us." After all this, the president looked at me—only me—and mulling over her message to the campus, said, "Okay, fine, just tell me what to say then." My White words fell on clogged White ears. That was back in 2017.

On the Zoom call, James was finishing his overview. He looked tired. Later I found out that he and other non-White staff members had received a volume of e-mail from students complaining that the administration wasn't doing enough to address the safety of Black, Latinx, and other minority students. Students were scared and upset, and they wanted campus leaders to do something meaningful. James hadn't been sleeping. The diversity workers who were doing the most were receiving the most pushback. As visible and vocal minorities, these diversity workers were expected to drive the bus they were being thrown under.

The purpose of the Zoom call was now clear. It was a rehash of 2017. The president wanted Black and Latinx voices to be her conscience. The subtext was the same: "I heard you. Fine. Now, just tell me what I'm supposed to say to the campus." But she didn't hear.

The president's behavior in these two diversity meetings, three years apart, embodies a common failure of White listening. Whites often ignore the voices of non-White people. Then, in moments of White crisis, they often turn to non-Whites and say, "I'm sorry I didn't listen before. I'm all ears. Just tell me what I should say."

To some, it comes as a surprise that asking non-White people, "What should I say?" is a condescending listening orientation. In White culture, listening is broadly understood as an act of respect. Talking over someone is rude; listening quietly is polite. But when Whites start listening after long periods of silence, and when Whites start openly feeling a crisis in their identity, expressed by feelings about how they've failed to listen to Black voices, we need to step back and ask several things.

(1) Why do we Whites care *now*, when we didn't seem to care in the past? White violence against Black people in the United States is chronic. Yet, Whites only episodically care about White violence. What is the motivation driving these moments of White awareness? If the motivation is White shame that suggests that White listening is performed as an act of absolution for White guilt.

(2) To whom are we Whites now listening? Like those on the diversity Zoom call, the question is why some particular people are being called to the table and listened to, while others are not. In PWIs, people of color should not be turned into the "diversity conscience" of us White people.

Lastly, (3) Why does the White listener think that fixing Whiteness and knowing "what to say" about White violence is the expertise of people of color? It is patronizing for White people to ask people of color to tell us how to address racism. This tendency is part of the old trend of problematizing minority existence rather than problematizing White majority existence. For years, Whites have expected Black people to solve anti-Black racism. White Anglo-Saxon Protestants have expected Jews to fix anti-semitism. Whites routinely expect people of color to do the diversity work at our universities. We think that hiring people of color will automatically solve our institutional White problem. These attitudes assume that once Whites become aware of Whiteness—through an experience of White shame, anxiety, and estrangement—all that is necessary is to for us to listen to non-Whites tell us how to *fix* Whiteness. "Just tell me what I should say . . ."

Variations of the Zoom call at my campus played out at hundreds of other PWIs in the United States. *Inside Higher Ed* published a piece, "Words Matter for College Presidents," with the pullquote: "Many higher education leaders called for change in response to the killing of George Floyd, but few shared ideas on how to enact it. Observers want them to do more."[2] Another article contained twenty statements from various presidents, provosts, and diversity teams. Most of them were lukewarm and failed to name the specific problem of systematic White police brutality against Black people. A few campus presidents marched with the thousands of Black Lives Matter activists who flooded American streets for the largest civil rights uprising since the 1960s, but most didn't.

The murders of Breonna Taylor and George Floyd caused a crisis in White listening. How long this particular crisis of White listening will last, and what its real effects are, we have yet to see. Floyd cried, "I can't breathe," and a chunk of White Americans who had ignored Black voices listened. For some reason, in 2020, Whites in the United States heard the cry "I can't breathe" as calling out to us. Was it because, unlike the killings of Tamir Rice, Trayvon Martin, and Michael Brown, the White public *literally heard* the dying screams of Floyd through cell phone recordings?[3]

When I attended the "We Shall Not Go Back" march in Staten Island in protest of the killing of Eric Garner in 2014, there were about three thousand people. Most of the protestors were people of color, and there were not large protests in multiple cities for multiple nights, as there were for Breonna Taylor and George Floyd. I'm not entirely sure why Garner's cry of "I can't breathe" fell on clogged White ears, while many Whites in 2020 have felt implicated by Floyd's words. One factor is that with the United States shut down due to COVID-19, everybody was homebound and glued to the media coverage of Taylor's and Floyd's deaths. Factor in four years of frustration with Trump's White mediocrity and an economic crash, and we get the conditions for White estrangement.

In the multiple Black Lives Matter demonstrations in my community in reaction to Taylor and Floyd's deaths, the demographic was overwhelming young (high school to college age), and split about fifty-fifty between White and non-White participants. I was struck by how many Whites carried signs that were related to White listening. "White Silence Is Violence." "White Silence Is Betrayal." "I'm Not Black, But I See You, I Hear You, I Mourn with You." "Neutrality Is Complicity." "I Get That I Will Never Get It, But I Stand by You."

The young White protestors who carried these signs and chanted the call-and-response, "Say her name—Breonna Taylor; say his name—George Floyd," engaged in street-level political action aimed at reducing White supremacy and rectifying the White problem of police brutality against Black people. These protest signs indicate a different pattern of listening from that of my university president. Her White anxiety led her to a condescending form of White listening in which she asked her "Black friends" to tell her how to react to the deaths of Breonna Taylor and George Floyd. The White protestors in the street were saying something very different. They, too, were experiencing White anxiety, but they explicitly owned their White anxiety and White ignorance. They joined the Black Lives Matter movement as Whites, but not as saviors or advocates of colorblindness.

The call-and-response injunctions "Say her name! Breonna Taylor; say his name! George Floyd," were the rally cries of the Black Lives Matter protests in the United States in the summer of 2020. These protest slogans express a demand for better listening, and they are aimed especially at us White people. Better listening is not an end in itself, but a means by which to reduce White supremacy, in the boardroom, in the classroom, in the concert hall, on Twitter, in diversity meetings, and in the streets.

Notes

PREFACE

1. https://www.berklee.edu/ear-training. Emphasis added. The Berklee School of Music is in the United States, in Boston, MA.

2. "[P]rolonged, repeated, and attentive listening affords the development of certain personal qualities in the listener, qualities that have wider usage than in just the kinds of musical experiences from which they are derived." Antony Gritten, "Empathic Listening as a Transferable Skill," *Empirical Musicology Review* 10, no. 1/2 (2015): 23–29.

3. Larissa E. Hopkins and Andrea D. Domingue, "From Awareness to Action: College Student's Skill Development in Intergroup Dialogue," *Equity & Excellence in Education* 48, no. 3 (2015): 392–402.

4. Biren A. Nagda and Patricia Gurin, "Intergroup Dialogue: A Critical-Dialogical Approach to Learning about Difference, Inequality, and Social Justice," *New Directions for Teaching and Learning*, 2007, no. 111 (Fall 2007): 35–45.

5. *Rhymes, Beats and Classroom Life: Hip Hop Pedagogy and the Politics of Identity* (New York: Teachers College Press, 2009), 2.

6. *Digging: The Afro-American Soul of American Classical Music* (Berkeley: University of California Press, 2009), Kindle edition, location 1392.

7. New York: Manhattan Music, 1994.

CHAPTER 1

1. On the notion of becoming white, see Noel Ignatiev, *How the Irish became White* (New York: Routledge, 2009), and Karen Brodkin, *How Jews became White Folks and What that Says about Race in America* (New Brunswick: Rutgers University Press, 1998).

2. *The Transit of Empire: Indigenous Critiques of Colonialism* (Minneapolis: University of Minnesota Press, 2011), 41.

3. Byrd, *The Transit of Empire*, 39. I am drawn to Byrd's concept of "cacophony," which she proposes as a strategy for "discern[ing] how the noise of competing claims, recognitions, and remediations function to naturalize possession." See chapter 2 of *Transit of Empire*, "'This Island's Mine': The Parallax Logics of Caliban's Cacophony."

4. *Being Apart: Theoretical and Existential Resistance in Africana Literature* (Charlottesville: University of Virginia Press, 2015), Kindle, location 308.

5. "The Souls of White Folk," in *Darkwater* (Originally published in 1920 by Harcourt, Brace and Company, New York), online at Project Gutenberg, https://www.gutenberg.org/files/15210/15210-h/15210-h.htm.

6. See Parris's "Introduction" to *Being Apart*.

7. *An Introduction to Africana Philosophy* (Cambridge: Cambridge University Press, 2008), 1–12.

8. Lanham: Rowman & Littlefield, 2021, viii.

9. Linda Martín Alcoff, *The Future of Whiteness* (University Park: Penn State University Press, 2015).

10. Studies of Whiteness are growing in the United States and in the UK. I return often to Sara Ahmed's path-breaking 2007 paper, "A Phenomenology of Whiteness," with its injunction: "If Whiteness gains currency by being unnoticed, then what does it mean to notice Whiteness?" (*Feminist Theory* [8] 2, August 2007, 149). Ahmed analyzes Whiteness in *Queer Phenomenology* (Durham: Duke University Press, 2006); *The Promise of Happiness* (Durham: Duke University Press, 2010); *Living a Feminist Life* (Durham: Duke University Press, 2017); and in her blog, *Feminiskilljoys.com*. Richard Dyer's book *White Essays on Race and Culture* (Abingdon: Routledge, 1997) is well-known. *Critical Race Theory in England* (Abingdon: Routledge, 2014), edited by Namita Chakrabarty, Lorna Roberts and John Preston asks if critical race theory imposes American categories to Europe. Shona Hunter's webpage *whitepages.org* is a resource featuring a preview of the *Routledge Handbook of Critical Whiteness Studies*, which she is co-editing with Christi van der Westhuizen. Besides those mentioned already, a large number of thinkers in the United States have made contributions to the analysis of Whiteness. These include Nell Irvin Painter, Dorothy Roberts, David Roediger, Michael Monahan, Veronica Watson, George Yancy, Shannon Sullivan, Tim Wise, Charles Mills, Naomi Zack, Richard Delgado, and Jean Stefancic, to name only a few. For an overview see Tim Engles, "Towards a Biography of Critical Whiteness Studies," *The Keep: Eastern Illinois Library*, November 2006.

11. Mabogo P. More, *Looking through Philosophy in Black* (Lanham: Rowman & Littlefield International, 2018), 146.

12. Roxanne Dunbar-Ortiz writes, "I refrain from using "America" and "American" when referring only to the United States and its citizens. Those blatantly imperialistic terms annoy people in the rest of the Western Hemisphere, who are, after all, also Americans. I use . . . 'US Americans' for its citizens." *An Indigenous People's History of the United States* (Boston: Beacon Press, 2014).

13. "Like everyone else, I really discovered jazz in America. Some countries have a national pastime and some do not. …. I learned in New York that jazz is a national pastime." Jean-Paul Sartre, "I Discovered Jazz in America," *Saturday Review*, November 29, 1947.

14. *Fugitive Tapes: Poetics of the Black Sonic Imagination* (unpublished manuscript, manuscript cited with permission of author), 200.

15. For a book that is closer to my theme of listening Whitely, see Loren Kajikawa's *Sounding Race in Rap Songs* (Oakland: University of California Press, 2015).

16. See Gene Santoro, *Myself When I Am Real: The Life and Music of Charles Mingus* (Oxford: Oxford University Press, 2000), 145.

17. See *Bad Faith and Anti-Black Racism* (Amherst: Humanity Books, 1995); *Her Majesty's Other Children* (Lanham: Rowman & Littlefield, 1997); *Existentia Africana: Understanding Africana Existential Thought* (Abingdon: Routledge, 2000); and *An Introduction to Africana Philosophy* (Cambridge: Cambridge University Press, 2008); and *What Fanon Said* (New York: Fordham Press, 2015).

18. *The Second Sex* (New York: Penguin, 1972), Introduction.

19. *Black Skins, White Masks* (London: Pluto Press, 1986), 36.

20. "Questions of Multiculturalism," in *The Postcolonial Critic: Interviews Strategies, Dialogues*, edited by Sarah Harasym, (Abingdon: Routledge, 1986), 59.

21. Beauvoir, *The Second Sex*, Introduction.

22. More, *Sartre on Contingency*, (Lanham: Rowman & Littlefield, 2021), 113.

23. Ibid.

24. "Négritude," *The Stanford Encyclopedia of Philosophy* (Summer 2018 Edition), Edward N. Zalta (ed.), https://plato.stanford.edu/archives/sum2018/entries/negritude/.

25. New York: French & European Publications, 2003, 13.

26. I was introduced to Manganyi's thought through More's treatment of him as an existential philosopher in *Sartre on Contingency*.

27. On the inadequacy of the notion of white "privilege," see Naomi Zack, *White Privilege and Black Rights: The Injustice of U.S. Police Racial Profiling and Homicide* (Lanham: Rowman & Littlefield, 2015), 3.

28. Du Bois, *Darkwater*, chapter two "The Souls of White Folk," at project Gutenberg, https://www.gutenberg.org/files/15210/15210-h/15210-h.htm.

29. *Wretched of the Earth* (New York: Grove Press, 2004), 5.

30. *Philosophy of Antifascism: Punching Nazis and Fighting White Supremacy* (Lanham: Rowman & Littlefield International, 2020), 13.

31. New York: Vintage, 1989.

32. Davis, *Blues People*, 141.

33. Sithole, *Fugitive Tapes*, 64.

34. Sithole, *Fugitive Tapes*, 110.

35. Quoted in Gene Santoro, *Myself When I Am Real: The Life and Music of Charles Mingus* (Oxford: Oxford University Press, 2000), 145.

36. Ibid.

37. I want to thank Michael Monahan for first suggesting to me the phrase "listening Whitely."

38. Fumi Okiji, *Jazz as Critique: Adorno and Black Expression Revisited* (Stanford: Stanford University Press, 2018). Kindle edition, Chapter 3.

39. Sara Ahmed, "A Phenomenology of Whiteness," *Feminist Theory* 8, no. 2 (August 2007): 149–68.

40. Durham: Duke University Press, 2006, 159.

41. Ahmed, "A Phenomenology of Whiteness," 150.

42. Ahmed, "Complaint as Diversity Work," November 11, 2017, https://feministkilljoys.com/2017/11/10/complaint-as-diversity-work/.

43. Ibid. In her speaking tours in 2018–2019, Ahmed further articulates the idea that complaint is diversity work; multiple versions of her talk are on YouTube.

44. Ahmed, "Complaint as Diversity Work," 2017.

45. http://nationalhumanitiescenter.org/pds/maai3/protest/text10/lockeartorpropaganda.pdf.

46. *Phenomenology of Chicana Experience & Identity: Communication and Transformation in Praxis* (Lanham: Rowman and Littlefield, 2000), ix.

47. Martinez, *Phenomenology of Chicana Experience*, xi.

48. Ibid.

49. Ibid.

50. Ibid.

51. Ibid.

52. *Listening and Voice* (Albany: SUNY Press, 1976/2007).

53. *Nose: The Political Economy of Music* (Minneapolis: University of Minnesota Press, 1977).

54. *Downcast Eyes* (Berkley: University of California Press, 1993).

55. *The Audible Past* (Durham: Duke University Press, 2003).

56. Ithaca: Cornell University Press, 1998.

57. *Blackness Visible: Essays on Philosophy and Race* (Ithaca: Cornell University Press, 1998).

58. Mills, *Blackness Visible*, 41. (Emphasis added)

59. Mills, *Blackness Visible*, 47.

60. Mills, *Blackness Visible*, 51.

61. Oxford: Oxford University Press, 2005.

62. Alcoff, *Visible Identities*, (Oxford: Oxford University Press, 2005), 51.

63. Cambridge: Polity, 2004.

64. Taylor, *Black Is Beautiful* (Oxford: Blackwell, 2016), 36.

65. Taylor, *Black Is Beautiful*, 45 and 48.

66. Lewis R. Gordon writes: "The dynamics of visibility and invisibility play important roles not only in Fanon's thought, but also in the whole corpus of phenomenological efforts to describe social reality." *Fanon and the Crisis of European Man* (New York: Routledge, 1995), 17.

67. Taylor, *Black Is Beautiful*, 48.

68. Baltimore: Johns Hopkins University Press, 2012.

69. Kara Keeling and Josh Kun, *Sound Clash* (Baltimore: Johns Hopkins University Press, 2012), 2.

70. Ibid.

71. Ibid.
72. Durham: Duke University Press, 2019.
73. Nina Sun Eidsheim, "Marian Anderson and 'Sonic Blackness' in American Opera," in *Sound Clash*, edited by Kara Keeling and Josh Kun, 221.
74. Sterne, *The Audible Past*, 14.
75. Ibid.
76. Sterne, *The Audible Past*, 22.
77. Sterne, *The Audible Past*, 33.
78. See Jean-Paul Sartre, *Critique of Dialectical Reason, Vol. 1* (London: Verso, 2006).
79. Sterne, *The Audible Past*, 14.
80. Sterne, *The Audible Past*, 15.
81. Keeling and Kun, *Sound Clash*, 6.
82. Germany: Springer-Verlag, 2012.
83. Navas, *Remix Theory*, 61.
84. Hebdige, Cut-n-Mix: *Culture, Identity and Caribbean Music* (Oxon: Comedia, 1987), 10.
85. Hebdige, *Cut-n-Mix*, 12.
86. Navas, *Remix Theory*, 14.
87. T Storm Heter, "Jazz," in *The Routledge Companion to Remix Studies*, edited by Eduardo Navas, Owen Gallagher, and xtine burrough (Abingdon: Routledge, 2015).
88. Tashima Thomas, "Race and Remix," in *The Routledge Companion to Remix Studies*.
89. Lanham: Lexington, 2010.
90. James, *The Conjectural Body*, 3.
91. James, *The Conjectural Body*, see chapter one.
92. Hampshire: Zero Books, 2015.
93. James, *Resistance and Melancholy*, 24.
94. James, *The Conjectural Body*, chapter one.
95. Ibid.
96. *Philosophy Compass*, January 18, 2013. https://doi.org/10.1111/phc3.12002.
97. James, "Oppression, Privilege, & Aesthetics."
98. James, "Oppression, Privilege, & Aesthetics."
99. Durham: Duke University Press, 2019.
100. James, *The Sonic Episteme*, chapter one.
101. Ibid.
102. Chicago: University of Chicago Press, 1996.
103. Monson, *Saying Something* (Chicago: University of Chicago Press, 1996), 102.
104. Oxford: Oxford University Press, 2007.
105. Monson, *Freedom Sounds* (Oxford: Oxford University Press, 2007), 246.
106. Cambridge: Cambridge University Press, 2003.
107. See Paul Austerlitz, "Jazz Consciousness," in *A Companion to African-American Studies*, edited by Lewis Gordon and Jane Anna Gordon (Malden: Blackwell, 2006). Austerlitz writes: "Bach and Mozart were both improvisers as well as composers," 211. In *Her Majesty's Other Children*, Lewis Gordon writes, "Bach,

in spite of the complexity of his fugues, wrote many of them spontaneously and grooved. Mozart and Beethoven did the same. But European classical music eventually collapsed, in European society's quest for order, into a leader-led relation," 220.

108. There are many cases, but to take one: Agustín Barrios Mangoré (1885–1944) the Paraguayan composer and classical guitarist virtuoso, often improvised during his live guitar performances. There are improvisational practices in many classical, nonclassical, popular, religious, and folk musical forms coming out of the North American, Afro-Caribbean, Caribbean, Latin American, and African contexts, to name only those in the Atlantic world.

109. New York: Routledge, 2018.

110. Gracyk, Brown, and Goldblatt, *Jazz and the Philosophy of Art*, 123.

111. Gracyk, Brown, and Goldblatt, *Jazz and the Philosophy of Art*, 132.

112. Gracyk, Brown, and Goldblatt, *Jazz and the Philosophy of Art*, 98.

113. "They quote the White onlooker from 1825: "Ajona, [was] a lithe, tall Black woman, with a body waving and undulating like Zoso's snake. …. Under the passion of the hour, the women tore off their garments, and entirely nude, went on dancing, but wriggling like snakes." Gracyk, Brown, and Goldblatt, *Jazz and the Philosophy of Art*, 98.

114. *Different Drummers: Rhythm & Race in the Americas* (Berkeley: University of California Press, 2010).

115. Munro, *Different Drummers*, 98.

116. Munro, *Different Drummers*, 24.

117. I draw extensively on Kathy J. Ogren's book *The Jazz Revolution: Twenties America and the Meaning of Jazz* (Oxford: Oxford University Press, 1992), which traces the moral panic over jazz expressed in White journalism of the 1920s. Ogren has deeply informed my understanding of the White public's navigation of the birth of jazz.

118. Ted Gioia, "Jazz and the Primitivist Myth," *Musical Quarterly* 73, no. 1 (1989): 130–43.

119. *Culture on the Margins: The Black Spiritual and the Rise of American Cultural Interpretation* (New Brunswick: Princeton University Press, 1999).

120. *Lying Up a Nation: Race and Black Music* (Chicago: University of Chicago, 2003).

121. *Race Music: Black Cultures from Bebop to Hip-Hop* (Berkeley: University of California Press, 2003).

122. *Phonographies* (Durham: Duke University Press, 2005).

123. *Segregating Sound* (Durham: Duke University Press, 2010).

124. Oxford: Oxford University Press, 1993.

125. Disidentification is, of course, Munoz's term, not Lott's. See *Disidentifications*, José Esteban Muñoz (Minneapolis: University of Minnesota Press, 1999).

126. Urbana: University of Illinois Press, 2008.

127. Fanon, *Black Skin, White Masks* (New York: Grove Press, 2008), 10.

128. *The Man Who Adores the Negro* (Urbana: University of Illinois Press, 2008), 177.

129. Cambridge, MA: Harvard University Press, 2012.

130. Kelley, *Africa Speaks* (Cambridge, MA: Harvard University Press, 2012), 5.

131. New York: The Free Press, 2010.

132. Kelley, *Thelonious Monk* (New York: The Free Press, 2010), Prelude.
133. Middletown: Wesleyan University Press, 1994.
134. New York: Basic Books, 2008.
135. Rose, *The Hip Hop Wars*, 5.
136. Sterne, *The Audible Past*, 4.
137. Fanon, *Black Skin, White Mask*, 109.
138. Fanon, *Black Skin, White Mask*, 110.
139. Minneapolis: University of Minnesota Press, 2014.
140. London: Pluto Press, 2011.
141. Dabashi, *Brown Skin, White Masks*, 6.
142. Dabashi, *Brown Skin, White Masks*, 36.
143. Oforlea, "[Un]veiling the White Gaze," *Western Journal of Black Studies* 36, no. 4 (2012): 290.
144. Oforlea, "[Un]veiling the White Gaze," 291.
145. New York: Schocken, 1995.
146. Gordon, *Fanon and the Crisis of European Man*, 27.
147. *White Privilege and Black Rights* (Lanham: Rowman and Littlefield, 2015), 8–9.
148. *Faulkner, Mississippi* (Chicago: University of Chicago Press, 2000), 30.
149. Berkeley: University of California Press, 1950.
150. Cambridge: Da Capo Press, 1960.
151. *Creolizing Political Theory: Reading Rousseau through Fanon* (New York: Fordham University Press, 2011).
152. *The Creolizing Subject* (New York: Fordham Press, 2011).
153. See the homepage of the book series here: https://www.rowmaninternational.com/our-books/series/creolizing-the-canon.
154. "Kansas City, Missouri, a cradle of jazz, along with New Orleans, Chicago, and New York, bred a distinct style of jazz that swiftly grew from ragtime to bebop. …. Surprisingly little scholarship has been devoted to the developments of Kansas City jazz." Fank Driggs and Chuck Haddix, *Kansas City Jazz: From Ragtime to Bebop* (Oxford: Oxford University Press, 2005), ix.
155. *Faulkner, Mississippi* (Chicago: University of Chicago Press, 2000), 196.
156. Charlottesville: University of Virginia Press, 2015, Kindle edition, chapter 4, location 3081.
157. *Caribbean Discourse: Selected Essays* (Charlottesville: University of Virginia Press), 140–1.
158. Durham: Duke University Press, 1997.
159. Glissant, *Faulkner Mississippi,* 196.
160. "Caribbean and Creole in New Orleans," in *American Creoles: The Francophone Caribbean and the American South*, edited by Martin Munro and Celia Britton (Liverpool: Liverpool University Press, 2012).
161. New York: Harper Perennial, 1999.
162. In Jacqueline Emry, "Writing to Belong," *Legacy: A Journal of American Women Writers* 33, no. 2 (2016): 286–309.
163. Omaha: Backwaters Press, 2011, 1.

164. Low, *Natural Theologies*, 10.
165. Charlottesville: University of Virginia Press, 2015, Kindle edition, chapter 4, location 2677.
166. *Being and Insurrection: Existential Liberation Critique, Sketches and Ruptures* (New York: Cannae Press, 2019), 72.
167. In 1982 she coedited the Black feminist anthology *All the Women Are White, All the Blacks Are Men, But Some of Us Are Brave* (New York: The Feminist Press at CUNY, 1993) along with Patricia Bell-Scott, and Barbara Smith.

CHAPTER 2

1. Dorothy Roberts, *Fatal Invention: How Science, Politics, and Big Business Re-Create Race in the Twenty-First Century* (New York and London: The New Press, 2012).
2. See Amiri Baraka's piece "Classical American Music," in *Digging: The Afro-American Soul of American Classical Music* (Berkeley: University of California Press, 2009).
3. Jon Panish, *The Color of Jazz: Race and Representation in Postwar American Culture* (Jackson: University of Mississippi Press, 1997), iv.
4. Ibid.
5. Du Bois, *Darkwater*, chapter 2 "The Souls of White Folk," at project Gutenberg, https://www.gutenberg.org/files/15210/15210-h/15210-h.htm.
6. *Sound Clash: Listening to American Studies* (Baltimore: The Johns Hopkins University Press, 2012), 2.
7. Morroe Berger, "Resistance to the Diffusion of a Culture-Pattern," *Journal of Negro History* 32, no. 4 (October 1947): 470.
8. David Grazian, *Blue Chicago: The Search for Authenticity in Urban Blues Clubs* (Chicago: University of Chicago Press, 2003), 29.
9. In Kathy J. Ogren, *The Jazz Revolution* (Oxford: Oxford University Press, 1898), 474.
10. Ibid.
11. Berger, "Resistance to the Diffusion of a Culture-Pattern."
12. *Look, a White! Philosophical Essays on Whiteness* (Philadelphia: Temple University Press, 2012), 5.
13. Ogren, *The Jazz Revolution*, 77.
14. Quoted in Eric Lott, "Mr. Clemens and Jim Crow: Twain, Race and Blackface," in *The Cambridge Companion to Mark Twain*, edited by Forrest G. Robinson (Cambridge: Cambridge University Press, 1995), 129.
15. In Lawrence Gushee, *Pioneers of Jazz: The Story of the Creole Band* (Oxford: Oxford University Press, 2005), 105.
16. In Gushee, *Pioneers of Jazz*, 129.
17. In Gushee, *Pioneers of Jazz*, 105.
18. Ibid.
19. In Gushee, *Pioneers of Jazz*, 107.

20. In Gushee, *Pioneers of Jazz*, 187.
21. In Gushee, *Pioneers of Jazz*, 112.
22. *Humbug: The Art of P.T. Barnum* (Chicago: University of Chicago Press, 1973).
23. Gushee, *Pioneers of Jazz*, 202.
24. Gushee, *Pioneers of Jazz*, 230.
25. Ibid.
26. Ibid.
27. Gushee, *Pioneers of Jazz*, 202.
28. Ibid.
29. Ibid.
30. Gushee, *Pioneers of Jazz*, 142.
31. Sieglinde Lemnke, *Primitivist Modernism: Black Culture and the Origins of Transatlantic Modernism* (Oxford: Oxford University Press, 1998), 67.
32. David Meltzer, *Reading Jazz* (San Francisco: Mercury House, 1993), 117.
33. Lawrence W. Levine, *Highbrow/Lowbrow* (Cambridge, MA: Harvard University Press, 1988), 134.
34. Neil Leonard, *Jazz and the White Americans: The Acceptance of a New Art Form* (Chicago: University of Chicago Press, 1962), 79.
35. Leonard, *Jazz and the White Americans*, 79.
36. William H. Kenney, *Chicago Jazz: A Cultural History, 1904–1930* (New York: Oxford University Press, 1993), 79.
37. Paul Allen Anderson, *Deep River: Music and Memory in Harlem Renaissance Thought* (Durham: Duke University Press, 2001), 233.
38. Jeffrey Magee, *The Uncrowned King of Swing: Fletcher Henderson and Big Band Jazz* (Oxford: Oxford University Press, 2005), 37.
39. Ogren, *The Jazz Revolution*, 155.
40. Anderson, *Deep River*, 245.
41. Leonard, *Jazz and the White Americans*, 85.
42. "On Intersectionality and Cultural Appropriation: The Case of Postmillenial Black Hipness," *Journal of Black Masculinity* 1, no. 2 (2011).
43. *No Respect: Intellectuals and Popular Culture* (Abington: Routledge, 1989).
44. "The Problem with White Hipness: Race, Gender, and Cultural Conceptions in Jazz Historical Discourse," *Journal of the American Musicological Society* 48, no. 3 (Autumn 1995): 396–422.
45. Mezz Mezzrow and Bernard Wolf, *Really the Blues* (New York: Random House, 1946), 53.
46. Mezzrow, *Really the Blues*, 112.
47. Mezzrow, *Really the Blues*, 18.
48. Mezzrow, *Really the Blues*, 204.
49. Mezzrow, *Really the Blues*, 18.
50. Mezzrow, *Really the Blues*, 83.
51. https://books.google.com/ngrams/graph?corpus=26&content=corny&smoothing=3&year_end=2019&year_start=1800&direct_url=t1%3B%2Ccorny%3B%2Cc0#t1%3B%2Ccorny%3B%2Cc00.

52. https://www.etymonline.com/word/corny.
53. Mezzrow, *Really the Blues*, 54.
54. Mezzrow, *Really the Blues*, 14.
55. Mezzrow, *Really the Blues*, 14 and 146.
56. Mezzrow, *Really the Blues*, 146.
57. Gillian Mitchel, *The North American Folk Music Revival* (Farnham: Ashgate, 2016). See the Introduction.
58. *Last Cavalier: The Life and Times of John A. Lomax* (Champaign: University of Illinois Press, 2001).
59. Porterfield, *Last Cavalier*, 342.
60. https://en.wikipedia.org/wiki/Skip_James (accessed 7/17/20).
61. Katy Martin, "The Preoccupations of Mr. Lomax Inventor of the 'Inventor of Jazz,'" *Popular Music and Society* 36, no. 1 (2013), 30–39.
62. *The Creolizing Subject: Race, Reason, and the Politics of Purity* (New York: Fordham University Press, 2011).
63. *Mister Jelly Roll: The Fortunes of Jelly Roll Morton, New Orleans Creole and "Inventor of Jazz"* (Berkeley: University of California Press, 1950).
64. Aaron Oforlea, "[Un]veiling the White Gaze: Revealing Self and Other in the Land Where the Blues Began," *Western Journal of Black Studies* 36, no. 4 (2012), 289–94.
65. Oforlea, "[Un]veiling the White Gaze," 291.
66. Oforlea, "[Un]veiling the White Gaze," 299.
67. Antoinette Burton, *Archive Stories: Facts, Fictions and the Writing of History* (Durham: Duke University Press, 2005), 8.
68. Burton, *Archive Stories*, 8.
69. Burton, *Archive Stories*, 7.
70. Ibid.
71. Lomax, *Mister Jelly Roll*, 299.
72. Champaign: University of Illinois Press, 2008.
73. Mullen, *The Man Who Adores the Negro*, 66–7.
74. Burton, *Archive Stories*, 7.
75. Burton, *Archive Stories*, 8.
76. Burton, *Archive Stories*, 9.
77. Oforlea, "[Un]veiling the White Gaze," 299.
78. Leonard Feather, *The Book of Jazz* (New York: Random House, 1976), 40–41.
79. Feather, *The Book of Jazz*, 124–29.
80. Ibid.
81. Feather, *The Book of Jazz*, 129.
82. Ibid.
83. Feather, *The Book of Jazz*, 111, emphasis in original.
84. Feather, *The Book of Jazz*, 129.
85. Feather, *The Book of Jazz*, 48.
86. Ibid.
87. Ibid.

88. Richard M. Sudhalter, *Lost Chords: White Musicians and Their Contributions to Jazz, 1915–1945* (New York: Oxford University Press, 1999).

89. Randall Sandke, *Where the Dark and the Light Folks Meet* (Lanham: The Scarecrow Press, 2010).

90. Sudhalter, *Lost Chords*, 7.

91. William H. Youngren, "Black and White Intertwined," *Atlantic* 283, no. 2 (February 1999): 86–88.

92. John Hoberman, "Darwin's Athletes," in *Doing Real World Research in Sports Studies*, edited by Andy Smith and Ivan Wadddington (London: Routledge, 2014), 45.

93. Sudhalter, *Lost Chords*, vxii.

94. Sudhalter, *Lost Chords*, xvi.

95. Ibid.

96. Sudhalter, *Lost Chords*, 11.

97. Sudhalter, *Lost Chords*, 746.

98. Randke, *Where the Dark and the Light Folks Meet*, 6.

99. *The Signifying Monkey: A Theory of African-American Literary Criticism* (Oxford: Oxford University Press, 1988).

100. Baraka shows that the call-and-response of Black mu—work songs, blues, jazz, and spirituals—was rooted in an older tradition of oral communication in West Africa. He suggests how the call-and-response was an improvisatory structure of music and communication in which "answers are usually comments on the leader's theme or comments on the answers themselves in the improvised verses. The amount of improvisation depends on how long the chorus wishes to continue," Baraka, *Blues People* (New York: Harper Collins, 1999), 26.

101. Gilroy writes that call-and-response is "the structure that hosts" the "intense and often bitter dialogues which make the black arts movement move." Paul Gilroy, *The Black Atlantic: Modernity and Double Consciousness* (Cambridge, MA: Harvard University Press, 2000), 79.

102. David W. Music and Paul Akers Richardson, *"I Will Sing the Wondrous Story": A History of Baptist Hymnody in North America*, 1st ed. (Macon, GA: Mercer University Press, 2008), 88–89.

103. Ibid.

104. Ihde, *Listening and Voice: Phenomenologies of Sound* (Albany: State University of New York Press, 2007), 229.

105. Vivian Sobchak, "Simple Grounds: At Home in Experience," in *Postphenomenology: A Critical Companion to Ihde*, edited by Evan Selinger (Albany: State University of New York Press), 13.

106. Ihde, *Listening and Voice*, 16.

107. Ibid.

108. Cambridge: Belknap Press of Harvard, 1989.

109. Tricia Rose, *Black Noise: Rap Music and Black Culture in Contemporary America* (Middletown: Wesleyan University Press, 1994).

110. Ihde, *Listening and Voice*, 217.

111. Ihde, *Listening and Voice*, 78.

112. Ibid.

113. I admit that there are also many counter-examples to my claim that jazz requires noisy listening, such as the "please do not speak during the performance" signs that recently appeared on every table at my local jazz club, The Deerhead Inn in Water Gap, Pennsylvania. *The Green Mill* in Chicago also has a rigid policy on not talking during performances, enforced by a bouncer.

114. Katharine S. Bullard, *Civilizing the Child: Discourses of Race, Nation and Child Welfare in America* (Lanham: Lexington, 2013). See also Seth Koven, *Slumming: Sexual and Social Politics in Victorian London* (Princeton: Princeton University Press, 2004).

115. Bullard, *Civilizing the Child*, 1–8.

116. *Imperial Eyes: Travel Writing and Transculturation* (London: Routledge, 1992), 4.

117. Lanham: Lexington, 2019, Kindle Edition, location 42.

118. Nya, *Simone de Beauvoir and the Colonial Experience*, 190.

119. *Civilizing the Child: Discourses of Race, Nation and, Child Welfare in America* (Lexington: Lexington Books, 2012), 12.

120. *Burdens of Empire: British Feminists, Indian Women, and Imperial Culture, 1865–1915* (Chapel Hill: University of North Carolina Press, 1994), 1.

121. *A Small Place* (New York: Macmillan 1988).

122. I worked with two translations of Beauvoir, the older being *America Day by Day*, translated by Patrick Dudley (London: Gerald Duckworth & Co, 1952), and also the updated translation by Carol Cosman (Berkeley: University of California Press, 1999). I will indicate which quotes from which translation. Dudley translation, 15.

123. Beauvoir, *America Day by Day*, Dudley translation, 32.

124. Margaret A. Simons, "Beauvoir and the Problem of Racism," in *Philosophers on Race: Critical Issues*, edited by Julie K. Ward and Tommy L. Lott (Oxford: Blackwell, 2002).

125. Simone de Beauvoir, *The Second Sex* (New York: Vintage, 1949), 8–9.

126. Kathryn Sophia Belle (Kathryn T. Gines), "Sartre, Beauvoir, and the Race/Gender Analogy: A Case for Black Feminist Philosophy," in *Convergences: Black Feminism and Continental Philosophy*, edited by Maria del Guadalupe Davidson, Kathryn Sophia Belle (Kathryn T. Gines), Donna-Dale Marcano Albany: State University of New York, 2010), 59.

127. *Sartre Studies International* (2003) Vol. 9, no. 2: 55–67.

128. *Converges: Black Feminism and Continental Philosophy*, edited by Maria del Guadalupe Davidson, Kathryn T. Gines, and Donna-Dale L. Marcano (Albany: State University of New York Press, 2010), 51.

129. *Sartre Studies International* 17, no. 2 (2011): 42–59.

130. *Hannah Arendt and the Negro Question* (Bloomington: Indiana University Press, 2014).

131. Belle, *Hannah Arendt and the Negro Question*, 2.

132. Beauvoir, *America Day by Day*, Dudley translation, 186.

133. Beauvoir, *America Day by Day*, Dudley translation, 50.

134. Beauvoir, *America Day by Day*, Dudley translation, 33.

135. Ibid.
136. Linda Martín Alcoff, *The Future of Whiteness* (Hoboken: Wiley, 2015), 139.
137. Sara Ahmed, *Living a Feminist Life* (Durham: Duke University Press, 2017), "Conclusion 2: A Killjoy Manifesto." See also Ahmed's entry "Smile!" at her blog: https://feministkilljoys.com/2017/02/02/smile/.
138. Beauvoir, *America Day by Day*, Cosman translation, 34.
139. Beauvoir, *America Day by Day*, Cosman translation, 245.
140. I have written about this elsewhere. See my piece "Beauvoir's White Problem," published at the blog *Chère Simone de Beauvoir* on January 24, 2021. https://lirecrire.hypotheses.org/3404. I thank Marine Rouch for her insights and help on this topic.
141. Beauvoir, *America Day by Day*, Dudley translation, 45.
142. Ibid.
143. Beauvoir, *America Day by Day*, Dudley translation, 60.
144. Beauvoir, *America Day by Day*, Dudley translation, 205.
145. Ibid.
146. Beauvoir, *America Day by Day*, Dudley translation, 60.
147. Beauvoir, *America Day by Day*, Dudley translation, 45.
148. Beauvoir, *America Day by Day*, Dudley translation, 205.
149. Ibid.
150. Ibid.
151. Ibid.
152. Ibid.
153. Beauvoir, *America Day by Day*, Dudley translation, 35.
154. Beauvoir, *America Day by Day*, Dudley translation, 34.
155. Ibid.
156. Ibid.
157. Ibid.
158. Beauvoir, *America Day by Day*, Dudley translation, 35.
159. Ibid.
160. Beauvoir, *America Day by Day*, Dudley translation, 211.
161. Ibid.
162. New York: Farrar, Strauss and Giroux, 2016 [1997].
163. Williams, *Seeing a Colorblind Future* (New York: Farrar, Strauss and Giroux, 2016 [1997]), 28.
164. Williams, *Seeing a Colorblind Future*, 24.
165. Alcoff, *The Future of Whiteness*, 170.
166. Alcoff, *The Future of Whiteness*, 154.

LISTENING EXERCISES FOR CHAPTER 2

1. Famously the jazz musician Bill Evans who composed "Take Five," one of the first songs to introduce mainstream White audiences to complex meter, was inspired by folk musicians improvising in five during a tour of Europe.

2. *Riddim: Claves of African Origin* (Columbus: Music in Motion Films, Ltd., 2008).
3. Maurice Peress, *Dvorak to Duke Ellington: A Conductor Explores America's Music and Its African American Roots* (Oxford: Oxford University Press, 2008), 86.
4. "Space invader" is Nirmal Puwar's excellent term. Nirmal Puwar, *Space Invaders: Race, Gender and Bodies Out of Place* (Oxford: Berg, 2004).
5. This quote is from an episode of Questlove's podcast, *Questlove Supreme*. https://www.iheart.com/podcast/1119-questlove-supreme-53194211/episode/robert-glasper-71208792/.
6. Ken Burns, *Jazz*, miniseries on PBS, 2001.
7. https://www.youtube.com/watch?v=kIf6POCfRZg&t=70s.
8. https://www.youtube.com/watch?v=Zdj0pmQMTQI.
9. Ibid.

CHAPTER 3

1. Bechet, *Treat It Gentle* (Cambridge: Da Capo Press, 1960). Kindle edition, Location 2777. I thank Lewis Gordon in personal conversation for emphasizing the importance of treating Africana and Creole thinkers as existentialists and theorists in their own right, rather than thinking of them as derivative from European existential thinkers.
2. http://davidliebman.com/home/new_releases/petite-fleur-the-music-of-sidney-bechet/.
3. *Lost Sounds: Blacks and the Birth of the Recording Industry, 1890–1919* (Urbana: University of Illinois Press, 2010).
4. Bechet, *Treat It Gentle*, 2272.
5. Ibid.
6. Bechet, *Treat It Gentle*, 2777.
7. Bechet, *Treat It Gentle*, 73.
8. Ibid.
9. Ibid.
10. Bechet, *Treat It Gentle*, 74.
11. Bechet, *Treat It Gentle*, 1319.
12. bell hooks, *Black Looks: Race and Representation* (Boston: South End Press, 1992).
13. Bechet, *Treat It Gentle*, 73.
14. Ibid.
15. Bechet, *Treat It Gentle*, 97.
16. *Blues People: Negro Music in White America* (New York: Harper, 1999), 142.
17. Robin Kelley, "Notes on Deconstructing 'The Folk,'" *American Historical Review* 97, no. 5 (December 1992): 1402.
18. New York: Humanity Books, 1999.
19. Ahmed, *Queer Phenomenology* (New York: Humanity Books, 1999), 24.
20. Bechet, *Treat It Gentle*, 234.

21. Ibid.
22. Ibid.
23. Ahmed, *Queer Phenomenology*, 83.
24. Martin Munro, *Different Drummers: Rhythm & Race in the Americas* (Berkley: University of California Press, 2013), 43.
25. Martin Munro, *Different Drummers*, 44.
26. Sara Ahmed, *The Promise of Happiness* (Durham: Duke University Press, 2010), 29.
27. Bechet, *Treat It Gentle*, 555.
28. Ibid.
29. Bechet, *Treat It Gentle*, 540.
30. Ibid.
31. Ibid.
32. John McCusker, *Creole Trombone: Kid Ory and the Early Years of Jazz* (Jackson: University of Mississippi Press, 2012), 151.
33. McCusker, *Creole Trombone*, 69.
34. McCusker, *Creole Trombone*, 16.
35. McCusker, *Creole Trombone*, 108.
36. . McCusker, *Creole Trombone*, 130.
37. Gushee, *Jazz Pioneers*, 85.
38. Gushee, *Jazz Pioneers*, 139.
39. McCusker, *Creole Trombone*, 135.
40. McCusker, *Creole Trombone*, 159–61.
41. McCusker, *Creole Trombone*, 159.
42. McCusker, *Creole Trombone*, 19.
43. Ibid.
44. McCusker, *Creole Trombone*, 37.
45. McCusker, *Creole Trombone*, 41.
46. McCusker, *Creole Trombone*, 48.
47. Ibid.
48. Chicago: University of Chicago Press, 2015.
49. Kid Ory and his Creole Jazz Band, October 12, 1946. Columbia Records 37275.
50. https://archives.library.illinois.edu/archon/?p=creators/creator&id=2892.
51. John Chilton, *Sidney Bechet: Wizard of Jazz* (New York: Da Capo Press, 1996), 30.
52. McCusker, *Creole Trombone*, 12.
53. Gushee, *Pioneers of Jazz* (Oxford: Oxford University Press, 2010), 187.
54. Gushee, *Pioneers of Jazz*, 186.
55. Cambridge: Belknap Press of Harvard, 2017.
56. Gushee, *Pioneers of Jazz*, 281–2.
57. Rein T. Fertel, *Imagining the Creole City* (Baton Rouge: Louisiana State University Press, 2014), 12.
58. http://nobee.jplibrary.net. The library has issues of the *Bee* from September 1827 to December 1923.

59. The archives of the Bee are here: https://web.archive.org/web/20090427135557/; http://www.lib.lsu.edu/special/exhibits/creole/Institution/institution.html.
60. Gretna: Firebird Press, 1929.
61. Caulfeild, *The French Literature of Louisiana* (Gretna: Firebird Press, 1929), xi.
62. Édouard Glissant, *Faulkner/Mississippi* (Chicago: University of Chicago, 2000), 29.
63. J. Michael Dash, "Relating Islands: The South of the South in Americas," *Southern Quarterly* 55, no. 4 (Summer 2018): 130–42.
64. New York: Fordham University Press, 2011.
65. Glissant, *Faulkner/Mississippi*, 79.
66. Glissant, *Faulkner/Mississippi*, 69.
67. The subtitle of Monahan's book *The Creolizing Subject: Race, Reason and the Politics of Purity*.
68. Glissant, *Faulkner/Mississippi*, 197.
69. Glissant, *Faulkner/Mississippi*, 85.
70. Glissant, *Faulkner/Mississippi*, 86.
71. Glissant, *Poetics of Relation*, 29.
72. Charlottesville: University Press of Virginia, 1989.
73. Ann Arbor: University of Michigan Press, 1997.
74. Glissant, *Caribbean Discourse*, 111.
75. Glissant, *Caribbean Discourse*, 140–41.
76. Glissant, *Poetics of Relation*, 35.
77. Ibid.
78. Glissant, *Poetics of Relation*, 68.
79. Guillermina De Ferrrari, "The Ship, the Plantation, and the Polis: Reading Gilroy and Glissant as Moral Philosophy," *Comparative Literature Studies* 49, no. 2 (2012): 186.
80. Glissant, *Poetics of Relation*, 69.
81. Glissant, *Poetics of Relation*, 73.
82. "These musical expressions born of silence: Negro spirituals and blues, persisting in towns and growing cities; jazz, biguines, and calypsos, bursting into barrios and shantytowns; salsas and reggaes, assembled everything blunt and direct, painfully stifled, and patiently differed into this varied speech. This was the cry of the Plantation, transfigured into the speech of the world." Glissant, *Poetics of Relation*, 73.
83. Ibid.

LISTENING EXERCISES FOR CHAPTER 3

1. *Cut 'n' Mix: Culture, Identity and Caribbean Music* (London: Comedia/Metheun, 1987).
2. https://www.youtube.com/watch?v=CVozz4HOL8A&list=RDxQkSfXnljvM&index=7.

3. *Remix Theory: The Aesthetics of Sampling* (New York: Springer, 2012), 155.
4. Blogpost, "Hey Pat, What Do You Think of Kenny G," https://blogcritics.org/hey-pat-what-do-you-think/.
5. Ibid.
6. https://www.youtube.com/watch?v=xQkSfXnljvM.
7. https://www.loc.gov/resource/gottlieb.09731.0?r=-0.912,-0.068,2.824,1.145,0.

CHAPTER 4

1. London: Routledge, 2006, preface.
2. Ibid.
3. Jane Anna Gordon and Lewis R. Gordon, *Not Only the Master's Tools* (London: Routledge, 2006), preface.
4. Ibid.
5. Ibid.
6. Charlottesville: University of Virginia Press, 2015, see chapter three.
7. "Worlds and Knowledges Otherwise," *Volume One: Dossier Three: Post-Continental Philosophy*, October 1, 2006, 5. (Originally published in *CLR James Journal*, Volume 1: Number 11, Summer 2005.)
8. Ibid.
9. Lewis R. Gordon, *Fanon and the Crisis of European Man* (New York: Routledge, 1995), 44.
10. Ibid.
11. Du Bois, *Darkwater*, chapter two, "The Souls of White Folk," at Project Gutenberg, https://www.gutenberg.org/files/15210/15210-h/15210-h.htm.
12. Gordon, *Fanon and the Crisis of European Man*, 27.
13. Frantz Fanon, *Black Skin, White Masks* (New York: Grove Press, 2008), 73. Italics in the original.
14. Gordon, *Fanon and the Crisis of European Man*, 26.
15. See Mabogo Percy More, *Biko: Philosophy, Identity and Liberation* (Cape Town: HSRC Press, 2017).
16. Lewis R. Gordon, "Hansberry's Tragic Search for Postcoloniality," *Her Majesty's Other Children: Sketches of Racism from a Neocolonial Age* (Lanham: Rowman & Littlefield, 1997), 153.
17. *Ebony*, August 1965, 29–34.
18. More, *Biko*, 116.
19. More, *Biko*, 117.
20. Ibid.
21. Du Bois, *The Souls of Black Folk* (New York: Penguin Books, 1996), "The Afterthought."
22. Parris, *Being Apart* (Charlottesville: University of Virginia Press, 2015), 211.
23. This same pattern can be seen in professional sports in the United States, where Black athletes are praised for their "gifts" and White athletes are praised for their "hard work."

24. London: Humanity, 1995, 15.
25. More, *Sartre on Contingency* (Lanham: Rowman & Littlefield, 2021), 118.
26. More, *Sartre on Contingency*, 117.
27. Lewis Gordon, *Her Majesty's Other Children*, 216.
28. Ibid.
29. Gordon, *Her Majesty's Other Children*, 219.
30. Gordon, *Her Majesty's Other Children*, 235.
31. Gordon, *Her Majesty's Other Children*, 217.
32. Ibid.
33. Lanham: Rowman & Littlefield International, 2019, 138. Emphasis added.
34. More, *Looking through Philosophy in Black* (Lanham: Rowman & Littlefield International, 2019), 147.
35. *The Souls of White Folk* (Jackson: University Press of Mississippi, 2013), Introduction.
36. Du Bois, *Darkwater*, chapter two "The Souls of White Folk," at Project Gutenberg, https://www.gutenberg.org/files/15210/15210-h/15210-h.htm.
37. Du Bois, *Darkwater*, chapter two, "The Souls of White Folk."
38. Ibid.
39. Ibid.
40. Ibid.
41. Ibid.
42. Ibid.
43. Ibid.
44. Ibid.
45. Du Bois, *Souls*, Afterthought.
46. Du Bois, *Souls*, 148.
47. Du Bois, *Souls*, 3.
48. Du Bois, *Souls*, 148.
49. Ibid.
50. Du Bois, *Souls*, 150.
51. Du Bois, *Souls*, 133.
52. Ibid.
53. Du Bois, *Souls*, 3.
54. "He hears so little that there almost seems to be a conspiracy of silence; the morning papers seldom mention it" (Du Bois, *Souls*, 148).
55. Ibid.
56. Nirmal Puwar, *Space Invaders: Race, Gender and Bodies Out of Place* (Oxford: Berg Publishers, 2004).
57. Du Bois, *Souls*, 185.
58. Fanon, *Black Skin, White Masks*, 154.
59. Frantz Fanon, *Wretched of the Earth* (New York: Grove Press, 1963), 243.
60. Fanon, *Black Skin, White Masks*, 117.
61. Fanon, *Black Skin, White Masks*, 161.
62. Fanon, *Black Skin, White Masks*, 96.
63. Sara Ahmed, *On Being Included: Racism and Diversity in Institutional Life* (Durham: Duke University Press, 2012), 33.

64. Ahmed, *On Being Included*, 170.
65. https://cdn.ymaws.com/www.apaonline.org/resource/resmgr/data_on_profession/fy2018-demographic_statistic.pdf.
66. Philadelphia: Temple University Press, 2012.
67. *The Black Register: Essays on Blackness and the Politics of Being* (Cambridge: Polity, 2020), 180.
68. New York: Vintage Books, 1998.
69. Frederick Douglass and Angela Y. Davis, *Narrative of the Life of Frederick Douglass, an American Slave, Written by Himself* (San Francisco: City Lights Books, 2010), 46.
70. *Notebooks for an Ethics* (Chicago: University of Chicago Press, 1992), Sartre makes "the appeal" a cornerstone of his analysis of human relations and obligations to others. Craig Materrese notes that "Sartre describes the way musicians seem to be addressing the audience: 'They are speaking to best part of you, the toughest, the freest.'" Craig Materrese, "Jazz Is Like a Banana." In *Severally Seeking Sartre*, edited by Benedict O'Donohoe (Newcastle upon Tyne: Cambridge Scholars Press, 2012), 57.
71. Davis, *Blues Legacies and Black Feminism* (New York: Vintage Books, 1998), xii.
72. Ibid.
73. Davis, *Blues Legacies and Black Feminism*, xvii.
74. Davis, *Blues Legacies and Black Feminism*, 141. Emphasis added.
75. Robin Kelley, "Notes on Deconstructing 'The Folk,'" *American Historical Review* 97, no. 5 (December 1992): 1406.
76. bell hooks, *Black Looks* (Boston: South End Press, 1992).
77. hooks, *Black Looks*, 165.
78. Watson, *The Souls of White Folk*, 2768.
79. hooks, *Black Looks*, 30.
80. hooks, *Black Looks*, 16.
81. hooks, *Black Looks*, 21.
82. hooks, *Black Looks*, 166.
83. hooks, *Black Looks*, 29.
84. hooks, *Black Looks*, 26.
85. Frederick Douglass, Philip Sheldon Foner, and Yuval Taylor, *Frederick Douglass: Selected Speeches and Writings* (Chicago: Lawrence Hill Books, 1999).
86. Paul Allen Anderson, *Deep River: Music and Memory in Harlem Renaissance Thought* (Durham: Duke University Press, 2001), 221.
87. Alain Locke, *The Negro and His Music* (Washington: The Publication in Negro Folk Education, 1936), 70.
88. Locke, *The Negro and His Music*, 9.
89. Locke, *The Negro and His Music*, 112.
90. Locke, *The Negro and His Music*, 89.
91. Locke, *The Negro and His Music*, 87.
92. Locke, *The Negro and His Music*, 134.
93. Ibid.
94. Locke, *The Negro and His Music*, 135.

95. Ibid.
96. Locke, *The Negro and His Music*, 90.
97. Leonard Harris, "The Great Debate: W. E. B. Du Bois vs. Alain Locke on the Aesthetic," *Philosophia Africana* 7, no. 1 (March 2004): 15–39.
98. Locke, *The Negro and His Music*, 88.
99. Locke, *The Negro and His Music*, 259.
100. Locke, *The Negro and His Music*, 261.
101. Locke, *The Negro and His Music*, 210.
102. Locke, *The Negro and His Music*, 8.
103. Ibid.
104. Ibid.
105. Locke, *The Negro and His Music*, 132.
106. Ibid.
107. Alain Locke, ed., *The New Negro* (New York: Simon & Schuster, 1992), 254.
108. Locke, *The Negro and His Music*, 82.
109. Locke, *The Negro and His Music*, 85–86.
110. Locke, *The Negro and His Music*, 119.
111. Locke, *The Negro and His Music*, 61.
112. Locke, *The Negro and His Music*, 118.
113. Ibid. Emphasis added.
114. "The Negro-Art Hokum," *Nation* 122, June 16, 1926, 662–3.
115. Locke, *The Negro and His Music*, 118.
116. Harris, "The Great Debate," 30.
117. http://nationalhumanitiescenter.org/pds/maai3/protest/text10/lockeartpropaganda.pdf.
118. Ibid.
119. Harris, "The Great Debate," 16.
120. Hurston, *The Sanctified Church* (Lebanon: Da Capo Press, 1998), 64.
121. Ibid.
122. Ibid.
123. Hurston, *The Sanctified Church*, 80.
124. Hurston, *The Sanctified Church*, 66.
125. Hurston, *The Sanctified Church*, 56.
126. Hurston, *The Sanctified Church*, 58.
127. Ibid.
128. Ibid.
129. Oxford: Oxford University, 1998, 136.
130. Ogren, *The Jazz Revolution*, 131. Emphasis added.
131. Ogren, *The Jazz Revolution*, 132.
132. Ogren, *The Jazz Revolution*, 98.
133. Hurston, *The Sanctified Church*, 56.
134. "The Politics of Fiction, Anthropology, and the Folk: Zora Neale Hurtston," in *History and Memory in African-American Culture*, edited by Geneviève Fabre and Robert O'Meally (New York: Oxford University Press, 1994).
135. Hurston, *The Sanctified Church*, 62.

136. Hurston, *The Sanctified Church*, 62–63.
137. Hurston, *The Sanctified Church*, 63.
138. Ibid.
139. Hurston, *The Sanctified Church*, 64.
140. Ibid.
141. Ibid.
142. Hurston, *The Sanctified Church*, 66.
143. Ibid.
144. Ibid.
145. Lee B. Brown, "Postmodernist Jazz Theory: Afrocentrism, Old and New," *Journal of Aesthetics and Art Criticism* 57, no. 2, Aesthetics and Popular Culture (Spring 1999): 235–46.
146. Amiri Baraka, *Blues People* (New York: Harper Perennial, 1999), 148.
147. Hurston, *The Sanctified Church*, 67.
148. Hurston, *The Sanctified Church*, 80.
149. Hurston, *The Sanctified Church*, 67.
150. Hurston, *The Sanctified Church*, 79.
151. Ibid.
152. Hurston, *The Sanctified Church*, 80.
153. Hurston, *The Sanctified Church*, 81.
154. Hurston, *The Sanctified Church*, 106–07.
155. Jacqueline Emery, "Writing to Belong: Alice Dunbar-Nelson's Newspaper Columns in the African American Press," *Legacy: A Journal of American Women Writers* 33, no. 2 (2016): 286–309.
156. Judith Fetterley and Marjorie Pryse, *Writing Out of Place: Regionalism, Women, and American Literary Culture* (Urbana: University of Illinois Press, 2003). See their chapter on "Regionalism as 'Queer' Theory."
157. Alice Dunbar-Nelson, *The Works of Alice Dunbar-Nelson, Volume 1* (Oxford: Oxford University Press, 1994), 56.
158. Emery, "Writing to Belong," 303.
159. Elizabeth Ammons, *Conflicting Stories: American Women Writers at the Turn into the Twentieth* (Oxford: Oxford University Press, 1992), 66.
160. Katherine Adams, Sandra A. Zagarell, and Caroline Gebhard. "Recovering Alice Dunbar-Nelson for the Twenty-First Century: An Introduction," *Legacy: A Journal of American Women Writers* 33, no. 2 (2016): 236.
161. Emery, "Writing to Belong," 292.
162. Adams, Zagarell, and Gebhard, "Recovering Alice Dunbar-Nelson," 229.
163. Alice Dunbar-Nelson, *The Works of Alice Dunbar-Nelson*, 56.
164. *Writing Out of Place: Regionalism, Women, and American Literary Culture*, Judith Fetterley and Marjorie Pryse (Urbana: University of Illinois Press, 2003), in the chapter on "Regionalism as 'Queer' Theory," 334.
165. Dunbar-Nelson, *The Works of Alice Dunbar-Nelson*, 56.
166. Dunbar-Nelson, *The Works of Alice Dunbar-Nelson*, 62.
167. Ibid.
168. Ibid.

169. Ibid.
170. https://americanliterature.com/author/alice-dunbar-nelson/short-story/msieu-fortiers-violin.
171. Ibid.
172. *Indianapolis Freeman*, October 30, 1915.
173. Errol Hill, James V. Hatch, and Don Wilmeth, eds., *A History of American Theater* (Cambridge: Cambridge University Press, 2003), 209.
174. Gushee, *Pioneers of Jazz* (New York: Harper Perennial, 1999), 12.
175. *Indianapolis Freeman*, December 18, 1915, 5.
176. Carl R. Diton, "The Present Status of Negro American Musical Endeavor," *Indianapolis Freeman*, December 25, 1915, 20.
177. E. Azalia Hackley, *Indianapolis Freeman,* December 25, 1915, 25.
178. Clifford E. Watkins, *Showman: The Life and Music of Perry George Lowery* (Jackson: University of Mississippi Press, 2003), 18.
179. All my research was conducted through Google's archive of the *Freeman*, available here: https://news.google.com/newspapers?nid=FIkAGs9z2eEC.
180. *Indianapolis Freeman*, October 3, 1914, 5.
181. Ibid.
182. Ibid.
183. Ibid.
184. Ibid.
185. *Indianapolis Freeman*, January 3, 1910, 4.
186. Matt Sakakeeny, "New Orleans Music as a Circulatory System," *Black Music Research Journal* 31, no. 2 (Fall 2011): 291–325.
187. Aleen J. Ratzlaff, "Illustrated African American Journalism: Political Cartooning in the *Indianapolis Freeman*," in *Seeking a Voice: Images of Race and Gender in the 19th Century Press*, edited by David B. Sachsman, S. Kittrell Rushing, and Roy Morris (West Lafayette: Purdue University Press, 2009), 138.
188. Collier-Thomas, *A Treasury of African American Christmas Stories* (Boston: Beacon Press, 2018, edited by Bettye Collier-Thomas, 46.
189. *Indianapolis Freeman*, October 30, 1915, 6.
190. Ibid.
191. *Indianapolis Freeman*, July 31, 1915, 6.
192. Ibid.
193. Ibid.
194. *Indianapolis Freeman,* December 26, 1914, 7.
195. Ibid.
196. Ibid.
197. Ibid.
198. Ibid.
199. *Indianapolis Freeman*, October 30, 1915, 5.
200. Ibid.
201. *New York Age*, September 30, 1915, 3.
202. *Indianapolis Freeman*, December 26, 1914, 6.
203. *New York Age*, September 30, 1915, 3.

204. Ibid.
205. Ibid.
206. Ibid.
207. Ibid.
208. *Indianapolis Freeman*, December 25, 1915, 5.
209. Ibid.
210. Alcoff, *The Future of Whiteness*, 39.

LISTENING EXERCISES FOR CHAPTER 4

1. In many cases, the Discography of American Historical Recordings (DAHR) will have period recordings and valuable information about these records. For "Moten Stop, look here: https://adp.library.ucsb.edu/index.php/matrix/detail/800012934/BVE-38674-Moten_stomp. Check my YouTube channel for a compilation of the recordings I mention.
2. In his autobiography, Count Basie describes how he and Eddie Durham came up with "Moten Swing" (a related tune), which gives insight into the process. See *Good Morning Blues: The Autobiography of Count Basie (as Told to Albert Murray)* (New York: Random House, 1986), 126. The band needed a new instrumental number, so Basie and Durham adopted a pop song ("You're Driving Me Crazy"), while sitting at the piano, exchanging ideas, and drinking.
3. New York: Vintage Books, 1998.
4. Davis, *Blues Legacies* (New York: Vintage Books, 1998), 41.
5. Jeffrey Magee, *The Uncrowned King of Swing: Fletcher Henderson and Big Band Jazz* (Oxford: Oxford University Press, 2005), 23.
6. Magee, *Uncrowned King*, 24.
7. Bruce Crowther and Mike Pinfold, *Singing Jazz: The Singers and Their Styles* (San Francisco: Miller Freeman Books, 1997), 48.
8. *The Music of Black Americans: A History* (New York: Norton, 1971).
9. Southern, *Music of Black Americans*, 201, 212, and 213. Emphasis added.
10. Southern, *Music of Black Americans*, 214.

AFTERWORD

1. "What's in a Name? W. E. B. Du Bois vs. W.E.B. DeBois," *UC Press Blog*, accessed May 20, 2021, https://www.ucpress.edu/blog/25526/whats-in-a-name-w-e-b-du-bois-vs-w-e-b-debois/.
2. Lindsey McKenzie, "Words Matter for College Presidents, but so Will Actions," *Inside Higher Ed*, June 8, 2020. https://www.insidehighered.com/news/2020/06/08/searching-meaningful-response-college-leaders-killing-george-floyd.
3. I thank my colleague and mentor, Veronica Watson, for helping me formulate these thoughts.

References

Adams, Katherine, Sandra A. Zagarell, and Caroline Gebhard. "Recovering Alice Dunbar-Nelson for the Twenty-First Century: An Introduction." *Legacy: A Journal of American Women Writers* 33, no. 2 (2016): 236.
Ahmed, Sara. "A Phenomenology of Whiteness." *Feminist Theory* 8, no. 2 (August 2007): 149.
Ahmed, Sara. *Living a Feminist Life*. Durham: Duke University Press, 2017.
Ahmed, Sara. *Queer Phenomenology*. Durham: Duke University Press, 2006.
Ahmed, Sara. *The Promise of Happiness*. Durham: Duke University Press, 2010.
Alcoff, Linda Martín. *The Future of Whiteness*. Hoboken: Wiley, 2015.
Ammons, Elizabeth. *Conflicting Stories: American Women Writers at the Turn into the Twentieth*. Oxford: Oxford University Press, 1992.
Anderson, Paul Allen. *Deep River: Music and Memory in Harlem Renaissance Thought*. Durham: Duke University Press, 2001.
Attali, Jacques. *Noise: The Political Economy of Music*. Minneapolis: University of Minnesota Press, 1977.
Baraka, Amiri. *Blues People: Negro Music in White America*. New York: Harper Perennial, 1999.
Baraka, Amiri. *Digging: The Afro-American Soul of American Classical Music*. Berkeley: University of California Press, 2009.
Basie, Count. *Good Morning Blues: The Autobiography of Count Basie (as Told to Albert Murray)*. New York: Random House, 1986.
Beauvoir, Simone. *America Day by Day*, trans. Carol Cosman. Berkeley: University of California Press, 1999.
Beauvoir, Simone. *The Second Sex*. New York: Penguin, 1972.
Bechet, Sidney. *Treat it Gentle*. Cambridge: Da Capo Press, 1960.
Belle, Kathryn Sophia. "Fanon and Sartre 50 Years Later." *Sartre Studies International* 9, no. 2 (2003): 55–67.
Belle, Kathryn Sophia. (Formerly Kathryn T. Gines). *Hannah Arendt and the Negro Question*. Bloomington: Indiana University Press, 2014.

Belle, Kathryn Sophia. "Sartre, Beauvoir, and the Race/Gender Analogy: A Case for Black Feminist Philosophy." In *Convergences: Black Feminism and Continental Philosophy,* edited by Maria del Guadalupe Davidson, Kathryn Sophia Belle, and Donna-Dale Marcano. Albany: State University of New York, 2010.

Benítez-Rojo, Antonio. *The Repeating Island: The Caribbean and the Postmodern Perspective.* Durham: Duke University Press, 1997.

Benson, Bruce Ellis. *The Improvisation of Musical Dialogue: A Phenomenology of Music.* Cambridge: Cambridge University Press, 2003.

Berger, Morroe. "Resistance to the Diffusion of a Culture-Pattern." *The Journal of Negro History* 32, no. 4 (October 1947): 470.

Brodkin, Karen. *How Jews became White Folks and What that Says about Race in America.* New Brunswick: Rutgers University Press, 1998.

Brooks, Tim. *Lost Sounds: Blacks and the Birth of the Recording Industry, 1890–1919.* Urbana: University of Illinois Press, 2010.

Brown, Lee B. "Postmodernist Jazz Theory: Afrocentrism, Old and New." *Journal of Aesthetics and Art Criticism* 57, no. 2, Aesthetics and Popular Culture (Spring 1999): 235–46.

Bullard, Katharine S. *Civilizing the Child: Discourses of Race, Nation and Child Welfare in America.* Lanham: Lexington, 2013.

Burton, Antoinette. *Archive Stories: Facts, Fictions and the Writing of History.* Durham: Duke University Press, 2005.

Burton, Antoinette. *Burdens of Empire: British Feminists, Indian Women, and Imperial Culture, 1865–1915.* Chapel Hill: University of North Carolina Press, 1994.

Byrd, Jodi A. *The Transit of Empire: Indigenous Critiques of Colonialism.* Minneapolis: University of Minnesota Press, 2011.

Carby, Hazel. "The Politics of Fiction, Anthropology, and the Folk: Zora Neale Hurtston." In *History and Memory in African-American Culture,* edited by Geneviève Fabre and Robert O'Meally. New York: Oxford University Press, 1994.

Caulfeild, Ruby. *The French Literature of Louisiana.* Gretna: Firebird Press, 1929.

Chakrabarty, Namita, Lorna Roberts, and John Preston, eds. *Critical Race Theory in England.* Abingdon: Routledge, 2014.

Coulthard, Glen. *Red Skins, White Masks: Rejecting the Colonial Politics of Recognition.* Minneapolis: University of Minnesota Press, 2014.

Crowther, Bruce, and Mike Pinfold. *Singing Jazz: The Singers and Their Styles.* San Francisco: Miller Freeman Books, 1997.

Cruz, Jon. *Culture on the Margins: The Black Spiritual and the Rise of American Cultural Interpretation.* New Brunswick: Princeton University Press, 1999.

Dabashi, Hamid. *Brown Skin, White Masks.* London: Pluto Press, 2011.

Dash, J. Michael. "Relating Islands: The South of the South in Americas." *The Southern Quarterly* 55, no. 4 (Summer 2018): 130–42.

Davis, Angela. *Blues Legacies and Black Feminism.* New York: Vintage, 1989.

De Ferrrari, Guillermina. "The Ship, the Plantation, and the Polis: Reading Gilroy and Glissant as Moral Philosophy." *Comparative Literature Studies* 49, no. 2 (2012): 186.

Diagne, Souleymane Bachir. "Négritude." *The Stanford Encyclopedia of Philosophy*, Summer 2018 edition. https://plato.stanford.edu/archives/sum2018/entries/negritude/.

Douglass, Frederick, and Angela Y. Davis. *Narrative of the Life of Frederick Douglass, an American Slave, Written by Himself.* San Francisco: City Lights Books, 2010.

Douglass, Frederick, Philip Sheldon Foner, and Yuval Taylor, eds. *Frederick Douglass: Selected Speeches and Writings.* Chicago: Lawrence Hill Books, 1999.

Driggs, Fank, and Chuck Haddix. *Kansas City Jazz: From Ragtime to Bebop.* Oxford: Oxford University Press, 2005.

Du Bois, W. E. B. *The Souls of Black Folk.* New York: Penguin Books, 1996.

Du Bois, W. E. B. "The Souls of White Folk." In *Darkwater*. New York: Harcourt, Brace and Company, 1920 (923–938).

Dunbar-Nelson, Alice. *The Works of Alice Dunbar-Nelson, Volume 1.* Oxford: Oxford University Press, 1994.

Dunbar-Ortiz, Roxanne. *An Indigenous People's History of the United States.* Boston: Beacon Press, 2014.

Dyer, Richard. *White: Essays on Race and Culture.* Abingdon: Routledge, 1997.

Eidsheim, Nina Sun. "Marian Anderson and 'Sonic Blackness' in American Opera." In *Sound Clash: Listening to American Studies*, edited by Kara Keeling and Josh Kun. Baltimore: Johns Hopkins University Press, 2012.

Eidsheim, Nina Sun. *The Race of Sound: Listening, Timbre, and Vocality in African American Music.* Durham: Duke University Press, 2019.

Emery, Jacqueline, "Writing to Belong: Alice Dunbar-Nelson's Newspaper Columns in the African American Press." *Legacy: A Journal of American Women Writers* 33, no. 2 (2016): 286–309.

Engles, Tim. "Towards a Biography of Critical Whiteness Studies." *The Keep: Eastern Illinois Library*, November 2006.

Esteban, José Muñoz. *Disidentifications: Queers of Color and the Performance of Politics.* Minneapolis: University of Minnesota Press, 1999.

Fanon, Frantz. *Black Skins, White Masks.* London: Pluto Press, 1986.

Fanon, Frantz. *Wretched of the Earth.* New York: Grove Press, 2004.

Feather, Leonard. *The Book of Jazz.* New York: Random House, 1976.

Fertel, Rein T. *Imagining the Creole City.* Baton Rouge: Louisiana State University Press, 2014.

Fetterley, Judith, and Marjorie Pryse. *Writing Out of Place: Regionalism, Women, and American Literary Culture.* Urbana: University of Illinois Press, 2003.

Gates, Henry Lewis. *The Signifying Monkey: A Theory of African-American Literary Criticism.* Oxford: Oxford University Press, 1988.

Gilroy, Paul. *The Black Atlantic: Modernity and Double Consciousness.* Cambridge, MA: Harvard University Press, 2000.

Gioia, Ted. "Jazz and the Primitivist Myth." *Musical Quarterly* 73, no. 1 (1989): 130–43.

Glissant, Édouard. *Caribbean Discourse: Selected Essays.* Charlottesville: University of Virginia Press, 1991.

Glissant, Édouard. *Faulkner, Mississippi*. Chicago: University of Chicago Press, 2000.

Glissant, Édouard. *Poetics of Relation*. Ann Arbor: University of Michigan Press, 1997.

Gordon, Jane A. *Creolizing Political Theory: Reading Rousseau through Fanon*. New York: Fordham University Press, 2011.

Gordon, Jane Anna, and Lewis R. Gordon. *Not Only the Master's Tools: African American Studies in Theory and Practice*. London: Routledge, 2005.

Gordon, Lewis R. *An Introduction to Africana Philosophy*. Cambridge: Cambridge University Press, 2008.

Gordon, Lewis R. *Bad Faith and Anti-Black Racism*. Amherst: Humanity Books, 1995.

Gordon, Lewis R. *Existentia Africana: Understanding Africana Existential Thought*. Abingdon: Routledge, 2000.

Gordon, Lewis R. *Fanon and the Crisis of European Man*. New York: Routledge, 1995.

Gordon, Lewis R. *Her Majesty's Other Children*. Lanham: Rowman & Littlefield, 1997.

Gordon, Lewis R. *What Fanon Said*. New York: Fordham Press, 2015.

Gottlieb, William P. Portrait of Bob Wilber, Freddie Moore, Sidney Bechet, and Lloyd Phillips, Jimmy Ryan's Club, New York, N.Y., ca. June. United States, 1947. Monographic. Photograph. https://www.loc.gov/item/gottlieb.00581/.

Gracyk, Theodore, Lee Brown, and David Goldblatt. *Jazz and the Philosophy of Art*. New York: Routledge, 2018.

Gritten, Antony. "Empathic Listening as a Transferable Skill." *Empirical Musicology Review* 10, no. 1 (2015): 23–29.

Gushee, Lawrence. *Pioneers of Jazz: The Story of the Creole Band*. Oxford: Oxford University Press, 2005.

Harris, Leonard. "The Great Debate: W. E. B. Du Bois vs. Alain Locke on the Aesthetic." *Philosophia Africana* 7, no. 1 (March 2004): 15–39.

Harris, Neil. *Humbug: The Art of P.T. Barnum*. Chicago: University of Chicago Press, 1973.

Hebdige, Dick. *Cut-n-Mix: Culture, Identity and Caribbean Music*. Oxon: Comedia, 1987.

Heter, T Storm. "Jazz." In *The Routledge Companion to Remix Studies*, edited by Eduardo Navas, Owen Gallagher, and xtine burrough. Abingdon: Routledge, 2015.

Hill, Errol, James V. Hatch, and Don Wilmeth, eds. *A History of American Theater*. Cambridge: Cambridge University Press, 2003.

Hill, Marc Lamont. *Rhymes, Beats and Classroom Life: Hip Hop Pedagogy and the Politics of Identity*. New York: Teachers College Press, 2009.

Hoberman, John. "Darwin's Athletes." In *Doing Real World Research in Sports Studies*, edited by Andy Smith and Ivan Wadddington. London: Routledge, 2014.

hooks, bell. *Black Looks: Race and Representation*. Boston: South End Press, 1992.

Hopkins, Larissa E., and Andrea D. Domingue. "From Awareness to Action: College Student's Skill Development in Intergroup Dialogue." *Equity & Excellence in Education* 48, no. 3 (2015): 392–402.

Hull, Akahsa Gloria, Patricia Bell-Scott, and Barbara Smith, eds. *All the Women Are White, All the Blacks Are Men, but Some of Us Are Brave*. New York: The Feminist Press, 1993.

Hurston, Zora Neal. *The Sanctified Church.* Lebanon: Da Capo Press, 1998.
Ignatiev, Noel. *How the Irish became White.* New York: Routledge, 2009.
Ihde, Don. *Listening and Voice.* Albany: State University of New York Press, 2007.
James, Robin. "On Intersectionality and Cultural Appropriation: The Case of Postmillenial Black Hipness." *Journal of Black Masculinity* 1, no. 2 (2011): 121–130.
James, Robin. "Oppression, Privilege, & Aesthetics." *Philosophy Compass* 8, no. 2 (2013): 101–16.
James, Robin. *Resistance and Melancholy: Pop Music, Feminism, Neoliberalism.* Alresford: Zero Books, 2015.
James, Robin. *The Conjectural Body: Gender, Race, and the Philosophy of Music.* Lanham: Lexington, 2010.
James, Robin. *The Sonic Episteme: Acoustic Resonance, Neoliberalism, and Biopolitics.* Durham: Duke University Press, 2019.
Jay, Martin. *Downcast Eyes.* Berkley: University of California Press, 1993.
Kajikawa, Loren. *Sounding Race in Rap Songs.* Oakland: University of California Press, 2015.
Keeling, Kara, and Josh Kun, eds. *Sound Clash: Listening to American Studies.* Baltimore: Johns Hopkins University Press, 2012.
Kelley, Robin D. G. *Africa Speaks, America Answers: Modern Jazz in Revolutionary Time.* Cambridge, MA: Harvard University Press, 2012.
Kelley, Robin D. G. *Freedom Dreams: The Black Radical Imagination.* Boston: Beacon Press, 2002.
Kelley, Robin D. G. "Notes on Deconstructing 'The Folk'." *American Historical Review* 97, no. 5 (December 1992): 1402.
Kelley, Robin D. G. *Thelonious Monk: The Life and Times of an American Original.* New York: The Free Press, 2010.
Kenney, William H. *Chicago Jazz: A Cultural History, 1904–1930.* New York: Oxford University Press, 1993.
Kincaid, Jamaica. *A Small Place.* New York: Macmillan, 1988.
Koven, Seth. *Slumming: Sexual and Social Politics in Victorian London.* Princeton: Princeton University Press, 2004.
Lemnke, Sieglinde. *Primitivist Modernism: Black Culture and the Origins of Transatlantic Modernism.* Oxford: Oxford University Press, 1998.
Leonard, Neil. *Jazz and the White Americans: The Acceptance of a New Art Form.* Chicago: University of Chicago Press, 1962.
Levine, Lawrence W. *Highbrow/Lowbrow: The Emergence of Cultural Hierarchy in America.* Cambridge, MA: Harvard University Press, 1988.
Locke, Alain. *The Negro and His Music.* Washington: The Publication in Negro Folk Education, 1936.
Locke Alain, ed. *The New Negro.* New York: Simon & Schuster, 1992.
Lomax, Alan. *Mister Jelly Roll: The Fortunes of Jelly Roll Morton, New Orleans Creole and Inventory of the Blues.* Berkeley: University of California Press, 1950.
Lott, Eric. *Love and Theft: Blackface Minstrelsy and the American Working Class.* Oxford: Oxford University Press, 1993.

Lott, Eric. "Mr. Clemens and Jim Crow: Twain, Race and Blackface." In *The Cambridge Companion to Mark Twain*, edited by Forrest G. Robinson. Cambridge: Cambridge University Press, 1995.

Low, Denise. *Natural Theologies: Essay about Literature of the New Middle West*. Omaha: Backwaters Press, 2011.

Magee, Jeffrey. *The Uncrowned King of Swing: Fletcher Henderson and Big Band Jazz*. Oxford: Oxford University Press, 2005.

Martin, Billy. *Riddim: Claves of African Origin*. Columbus: Music in Motion Films, Ltd., 2008.

Martin, Katy. "The Preoccupations of Mr. Lomax Inventor of the 'Inventor of Jazz'." *Popular Music and Society* 36, no. 1 (2013): 30–39.

Martinez, Jacqueline M. *Phenomenology of Chicana Experience & Identity: Communication and Transformation in Praxis*. Lanham: Rowman and Littlefield, 2000.

McCusker, John. *Creole Trombone: Kid Ory and the Early Years of Jazz*. Jackson: University of Mississippi Press, 2012.

McKenzie, Lindsey. "Words Matter for College Presidents, but So Will Actions." *Inside Higher Ed*, June 8 (2020).

Meltzer, David. *Reading Jazz*. San Francisco: Mercury House, 1993.

Mezzrow, Mezz. *Really the Blues*. New York: Random House, 1946.

Miller, Karl Hagstom. *Segregating Sound: Inventing Folk and Pop Music in the Age of Jim Crow*. Durham: Duke University Press, 2010.

Mills, Charles W. *Blackness Visible: Essays on Philosophy and Race*. Ithaca: Cornell University Press, 1998.

Mitchel, Gillian. *The North American Folk Music Revival*. Farnham: Ashgate, 2016.

Monahan, Michael J. *The Creolizing Subject: Race, Reason and the Politics of Purity*. New York: Fordham Press, 2011.

Monson, Ingrid. *Freedom Sounds: Civil Rights Call Out to Jazz and Africa*. Oxford: Oxford University Press, 2007.

Monson, Ingrid. *Saying Something: Jazz Improvisation and Interaction*. Chicago: University of Chicago Press, 1996.

Monson, Ingrid. "The Problem with White Hipness: Race, Gender, and Cultural Conceptions in Jazz Historical Discourse." *Journal of the American Musicological Society* 48, no. 3 (Autumn 1995): 396–422.

More, Mabogo P. *Biko: Philosophy, Identity and Liberation*. Cape Town: HSRC Press, 2017.

More, Mabogo P. *Looking through Philosophy in Black*. Lanham: Rowman & Littlefield International, 2018.

More, Mabogo P. *Sartre on Contingency: Antiblack Racism and Embodiment*. Lanham: Rowman & Littlefield, 2021.

Mullen, Patrick B. *The Man Who Adores the Negro: Race and American Folklore*. Urbana: University of Illinois Press, 2008.

Munro, Martin. *Different Drummers: Rhythm & Race in the Americas*. Berkeley: University of California Press, 2010.

Munro, Martin, and Celia Britton, eds. *American Creoles: The Francophone Caribbean and the American South*. Liverpool: Liverpool University Press, 2012.

Music, David W., and Paul Akers Richardson. *"I Will Sing the Wondrous Story": A History of Baptist Hymnody in North America.* Macon: Mercer University Press, 2008.

Nagda, Biren A., and Patricia Gurin. "Intergroup Dialogue: A Critical-Dialogical Approach to Learning about Difference, Inequality, and Social Justice." *New Directions for Teaching and Learning*, no. 111 (Fall 2007): 35–45.

Navas, Eduardo. *Remix Theory: The Aesthetics of Sampling.* Germany: Springer-Verlag, 2012.

Nya, Nathalie. *Simone de Beauvoir and the Colonial Experience.* Lanham: Lexington, 2019, Kindle Edition.

Oforlea, Aaron. "[Un]veiling the White Gaze." *Western Journal of Black Studies* 36, no. 4 (2012): 290.

Ogren, Kathy J. *The Jazz Revolution: Twenties America and the Meaning of Jazz.* Oxford: Oxford University Press, 1992.

Okiji, Fumi. *Jazz as Critique: Adorno and Black Expression Revisited.* Stanford: Stanford University Press, 2018.

Panish, Jon. *The Color of Jazz: Race and Representation in Postwar American Culture.* Jackson: University of Mississippi Press, 1997.

Parris, La Rose T. *Being Apart: Theoretical and Existential Resistance in Africana Literature.* Charlottesville: University of Virginia Press, 2015.

Porterfield, Nolan. *Last Cavalier: The Life and Times of John A. Lomax.* Champaign: University of Illinois Press, 2001.

Pratt, Mary Louise. *Imperial Eyes: Travel Writing and Transculturation.* London: Routledge, 1992.

Puwar, Nirmal. *Space Invaders: Race, Gender and Bodies Out of Place.* Oxford: Berg, 2004.

Radano, Ronald. *Lying Up a Nation: Race and Black Music.* Chicago: University of Chicago, 2003.

Ramsey Jr., Guthrie P. *Race Music: Black Cultures from Bebop to Hip-Hop.* Berkeley: University of California Press, 2003.

Ratzlaff, Aleen J. "Illustrated African American Journalism: Political Cartooning in the *Indianapolis Freeman*." In *Seeking a Voice: Images of Race and Gender in the 19th Century Press*, edited by David B. Sachsman, S. Kittrell Rushing, and Roy Morris. West Lafayette: Purdue University Press, 2009.

Riley, John. *The Art of Bop Drumming.* New York: Manhattan Music, 1994.

Roberts, Dorothy. *Fatal Invention: How Science, Politics, and Big Business Re-Create Race in the Twenty-First Century.* New York: The New Press, 2012.

Roberts, Neil. *Freedom as Marronage.* Chicago: University of Chicago Press, 2015.

Rose, Tricia. *Black Noise: Rap Music and Black Culture in Contemporary America.* Middletown: Wesleyan University Press, 1994.

Rose, Tricia. *The Hip Hop Wars.* New York: Basic Books, 2008.

Ross, Andrew. *No Respect: Intellectuals and Popular Culture.* Abington: Routledge, 1989.

Sakakeeny, Matt. "New Orleans Music as a Circulatory System." *Black Music Research Journal* 31, no. 2 (Fall 2011): 291–325.

Sandke, Randall. *Where the Dark and the Light Folks Meet.* Lanham: The Scarecrow Press, 2010.
Santoro, Gene. *Myself When I Am Real: The Life and Music of Charles Mingus.* Oxford: Oxford University Press, 2000.
Sartre, Jean-Paul. *Critique of Dialectical Reason, Vol. 1.* London: Verso, 2006.
Sartre, Jean-Paul. *Notebooks for an Ethics.* Chicago: University of Chicago Press, 1992.
Schuyler, George S. "The Negro-Art Hokum." *Nation* 122, June 16 (1926): 662–3.
Shaw, Devin Z. *Philosophy of Antifascism: Punching Nazis and Fighting White Supremacy.* Lanham: Rowman & Littlefield International, 2020.
Simons, Margaret A. "Beauvoir and the Problem of Racism." In *Philosophers on Race: Critical Issues*, edited by Julie K. Ward and Tommy L. Lott. Oxford: Blackwell, 2002.
Sithole, Tendayi. *Fugitive Tapes: Poetics of the Black Sonic Imagination.* Unpublished mansucript, manuscript provided by author.
Sobchak, Vivian. "Simple Grounds: At Home in Experience." In *Postphenomenology: A Critical Companion to Ihde,* edited by Evan Selinger. Albany: State University of New York Press, 2008.
Southern, Eileen. *The Music of Black Americans: A History.* New York: Norton, 1971.
Spivak, Gayatri. "Questions of Multiculturalism." In *The Postcolonial Critic: Interviews Strategies, Dialogues,* , edited by Sarah Harasym. Abingdon: Routledge, 1986.
Sterne, Jonathan. *The Audible Past: Cultural Origins of Sound Reproduction.* Durham: Duke University Press, 2003.
Stover, A. Shahid. *Being and Insurrection: Existential Liberation Critique, Sketches and Ruptures.* New York: Cannae Press, 2019.
Sudhalter, Richard M. *Lost Chords: White Musicians and Their Contributions to Jazz, 1915–1945.* New York: Oxford University Press, 1999.
Taylor, Paul C. *Black Is Beautiful.* Oxford: Blackwell, 2016.
Taylor, Paul C. *Race: A Philosophical Introduction.* Oxford: Oxford University Press, 2005.
Thomas, Tashima. "Race and Remix." In *The Routledge Companion to Remix Studies*, edited by Eduardo Navas, Owen Gallagher, and xtine burrough. Abingdon: Routledge, 2015.
Watkins, Clifford E. *Showman: The Life and Music of Perry George Lowery.* Jackson: University of Mississippi Press, 2003.
Weheliye, Alex. *Phonographies: Grooves in Sonic Afro-Modernity.* Durham: Duke University Press, 2005.
Williams, Patricia J. *Seeing a Colorblind Future: The Paradox of Race.* New York: Farrar, Strauss and Giroux, 2016.
Yancy, George. *Look, a White! Philosophical Essays on Whiteness.* Philadelphia: Temple University Press, 2012.
Youngren, William H. "Black and White Intertwined." *Atlantic* 283, no. 2 (1999): 86–88.
Zack, Naomi. *White Privilege and Black Rights: The Injustice of U.S. Police Racial Profiling and Homicide.* Lanham: Rowman & Littlefield, 2015.

Index

Ahmed, Sara, 4, 8, 14, 24, 57, 69, 76–78, 112–13, 160
Alcoff, Linda, 2, 11, 14, 24, 56–57, 60, 138

bad faith, 17, 27–29, 46–48, 53–56, 60, 71, 76–77, 94, 97, 103, 106–7, 132, 138
Baraka, Amiri, xi, 22, 49, 50, 127–28
Basie, Count, 47, 142, 144, 181
Beauvoir, Simone, 3, 4, 18–19, 27, 53–60, 104–5, 112, 114, 141
Bechet, Sidney, 9, 10, 20, 22, 40, 57–58, 64, 67–79, 82, 85, 87, 88, 90–92, 96–97, 99–102, 106, 109, 110, 114, 125, 147
Belle, Kathryn Sophia, 27, 55–56
Black existentialism, 103–11
Byrd, Jodi A., 1

Carby, Hazel, 127–28
colorblind listening, 46–50, 65
Coulthard, Glen, 18
creolization, 20–22, 93–96
Critical Whiteness Studies, 1, 2, 112–13, 118–19

Davis, Angela, 6, 24, 79, 103, 107, 114–18, 120, 133, 139, 141, 144–46

Diagne, Souleyman Bachir, 4
digenesis, 21–22
Douglass, Frederick, 9, 68, 83, 104, 120
Du Bois, W.E.B., 2, 5, 19, 27–29, 31, 44, 60, 103–11, 114, 117, 120–25, 129–33, 137–38, 151
Dunbar-Nelson, Alice, 23–25, 120, 130–33, 138

ecstatic listening, 50–53, 65
Etude, the, 9, 29–31, 47, 138
Eurocentrism, 19, 69, 138
existentialism, 1, 3, 10, 18, 19, 22, 55, 56, 104, 111, 138

Fanon, Frantz, 3–5, 7, 17–20, 27, 41, 44, 46, 55, 73, 103–7, 111–14, 120, 125, 138
Feather, Leonard, 46–48
feminism, 4, 8, 18, 23, 54, 114–18, 141, 145
Floyd, George, 151–57
Freeman Indianapolis, 91, 133–38

Gioia, Ted, 16, 29
Glissant, Édouard, 20–22, 68, 85, 93–97, 126
Gordon, Jane A., 21, 94

Gordon, Lewis R., 2–3, 19, 20, 27, 76, 103–7, 114, 120, 125, 141
Gracyk, Theodore, 15
Gushee, Lawrence, 32, 88, 91

Harlem Renaissance, 9, 24, 28, 44, 103–4, 115, 120–30
Hill, Marc Lamont, xi
hipsters, 7, 16, 27, 31, 39–42, 58–60, 64, 116–17
hooks, bell, 24, 73, 103, 118–20, 133
Hull, Akahsa Gloria, 24
Hurston, Zora Neal, 24, 120–30, 132, 133, 149

Ihde, Don, 11, 50–53

James, Robin, 14–15, 18, 39, 43, 49
Judaism, 19

Kelley, Robin D. G., 17, 75, 117, 141
Kincaid, Jamaica, 55

Levine, Lawrence, 51
Locke Alain, 9, 44, 90, 103, 104, 122–25, 131–33, 138
Lomax, Alan, 19–21, 42, 44–46, 65
Lott, Eric, 16, 45, 90, 133

Martinez, Jacqueline M., 10, 24
Mezzrow, Mezz, 9, 39–43, 57, 58, 64, 142
Mingus, Charles, 3, 6–7
minstrelsy, 16, 22, 27–29, 32–35, 40, 41, 60, 63, 80–82, 88–90, 111, 121–24, 133–34, 138, 145
Monahan, Michael J., 21, 44, 94, 95, 160
Monson, Ingrid, 14, 15, 17, 39
More, Mabogo P., 2, 4, 5, 105–6, 113, 141
Morton, Jelly Roll, 22, 42, 44–45, 65, 67–79, 82
Mullen, Patrick B., 17, 45

Navas, Eduardo, 13, 101

Ogren, Kathy J., 16, 29, 31, 127, 164
The Original Creole Band, 9, 22, 32–35, 67, 81, 88–92, 134
Ory, Edward "Kid", 9, 22, 30, 40, 67, 68, 79–88

Parris, LaRose, 1, 21, 24, 104, 105, 141
phenomenology, 5, 6, 8–10, 12–14, 18, 22, 39–41, 44, 50–52, 55, 68–72, 75, 77, 79, 86, 99, 104, 107, 108, 110, 114–16, 118, 126, 130, 131, 136
polyrhythm, 61–62
Puwar, Nirmal, 172

race records, 141–50
remix, 5, 12–14, 52, 70, 72, 99, 101
revivalism, 42–46, 64, 71–79
Roberts, Neil, 21, 85, 94
Rose, Tricia, 17, 52

Sartre, Jean-Paul, 2–4, 13, 18–20, 27, 50, 55, 94, 104, 105, 107, 112–14, 141
savior listening, 35–39
Shaw, Devin Z., 5, 48
Simons, Margaret A., 24, 55
Sithole, Tendayi, 3, 6, 113, 141
sonic gaze, xii, 1–4, 6, 7, 16, 18–20, 23, 25, 44, 52, 68, 71, 78, 80, 85, 90, 95, 103, 107, 110, 111, 116, 141, 150, 152
sound studies, 5, 12–14
Spivak, Gayatri, 4, 5, 20, 23
Sterne, Jonathan, 11–13, 18
Stover, A. Shahid, 24

Taylor, Breonna, 151–57
Taylor Paul C., 11–12

vaudeville, 33–35, 39, 51, 80–82, 88–92, 103, 122, 124, 133–39

versioning, 13, 72–73, 99–100, 129, 141
visualism, 3, 11–12

Weheliye, Alex, 16
White problem, 2, 27, 29, 53, 55–56, 60, 103–7, 113, 120, 156
Whitney, Salem-Tutt, 124, 133–39

Williams, Patricia J., 59

Yancy, George, 31, 113, 160

Zack, Naomi, 19, 160

www.ingramcontent.com/pod-product-compliance
Lightning Source LLC
Chambersburg PA
CBHW031710230426
43668CB00006B/172